CUSTOMISING ELECTRIC & BASS GUITARS

The complete guide
to painting, staining, finishing
and body transformation

HAMMERITE
METAL PAINT

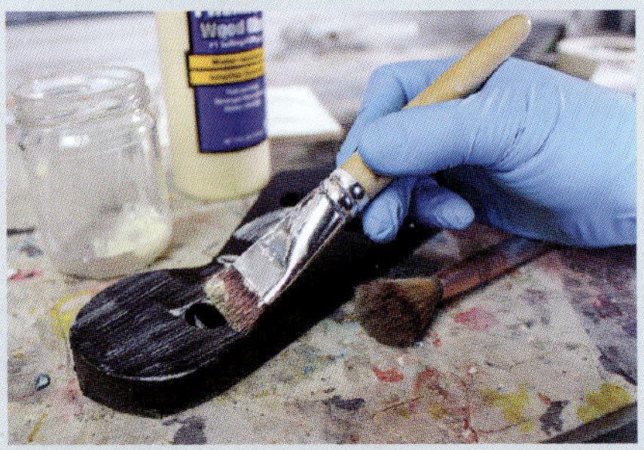
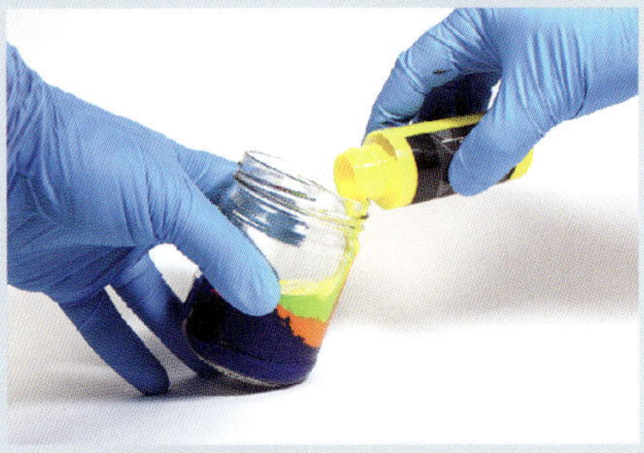
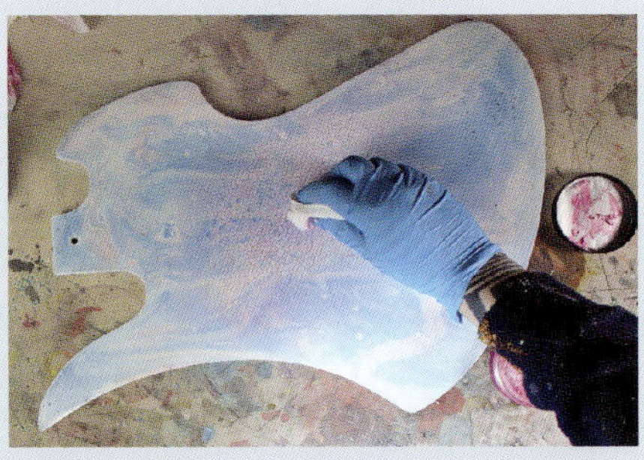

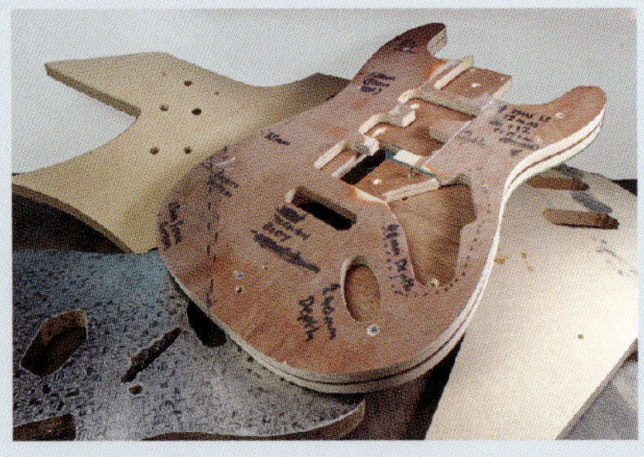
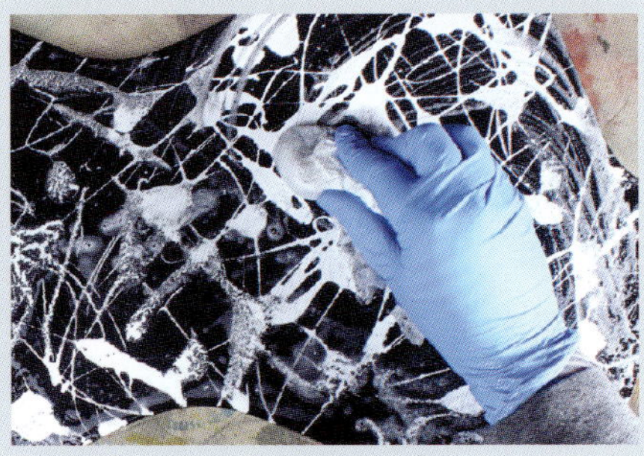

Daniel Wallis

CUSTOMISING ELECTRIC & BASS GUITARS

The complete guide
to painting, staining, finishing
and body transformation

THE CROWOOD PRESS

CONTENTS

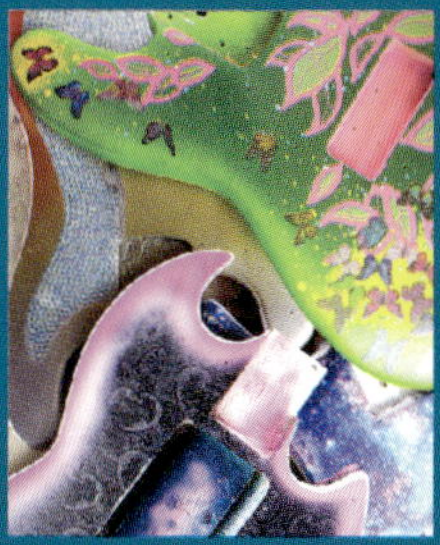

uni POSCA
uni POSCA
uni POSCA
cricut

INTRODUCTION

From a simple change of colour to an ornate paint job, a change of finish can transform your relationship with any guitar. I firmly believe that the way a guitar looks and feels will affect the way you play it. Imagine picking up your dream guitar and playing your go-to riff on it; you're picking notes that you have countless times before, but this time on the best instrument you have ever held. Picture yourself on stage with a guitar so cool that the audience isn't just impressed with your musical prowess, but also with your rock-star looks – you've blown them away. This concept is in the back of my mind every time I customise a guitar. I've had clients who love their guitars, but want them in more inspirational colours, or who want their guitar to match their music with the simple addition of a band logo, or who request a more complex transformation into the physical embodiment of the music they play on it. This book covers how you can do the same, by starting simple, then getting more complex, and with examples by artists and builders who inspire me, and I hope will you too.

HOW THE BOOK WORKS

Whether you're working on a second-hand guitar, a kit guitar, or building one from scratch, the journey is similar, with the end point determining the route you follow through the book. I recommend reading the entire book, as you may find inspiration from one technique or process to combine with another, or to use in a different way to make it uniquely yours.

This book starts with how to prepare your guitar for a custom paint job, stripping the current finish if necessary, and dealing with any dents and dings. I cover some basic information you'll need if you want to change the shape before introducing different types of paint, lacquer, stains, dyes and waxes. Most of these finishes can be applied in multiple ways. The one you select may be dictated by your set-up and workspace or tools you already have, but perhaps you'll be able to try multiple approaches and pick your favourite. I'm assuming here that once you've customised one guitar, you'll catch the bug and want to do more. I've still got the very first electric guitar my parents bought for me, a Squier Stratocaster in the early 1990s. It's now on its fourth finish.

Many of my clients come to me with vague ideas that require help to transform into real finishes on their guitar. The middle of the book covers some key elements to think about in your designs, how to find inspiration and creativity, and how to bring to life an idea.

There are sections covering a range of more artistic approaches to finishing that include examples by artists, luthiers and well-known guitars such as Eddie Van Halen's Frankenstrat as inspiration.

The book concludes with processes that allow you to customise other parts of the guitar, starting with the neck, fretboard and headstock, before moving on to the scratchplate and hardware.

PLAYABLE ART

I have included a few boxes of ideas, designed to trigger some inspiration, or a new way of looking at the techniques I cover. Key to my thinking when writing the book, and an idea you may want to consider, is that the guitar is a canvas and what you create is an artwork.

ABOUT ME

I started playing guitar in primary school when they ran out of space in the saxophone class, but hadn't yet filled up the guitar group. I haven't looked back since. Almost immediately, I tried refinishing an old guitar my grandparents had in their loft, though I never completed it. If only I'd had a book to guide me. Since then, I've worked as a magician entertaining at children's parties, studied art at university, had a twenty-year career in arts education and, as of writing this book, have officially been customising other people's guitars as a job for just over a decade.

My guitar customisation company was called Devil & Sons. I liked the idea of mixing the suggestion of an old family-run business, like the '... & Sons' shops around the east end of London where I grew up, with the legend of Robert Johnson. Instead of selling your soul to the devil to be able to play guitar, you could bring your guitar to the Devil & Sons crossroads for the creation of a guitar you would sell your soul for. Very early on, I started a YouTube channel to help teach people how to do this too, combining my love of teaching with the arts with guitars. This evolved into a podcast called The Guitar Builders Collective Chat. On the company's tenth anniversary, I split the company so that Devil & Sons is focused on the education work I do in maintaining, repairing, customising and building guitars. All the guitars I build and customise now bear a name that represents where I am in life, a proud father to two daughters. Look out for the Devil & Daughters logo on the guitars I have made, especially to demonstrate techniques throughout this book.

PRODUCTS AND PEOPLE

In this book, I only use products that I trust. Some are from companies I work with – some that I've used for years, while others are new but game-changing. Many products were bought in or donated by suppliers or manufacturers, and some are from my old stock from past customisation projects.

I have listed the brand and specific product name wherever possible. This helps you to use the same products if you want to replicate my work, but also allows you to compare them with other products online. I like to support small British-based companies, or buy specialised products as locally as possible (often mainland Europe) but there is a list of international suppliers at the end of the book. I sought advice from members of The Guitar Builders Collective to compile this list. The 'GBC' is a group of like-minded people from around the world who share a passion for guitars and guitar building. It includes professionals, hobbyists and people who are still to make or customise their first guitar. Links to it and all the inspirational artists I mention throughout the book can also be found at the end.

I recommend trying out different products over time if you are going to be customising a lot of guitars. This way, you can find what works best for you and your approach. Sometimes, this choice may be an environmental one, taking into account how and where the product is made and shipped from; sometimes, it may be finding a brand you like and want to support, while other times it may just be availability. As I use a lot of products, I often end up talking to the companies directly with the result that their customer support and staff play a role in my decision-making.

CASE STUDY: DEVIL & DAUGHTERS MODEL 666

In order to write this book, I potentially had to make a lot of guitars so that I could photograph and demonstrate each technique. To help keep everything under control, and to make sure it would all fit in my workshop, I used multiple process on each guitar. Dotted throughout the book will be case studies showing the finished guitars. I really hope these will act as inspiration, not just for guitars to copy techniques from, but also for ways of combining and evolving what I cover in the book into something unique to you.

This guitar started life as a second-hand Stratocaster style from Ashton that I bought it on eBay. There were a few parts missing and lots of big dents in the finish. The first stage for this guitar was to chop the sides of it and stick new wings on. This way, I could demonstrate what parts of the guitar are essential to make it work. I invented a new shape for it, too, which is covered in the section on using templates to shape a guitar. This is mainly a Gibson SG and Ibanez Iceman shape combined, with a bit of Fender to hold it all together.

The body has had a ceruse finish added with a wire brush, the pores being filled with the same-coloured wax that I applied to the neck. I used the top of the body to demonstrate the fabric-top and binding process and finished it all in a hard wax oil, so you'll see the body popping up a lot in the book.

A custom scratchplate was needed too. The pickups are all from my collection of leftovers gutted from past guitars, but the wiring is otherwise the same as the original. I also upgraded the bridge.

I was actually so inspired by the process of building this one that I'm using it as a basis for a series of guitars in this shape that I hope to make soon. I think that means I'll be keeping and not selling this one, the very first Devil & Daughters Model 666!

This finished guitar appears multiple times in the book to demonstrate a range of techniques.

The guitar looked like this when I first bought it from eBay.

DON'T MISS THESE WARNING BOXES!

I will be pointing out some important things to consider, both for your own safety, but also to ensure things don't go wrong. My first warning is that some of the processes covered in the book use machinery and power tools. It is vital that you know how to use these competently and have read the relevant safety guidelines that come with each tool.

A WORD OF ADVICE

Look out for these tip boxes for advice that will assist you with the various techniques I've written about. Often, I'll be trying to help you avoid any mistakes I have made. I could say that I'm an experienced luthier, but as Oscar Wilde said, 'Experience is simply the name we give to our mistakes.'

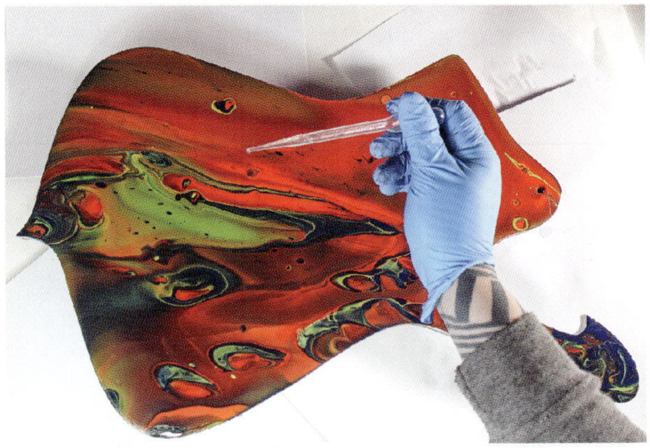

This bass appears throughout the book as it incorporates multiple techniques and processes.

INSPIRATION: BONVILLAIN DESIGN STUDIOS

Throughout the book I'll be including examples by people whose work is an inspiration to me. A takeaway from a cool guitar can be the finishing technique, the choice of paint, colour combinations, or changes to the overall design. Artists such as David from Bonvillain Design Studios are examples of what can be achieved when a guitar is treated as a canvas. It's an expression not just of the person who painted the instrument, but of the musician playing it.

David's swirls are unique and, despite the huge variety of finishes you can see here and on his website, they all have a definite style to them which is Bonvillian Design Studios signature. He describes his paint jobs as "intended to be out of this world bonkers. Traditional is not really our jam.". The fact that his guitars have also been played by such famous guitarists is an additional bonus for my love of them.

Before dipping the guitars, David runs through the paint with combs or objects that disrupt and distort the swirls.

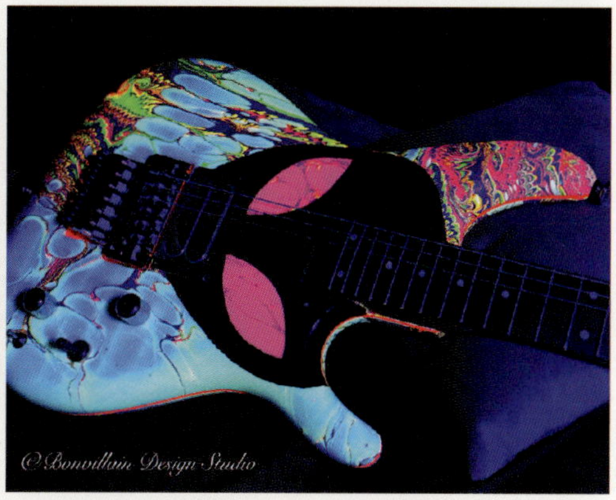

David's work is sometimes augmented with additional painting. I love how the glow in the dark paint complements the design.

Steve Vai and Kerry King are two of the artists to have guitars finished in David's work.

DEVIL &
DAUGHTERS
ERNIE BALL
CUSTOM GAUGE
10
ELECTRIC OR ACOUSTIC GUITAR STRING
1010

CHAPTER 1

UNDERSTANDING THE GUITAR

Before diving into customisation, it's crucial to understand the key features of a guitar. This knowledge will help you to make informed decisions and avoid potential pitfalls; there are parts that can be hacked off and parts that should not be changed. There are key features to how a guitar is assembled and set up that will dictate what can and can't be customised. As Scott from Bonehead Guitars, my cohost of The Guitar Builders Collective Chat podcast, often says, 'Guitarists know very little about how a guitar works' (though usually employing somewhat harsher language). Why do they need to know about neck angles and shielding? It doesn't necessarily help with playing. I didn't even know what intonation was until I customised my first guitar and then couldn't get it to tune up correctly, and I'd been playing for over a decade at that point. So, let's begin with a crash course in how a guitar is assembled from the perspective of someone wanting to repaint their guitar.

CHOICE OF WOOD

There is a current debate about tonewood and the concept that certain species of wood have qualities that are more beneficial to the overall sound of an instrument than others. For acoustic instruments this is undeniably true, but for electric guitars it's proven to have negligible, if any, effect on the output signal, most of which is dictated by strings and pickups, and then transformed through amps and processors. Wood choice can clearly affect the weight of the instrument and potentially the way the guitar feels and resonates against your body when playing. For anyone looking to customise a guitar, the wood choice can also affect the finish. Some of the processes in this book will use the grain of the wood as both a visual and textural feature. If changing the body shape, some woods are easier to work with. Some woods are more durable than others. For many of the techniques, the wood will be hidden under layers of paint or lacquer and will only make a difference in the preparation that goes into applying these.

In most cases, you will use the wood chosen by the guitar's manufacturer. However, some processes involve adding new wooden parts and for these I suggest sourcing local, second-hand, or renewable materials. A guitar made from an old butcher's block, a roof joist from your grandfather's house, or a piece of wood that's been in your shed for twenty years adds a unique story to your customisation.

PAINTS AND FINISHES

Paints and finishes are the primary focus of this book and I'll go into these in much more detail later. Suffice to say at this stage that you will not notice a difference in sound coming through the amp by changing the material used to finish your guitar. However, classic nitrocellulose laquer, modern polyurethane and wood oils feel different to the touch and I believe this can affect the playing; after all, a guitar is somewhat of a tactile instrument. If you're customising a guitar for a punk rock guitarist who likes to play topless, then a gloss polyurethane may stick to their sweaty skin in a way that a satin or oiled finish wouldn't (sorry if that picture is now stuck in your head). Lots of players prefer a satin or oiled finish for various reasons, although I've heard Mark, the guitar YouTuber from Pherotone Studios, say that he wishes all guitars had a nitrocellulose finish because he loves how it feels and it makes playing more pleasurable.

THE PARTS OF A GUITAR

Body

There is nothing about the shape of the body that affects the sounds that the guitar can make. The body simply must be long enough to fit the full length of the strings, deep enough to hold the pickups and electronics, and strong enough to resist warping due to the string tension. The rest is all a bonus, but often function and form are balanced in a great design. Any guitarist playing an odd-shaped guitar, or one with a light body, will have experienced neck dive (the neck pulling towards the ground) due to an unbalanced instrument. Locating where the strap attaches can help with this and the design of the shape may take this into account. Some guitars have arm bevels and curves that ergonomically contour to help with supporting the guitar better when playing. Some designs will take into account the positioning of the controls. When customising the body there are so many options, from changing the shape completely, to adding simple bevels and carves. In most cases, though, it's just a cool paint job that the guitars need.

Necks

Not all necks are the same. Some are bolt-on, others are set (glued) into place, while some are part of the same piece of wood as the body, or at least the middle length of the body, with wings stuck on either side. You can swap one bolt-on neck for another easily, but, in this book, I'm assuming you are customising a guitar with the neck that belongs on it. If you do change the neck, bear in mind there may be a difference in the heel size (the part that is clamped to the body by the bolts), both its width and its height. This means that a direct swap isn't always possible without some work done to adjust the neck pocket on the guitar body.

Necks come in different scale lengths, which affects the positioning of the frets. Even necks with the same scale length may have a different number of frets, causing them to sit differently in the neck pocket in relation to the bridge saddles. These variations can lead to intonation issues, preventing your guitar from being correctly in tune. I will delve deeper into scale length and intonation when explaining how to set up a guitar later in this chapter.

Truss rods

The truss rod runs through the guitar neck from the nut to the heel. It applies tension to the neck and can be adjusted to create a bow. If the neck bows upwards towards the strings, it will get in the way of the strings and stop them vibrating properly. Sometimes this is the cause of a string choking out when played. Normally a slight back bow to

A neck with the fretboard removed, revealing the truss rod.

the neck is required for everything to work properly. This adjustment often happens at the headstock end, via an opening which may or may not be concealed by a cover. Sometimes it's at the heel end via a visible wheel in the fretboard, or an opening that is accessible from the cavity where the pickups are. Adjusting this can require the pickguard to be removed. Annoyingly, some necks must be removed to make this adjustment.

Headstocks

This is the end of the neck where the strings attach. Some companies, such as Strandberg and Steinberger, are well known for producing guitars with headless necks. For some reason, whenever I post a video on YouTube about headless guitars, the haters join in the comments and complain. I actually quite like headless guitars, but there's less space to customise with cool paint jobs and logos.

Machine heads

The parts that grip and tighten the strings at the headstock to tune them can be known as tuners, gear heads, tuning pegs, tuning machines or, as I like to call them, machine heads. When I was first learning electric guitar, I had the tab book for Machine Head's *Burn My Eyes*, one of my favourite albums of the time – I remember it fondly whenever I use the term machine head. In most cases, you'll find the machine heads can go back in any order, although for a Les Paul style headstock you will have three per side of the headstock that point in a different way. It is pretty obvious which side is which, but you may want to mark the individual machine heads when you remove them, using a piece of masking tape.

A variety of guitar and bass machine heads.

When removing the machine heads, double-check the height of each shaft. Sometimes they are staggered, meaning that the one furthest from the nut is shorter. This allows for a larger break angle from the nut, which helps to prevent the string popping out of the nut. If this is the case, they need to be put back in the same order. This is not that common and is only needed on a headstock that is not angled back from the neck.

More expensive tuners may also have different gears on each machine head, resulting in the shafts rotating a different amount for the same turn of the knob. Graph Tech calls its system like this Ratio Balanced-Gear Tuning Technology. Each string is a different thickness; thicker strings are more sensitive to pitch change than thinner ones with each turn of a standard machine head. With the ratio systems one full turn of each knob is a change of pitch of around one tone when the correct machine head is assigned to the correct string. They are normally marked so that you can tell.

If you're thinking of upgrading machine heads you may find the holes in the headstock will need to be filled and redrilled if the shaft size is different, or the screws are in different places. I've found that most good machine heads come with a drill guide, or this is supplied on a website. I often swap out tuners like for like, but in a different finish to better fit the guitar customisation.

Bridges

There are so many types of bridges, but for this book it's not necessary to know about the differences, just what they have in common and how to remove your own one

Floating, or tremolo, bridges have a block that goes through the body. They can be found on guitars such as the Fender Stratocaster. The part of the bridge on top is either screwed down or held in place by being pulled against two pole pieces that are screwed into the body. The block will be connected to the body via springs that hook on to a claw that is screwed into the body.

Fixed bridges are simply screwed down. They can be found on guitars such as the Fender Telecaster. Some are top loading, meaning that the strings thread through the top of the bridge, over the saddles and along the neck to the machine heads. Some allow for the strings to go through the body and have a plate or ferrules on the back to stop the ball end of the string from passing all the way through the guitar.

A Tune-o-matic bridge is often in two parts, one where the saddles are and one where the end of the strings fit. It can be found on guitars such as the Gibson Les Paul. The parts both normally slip on to two studs. The studs are screwed into bushing that can be removed using a bolt with the same thread, long enough to screw into the body and for the bushing to ride up on.

when painting it. I won't be covering how to swap different bridge styles, but they are parts people often upgrade. I sometimes simply swap them for one of a different colour or finish, so as to match the customisation better. If you are swapping like for like it is still important to check the dimensions first, as you may need to plug some holes and drill new ones.

Scratchplate

A scratchplate's purpose is to stop the guitar body getting scratched during playing, but I see them as a mini canvas for customisation and there's a section on how to do that. They are sometimes referred to as pickguards, but I think that's a bit of a misnomer as they aren't made to guard your pick, but to guard against the damage your pick makes. Pedantic I know, but I like to be focused on the details!

ELECTRONICS AND SHIELDING

When customising a guitar using any of the techniques in this book it's going to be best to remove the electronics, so familiarising yourself with the basics is essential. There are countless options and combinations for how a guitar is wired in terms of the number and types of pickups, to the choice of controls that manipulate the output signal.

Pickups

Electromagnetic pickups (normally we drop the electromagnetic part) are connected to the guitar output jack, so that the signal they 'pick up' is sent to the amplifier. Pickups have a long coil of wire and magnets that work together to produce a magnetic field. When this field is disrupted by the plucked string, the mechanical energy of the string is transformed into electrical energy in the coil. This signal is sent via a guitar cable to the amplifier. There's no risk of electrocution, as the current in the amplifier doesn't feed back along the cable into the guitar and a pickup is unlikely to produce more than 1V. Some pickups are active, meaning that they are powered by an onboard battery (normally 9V).

These pickups are connected to the scratchplate, which has been removed to take the pickups out.

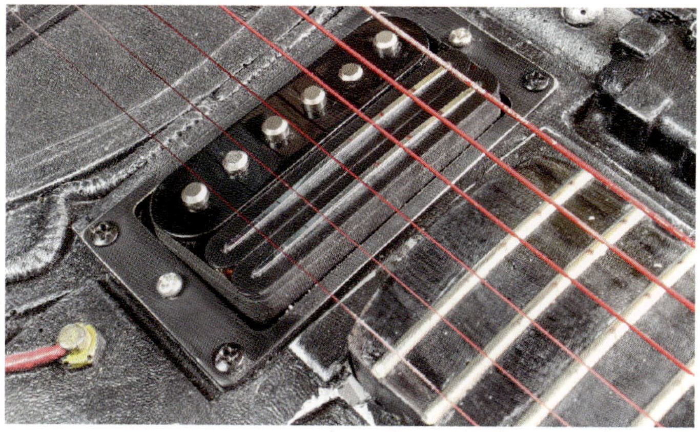

A pickup connected to a pickup surround, which is in turn screwed to the body.

A pickup directly mounted to the guitar body with screws.

Volume and tone-control circuits

In the guitar there will be some potentiometers and switches that manipulate the signal. There may be one master volume and tone, or one for each pickup, or a combination. These will all be linked together by wires that ground them.

Connected to the pickups is likely to be a switch that controls which pickups are in use at any one time. The style of the switch will vary in function (three-way and five-way selections being most common). There will also be an output jack connected to the circuit.

You will most likely find one or two additional wires coming from the back of one of the pots too; these are there to help with grounding. One will link to the bridge, either through a long drilled hole in the body that emerges under a screwed-down fixed bridge (where the bare end of the wire can make contact with the bridge), through to a bushing in the case of a Tune-o-matic style bridge, or soldered to the claw of a tremolo style bridge. The other wire is an optional one that most guitars won't have – it screws down to the cavity wall to connect the cavity shielding to the circuit.

The circuit is housed in a cavity that will be accessed either via a backplate that can be removed such as on a Gibson Les Paul, or hidden under the scratchplate in guitars such as the Fender Stratocaster. Some guitars, such as the Fender Telecaster, have their own control cavity plate. Normally the cavity is shielded either with some sort of tape, aluminium being a common choice, or painted with a specialised conductive paint. I prefer the latter.

A volume and tone circuit attached directly to the scratchplate of a Stratocaster.

This Les Paul has a separate cover for the control switch. The wires thread through to the control cavity via the pickup cavities.

KNOBS

I often change the knobs to ones that best match and complement the look of the customisation. This can be as simple as changing the colour while retaining the style associated with the guitar, but often I swap for a whole new look. There are lots of companies that sell knobs and often a search for potentiometer knobs online will come up with some good options, including those that aren't made specifically for guitars. Just double-check the diameter of the top of the potentiometer shaft when removing the current ones to make sure that the new ones will fit. 6mm or 6.35mm are common. The type of shaft will also have an impact on the knob choice.

Some shafts have a split in them; this allows for a push-on knob to fit securely. You can put a screw knob on, but the screw may damage the teeth and shaft.

If the shaft is solid and smooth you can use a knob with a screw. A push-on may fit, but will likely slip.

Knurled shafts fit the push-on knobs. You can get them with 18 or 36 teeth to match the knobs, but I find you can push a knob on to either.

If your pot has a D-shaped shaft tip it will need a knob with a matching D-hole, although a screw knob can lock in place if the screw is long enough.

SCREWS AND OTHER HARDWARE

Screws can easily be swapped for the same size in different colours, or for new ones if you're working on a used guitar. It would be a shame for a brand-new paint job to have old rusty screws unless that was a deliberate aesthetic choice. Many companies sell sets of screws for one complete guitar in packs, I've put a list of suppliers at the end of this book.

SETTING UP A GUITAR

I'm assuming that the guitar you are customising plays well and the electronics work; that you're simply customising it in some way, not repairing it. If you're not happy with any elements before you take the guitar apart, the chances are there will still be issues once you have completed your customisation magic and reassembled the guitar. For this reason, it's worth giving the guitar a full set-up to make sure it plays well before starting any work.

Following are five simple stages to cover a basic beginner set-up. You will find that you may have to repeat stages, as they can affect each other. The first time you do this it is easier to have the guitar lying flat on a soft surface that won't damage the body, but once you know what you are doing everything should be set up in the playing position. I will refer to the strings as the low string for the thickest bass string (the low E in standard tuning), and the high string for the thinnest treble one (high E in standard tuning).

Tuning

Begin with the guitar tuned so that the open, unfretted strings are pitched to your normal tuning. If you always play with an alternative to standard tuning, tune like that now.

Neck relief

Put a capo on the first fret and with your finger hold down the low string on the fret where the neck meets the body. This eliminates the nut and nut slot height from this test, so that you are measuring just the length of the neck that can flex. Use a feeler gauge to check the gap between the top of the seventh fret (roughly the halfway point between your finger and the capo) and the bottom of the low string – you want a gap of 0.254mm. Turning the truss rod will adjust this gap (counterclockwise to increase it). Repeat for the high string. This gap, relief or bow of the neck, is not a set gap. Some guitars and guitarists may require or prefer a bigger bow than others. As you learn what you like, you may end up using a different feeler gauge for a different sized gap. Remove the capo and retune your guitar after this stage.

Measuring the bow at the seventh fret using a feeler gauge.

String height

Different bridges and saddles work in different ways, but they essentially all do the same two things, which is to adjust the height of the strings from the guitar body and the length of the string between the nut and the saddle. The string height is also referred to as the action of the guitar. Shredders often want a low action, whereas slide players may prefer it high.

Adjust the string height so that the gap between the bottom of the low string and the top of the twelfth fret is 1.75mm. The height of the high string above the twelfth fret should be 1.25mm. I tend to adjust the strings so that

Measuring the string height.

the lowest two are 1.75mm, the next two are 1.5mm and the highest two are 1.25mm. There is no correct height for this, it's a personal preference which is often dictated by playing style. My suggested heights would be very average, neither a low nor high action. For bass, I aim for 2.5mm on the lowest string and 1.5mm on the highest. Play around until you know what you like. Don't forget to tune up again before proceeding with the set-up.

Intonation

To understand intonation, you need to know two things – how the length of the guitar strings and the spacing of the frets affect the tuning. The length of the string is measured from where it leaves the nut to where it touches the saddle, that is, the length of string that can vibrate when you pluck it. The space between frets gets smaller as you progress up the fret board. The twelfth fret is halfway along the length of the string length. When you play a note at the twelfth fret it is an octave higher than playing the same string unfretted. To put it in simple terms, this is because the note raises an octave as the string length halves. So halfway between the twelfth fret and the saddle is where the twenty fourth fret sits, which is the next octave. If your string is the wrong length, the frets simply won't produce the correct notes and will get further out of tune as you move up the fretboard.

FRET BUZZ AND CHOKING OUT

Fret, or string, buzz comes from the string lightly vibrating against a fret when plucked. A note choking out is when it doesn't ring for long after playing, or cuts off if bent. It may be something that can be fixed by adjusting the truss rod and/or the string height. A bigger back bow and a higher string height could eliminate these problems, as both move the strings away from the frets. Often, it's a bit of back and forth adjusting the saddles and the truss rod to eliminate the problem. If you are left with a guitar that doesn't suit your playing style due to the new action being too high, then you may need a repair. It's possible that a fret or frets may have come unseated or now be too high, but this book doesn't cover repairs. Just remember that a bit of string buzz isn't necessarily a problem, as it's not always transferred to the sound coming from the amp.

Adjusting the saddle position on a Stratocaster or Telecaster style bridge. Loosen the string first, so that you can raise the saddle whilst doing this and avoid scratching the bridge plate.

The saddle on a Les Paul is adjusted with these screws. This bridge doesn't have a stop bar and is known as a wrap-around bridge because the strings are attached to the underside instead of the stop bar.

You will have inferred from the above that the combination of string length and fret position is crucial to keeping your guitar in tune at every possible note. If only it were as simple as correctly placing the saddles when the guitar was built. The thickness or gauge of string actually affects this, so if you are playing with nines on your guitar (referring to a string set where the top string is 0.009in in diameter) the saddles will need to be in a slightly different place to if you are playing with twelves (0.012in in diameter).

The easiest way to check that the intonation is correct is to play an open string, then play the same string at the twelfth fret and compare the notes with a good electric tuner. If your fretted note is sharp, you need a longer string length; if it's flat, you need a shorter string length. The string length is adjusted by moving the saddle. To help me know which way to move them, I created the useful mnemonic: 'flat forwards, sharp back'.

Pickup height

The height of the pickups does affect the output; the closer they are to the strings, the louder the output is going to be. Often a pickup is angled so that the side under the low strings is a bit lower to compensate for the signal being stronger there. Play each string in turn, held down at the very last fret to make sure that the string isn't touching the pickup when you play. Then focus on one pickup only via the selector switch and play the high and low strings. Check that the sound coming through the amp is at the same level for both and compensate by raising or lowering the pickup height at the relevant side accordingly (raising it will bring it closer to the string and make the signal louder). Do this for all pickups. Then compare each pickup with the others and adjust the height so they are balanced. Now double-check that the pickups and strings are not interfering with each other.

BALANCING THE PICKUP OUTPUT

You may actually want one pickup to be louder than the others, perhaps if you switch to that one for solos. On my bass guitars I prefer the high string output to be louder because when I'm playing, I often don't play those strings as hard – testing the levels out by actually playing is the best solution. Try doing this with your amp at the volume settings you like. Small differences in volume output may be amplified as you increase the amp volume.

DO NOT CUSTOMISE YOUR GUITAR IF IT IS BROKEN

If you have a bigger problem, such as an issue with the nut, worn frets, or faulty pickups, it's worth getting that sorted now. In most cases things can be replaced easily. You may want to attempt the repair yourself, or take the guitar to a guitar shop or luthier. A good luthier can even fix problems like a warped neck. However, I'm a big fan of learning how to fix things yourself, so my YouTube channel is partly focused on giving people the skills and confidence to carry out these more minor repairs and fixes.

SCALE LENGTH

You may have heard the term scale length. Some people think it refers to the length of the strings, but, as you now know, this can vary slightly depending on the thickness of the strings. Technically, the scale length is the distance from the nut to the twelfth fret multiplied by two. This is, in theory, the distance from the nut to the saddle. Traditionally, it's measured in inches, with two common scale lengths being 25.5in on a Fender Stratocaster and 24.75in on a Gibson Les Paul.

To the ears of many, these instruments each have a unique sound, for many reasons including scale length. Longer scale lengths generally have a brighter, tighter sound due to the higher tension in the strings when compared to a shorter scale length with the same strings. With less tension comes a warmer tone and an ease to bending. A shorter scale length means closer together frets, which may be preferred by some.

Measuring the distance from the nut to the twelfth fret.

DISMANTLING A GUITAR

Dismantling a guitar for customisation is straightforward. While tools and steps may vary by model, the basics are the same. You will benefit from writing down some details for easier reassembly, which are highlighted below. It is also helpful to read about reassembling a guitar before starting. It's a good idea to document wire connections before resoldering.

I recommend putting all the parts into something as you remove them. I use baggies of different sizes. This separates the parts and offers a bit of protection from scratching when I then put everything into boxes.

Measure, measure, record and label

The key elements to take note of now are those that can easily be changed. I recommend taking multiple photos of these and writing down measurements (although I often just photograph them with a ruler next to them). Essentially, you need to record the placement of all the parts that move.

Here is a checklist:

* string height (at twelfth fret for all strings)
* saddle height and position (measure each if you can, although you may not have to alter this at all if you can remove the bridge in one piece)
* pickup height (it may be easier to measure the distance on each side from the high and low strings)
* pickups (label the back so you know which position and which way round they go)
* machine head order (if it matters)
* wiring (specifically the positioning of the potentiometers if they are removed and any wires you cut).

Removing the strings

Some people clip their strings off, but I prefer the less violent method of unstringing them. Sometimes it is necessary to clip the ends off where they have been bent in the machine heads. I keep the strings because, when I reassemble, I often first do it with the used strings. This way, I can make sure that everything lines up properly. Occasionally, I end up taking the guitar apart and doing some additional work, so it saves using new strings until the guitar is ready to go.

Label your potentiometers with a marker or masking tape and take a photo before removing them.

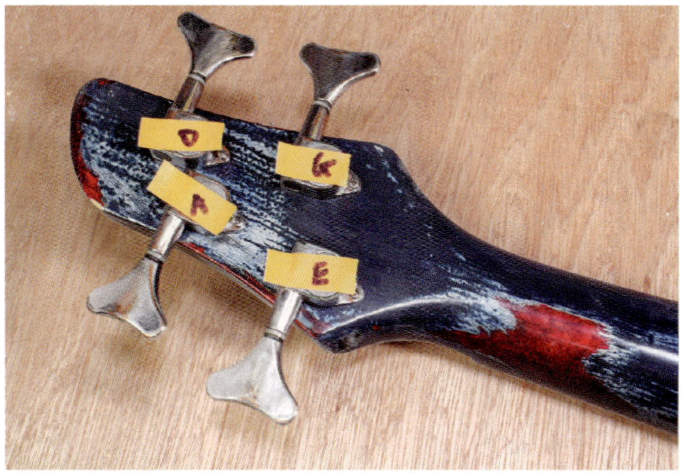

Put a small tab of masking tape on each machine head and label it with the string that goes on it.

Removing the neck

If you can remove the neck, that should be done next to make everything more compact. Partly loosen each screw in turn, then go back round and remove them. Do this without the strings on. Always remove the neck with the guitar on its back just in case there is a shim in the neck. Sometimes these fit the entire neck pocket, but often they are a small piece of material that runs the width of the pocket and pushed against the rear end of it. I've seen them made from thin wood veneer, business cards and food packaging.

A NOTE ON SHIMS

Shims adjust the neck angle to ensure that the strings run parallel with the neck, preventing string buzz and choking out, and achieving the correct action. While ideally unnecessary, shims are sometimes needed, especially for guitars with raised bridges like Tune-o-matics, where the neck must be angled to the body.

I did not mention shims in the set-up section because I'm assuming you have a guitar where this will have been sorted out at the build stage. If you are having issues with fret buzz and so on, you can try installing one, but it's too advanced a repair to cover in this book.

Removing hardware

All of the hardware should be easily removable simply by unscrewing it. Exceptions for certain types of bridges and how to remove their pole pieces and bushing were covered in the bridge section earlier in the chapter.

Removing the circuitry

Keep as much of the circuit connected as possible. If you unscrew the jack socket from the cover that holds it in place, you can often thread it back into the cavity and pop the whole thing out connected.

Where you must cut wires, for example the pickups, take photos first, then cut the wire close to the potentiometer end. You could desolder here, but often leaving a bit of wire helps with later matching up, especially if the wires are colour-coded. You could also tag them.

Unless you plan to paint the scratchplate or pickup surround, the pickup and wiring can be left attached. If there is a glued or taped-down shielding in the cavity, remove it instead of painting over it.

The middle tuning peg bushing is still in place on this headstock – you can see the bottom edge of it from this rear angle. It can normally be lightly tapped out from behind. Work around the bushing evenly. I use a nail punch to do it, but an old slotted screwdriver will do the job.

TAKING MEASUREMENTS

A good ruler really helps here, preferably one where the measurement scale goes right to the very end, rather than one where there is a gap before the markings start. The cheap guitar gauge shown in the photo works well, but I prefer a 15cm ruler with markings along both lengths (as opposed to centimetres on one side and inches on the other). The top ruler is a centre-finding ruler, where the numbers extend out from the middle in both directions; it is useful for lining parts up.

ASSEMBLING A GUITAR

Once you have taken a guitar apart, reassembly is straightforward. I suggest working in the following order:

1. Start with adding the strap pins back on the body. (I do this first as I once returned a guitar to a client and I'd forgotten to put them back on!)
2. Put all the electronics either back into the body, or attach to the scratchplate. If you've made a custom scratchplate, don't screw it in place yet. Make sure that any ground wires are threaded through to where the bridge goes.
3. Reattach the bridge.
4. Fit all the machine heads and related hardware to the headstock. Leave the string trees until the guitar is strung up, so that you can confirm they are in the correct place.
5. Put the neck into the neck pocket and ensure it fits snugly. If paint has got into the pocket during the customisation process or on the side of the neck heel, you may need to widen the pocket slightly with sandpaper. Do this in small passes and check-fit each time. Tighten the screws at the back one at a time halfway, so that the neck is held in place but potentially may have some give if the pocket fit is a bit wide.
6. Using string as a stand-in for the highest and lowest guitar strings, you can confirm that the neck is straight. If it isn't, you will need to push it into place and hold it whilst tightening the screws. You may have to sand the neck pocket sides slightly if there is a problem. Once satisfied, tighten the screws.
7. If you've made a new scratchplate, you can use the string as a guide; it should pass over the outer poles of the pickups. Adjust the scratchplate if necessary, drill pilot holes and screw down. If using an existing scratchplate, or the pickups are directly mounted in the body, they should be fine in their original position.
8. Screw in any remaining hardware except the truss rod cover, which goes on after the set-up.
9. Put the strings on, but not to full tension yet. Check that everything looks in line and return the saddles to their original place and height that you noted earlier. This is the same with any parts, such as the bridge, which can be adjusted.
10. Now tune up and go through the set-up procedure.

Use string to represent the highest and lowest guitar strings. Run it from the machine head along the neck, over the relevant saddle, through the bridge, back over the other saddle and back along the neck to the machine heads.

SHIELDING

Cavity shielding helps to reduce unwanted noise and hum in the guitar. I prefer to use shielding paint, which is essentially carbon black or graphite suspended in a paint, creating a conductive surface when painted on. You can also use a copper or aluminium tape. Most tapes have a glue that isn't conductive, so in order to ensure a surface that is connected into one continuous conductive area fold a piece in half and run it along the whole length, so that part of the metal of this strip is touching all others.

You will need a small tab of paint or tape that extends from the cavities to the body so that it can make contact with the scratchplate or control plate covering the cavity. The cover will also need to be shielded if it isn't metal; use tape for this purpose.

A strip of copper tape connects all of the aluminium strips together. I've used different tape only to help visually illustrate the process. Note the tabs overlapping the edges.

narex 20 8110 70

CHAPTER 2

PREPARATION

Any of the techniques in this book can be used on any electric guitar. Perhaps it's your own guitar, or a friend's, or maybe you are buying a guitar especially. If buying a guitar to experiment on, I suggest a good budget guitar over a second-hand one. Budget guitars can often be greatly improved with a good set-up. Second-hand guitars can seem like a bargain, but the ones I've bought on eBay often require a complete fret job, have badly damaged parts, or parts that need replacing.

I'm a big fan of kit guitars, I use two from The Guitar Fabrik in this book. They are guitars already dismantled and stripped of paint and ready to go.

Another option is to 3D-print some bodies for testing process on. This is a relatively cheap option if you have a 3D printer. I printed two bodies for this book from Tasmaniak Guitars, using a neck and hardware I had bought in. There's no reason I can't keep printing and painting bodies to swap the parts on to.

Rolls of aluminium oxide sandpaper. There are other types of sandpaper, but this is my preferred choice for sanding bare wood. I keep in stock 60, 180, 220 and 280 grit.

SANDING TOOLS

The processes throughout this book involve sanding. In most cases there are options as to how you sand, but some techniques require specific tools and types of sanding paper. Sandpaper comes in grades measured by the grit – the lower the numbers, the larger the abrasive particles. The photos show the three main types that I use.

I recently changed to using Abranet over wet & dry paper for most finishing of painted and lacquered surfaces, as it is less messy and also extremely effective.

Wet & dry paper is ideal for wet sanding, where debris is washed away whilst sanding and the paper is less prone to clogging. It can be used on any painted finish. I keep in stock 280, 320, 400, 600, 800 and 1000 grit.

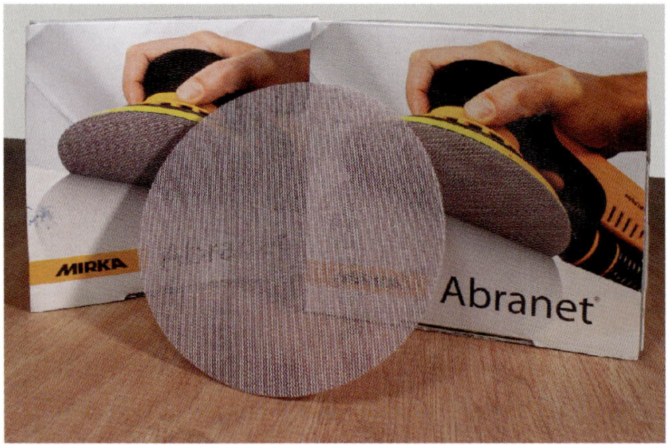

Abranet is a net-backed material designed for dust-free dry sanding. Along with Assilex, 3M Xtract and Cubitron, these modern sanding papers have changed the way I finish guitars.

Hard-backed sanding blocks. The yellow ones have a hook and loop system to hold matching backed sanding sheets. Paper is simply held in place on the cork blocks. The others bite into strips of paper. At the back are 3D-printed sanding sticks that paper is attached to with double-sided tape.

Soft-backed foam pads and blocks in different grits, indicated by their colour. A foam interface for the yellow block allows some flexibility in the paper attached to it. Note the stationery eraser, which is good for wrapping small bits of paper round.

Regular vacuuming is required to remove the build-up of dust in the Abranet surface. Wet & dry is still needed for some finishes, though, and is a cheaper option that still works really well.

There will be times when you need to use the paper with a hard-backed surface to ensure that you achieve a flat finish. In some situations, such as on guitar body curves and around edges, you will need a soft back to your sanding. You can use the sheets of paper on their own, or attach them to hard-backed blocks with a sponge interface. I prefer to use foam sanding pads and blocks, where the surface of the pad itself is abrasive.

I use a lot of hook and loop sanding sheets. They attach to sanding blocks and, most importantly, a random orbital sander. Over the years I've used various palm and mouse sanders, but a random orbital one is by far the most efficient way to sand back large areas with minimal sanding marks. When used with a vacuum, the efficiency increases, especially with Abranet or 3M Xtract papers.

A random orbital sander rotates and vibrates the sanding pad in an elliptical pattern, ensuring that no single part of the abrasive pad follows the same path twice.

PERSONAL PROTECTIVE EQUIPMENT

The dust from woods and especially from the paint you will be sanding back is hazardous to health. Always take precautions. A mask with a P3 filter is ideal for protecting against dust particles. Use an extractor wherever possible when sanding, especially with power tools and bench machinery. An air filter is a good addition to a workshop.

CLEANING SURFACES

It is essential that as you move from one stage of the customisation process to the next all dust and particles are cleaned from the guitar. Using a damp cloth isn't ideal, as water can be absorbed into the wood and take time to dry out. Instead, use something that evaporates quickly. Denatured alcohol is a common choice, as are isopropyl alcohol, naphtha and my miracle cleaning solution (*see* Tip Box). I also recommend the use of tack cloths, sticky cloths designed for picking up loose dust, dirt and lint from surfaces before painting.

Removing stickers

There's a good chance that a second-hand guitar is going to have stickers on it. Perhaps it's from a charity shop, like the guitar I'm using here (picked up for a bargain £5), or was covered in stickers by a punk. The laws of averages mean that many of the people reading this book will have done it. For tips on putting them on, there is a section later in the book, but for now we'll focus on how to remove them safely and cleanly (*see* the series of photos).

DANIEL'S MIRACLE CLEANING SOLUTION

A 1:1 mix of distilled vinegar and methylated spirits is great for cleaning the surfaces of dirty instruments and bare wood. I learnt this trick from person who taught me how to French polish; he was a furniture restorer and had used it for many years.

This is a window scraper, also sold for scraping ceramic hobs. Although good for scraping off large stickers, it can easily scratch the guitar. I use them to start the process, but don't worry about getting everything off. Alternatively, pull off what you can buy hand with no risk of damage to the guitar.

The meths-vinegar mix is great to use from the start, or after scraping off big stickers.

Hold a paper towel soaked in the solution over the sticker until it is wet through.

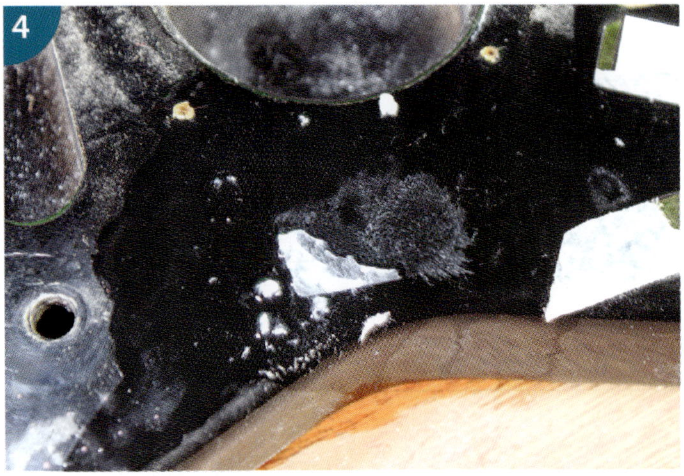

Most of the sticker will peel away, but a sticky residue will be left.

There will still be a smear left behind.

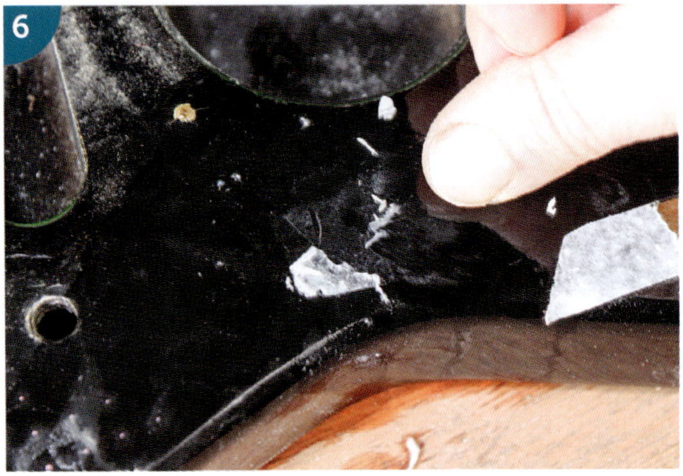

Rolling you thumb over the residue helps to pull it off.

A small amount of lighter fluid rubbed over the surface will remove the smear.

AN ALTERNATIVE

An alternative to lighter fluid is acetone. It's possibly even more effective and I use it sometimes in place of the meths-vinegar mix. However, it is a more dangerous substance, so only buy some if you plan to use it for other purposes too.

PREPPING A BODY FOR OVERSPRAY

There's no reason to strip back a guitar completely to repaint it if the body is in a good shape after a clean. Simply sand it all over with 600-grit paper. Use a block-backed paper to achieve a flat surface and a foam-backed one for the curves and contours. Make sure there are no visible scratches, dents or dings left in the surface. Most can be sanded away; any that can't need to be filled with the methods covered later.

You can see on this body how some wood has been revealed where I have sanded through the paint. This isn't a problem, as everything will be covered by the new finish.

DEALING WITH DENTS AND DINGS

If the body has dents and dings in it, some of these can be removed at this stage with sanding, but also easily missed. This example illustrates such a case, but also lets you know not to worry. These can be fixed in the priming stages explained later.

1 The corner has some paint chipped away and there are small chips and dents around it. These will show up when sprayed.

2 By sanding it smooth to the touch, the hard edges of chipped paint or dents appear to have been removed.

3 The primer coat has highlighted the dents; sanding alone didn't remove them.

4 I have sanded the top and point smooth, leaving the small dents on the closest edge.

5 A second coat of primer conceals the sanded area this time, but the dents I left are still visible.

6 With the colour added the dents ruin the finish, but there is no evidence of the ones I sanded.

STRIPPING A GUITAR

Some paints are not compatible with each other. This will be covered in the paint section later in the book. If you have any worries about the interaction between your new paint and the old paint, it will be best to strip the body completely. I would not advise the use of chemical strippers to remove the paint. I've tried a few different makes on a number of guitars and usually they have little or no effect because they are not designed for the types of paint that guitars are finished with.

I suggest you read the sections on how to finish the guitar before stripping off the paint because you will then have a better understanding of what you are removing. Sometimes the finish seems to peel away, but there's still a clear finish that was used to seal the wood. This will have to go if you want to stain the wood. When I heat-strip, the top colour coat will often pull away from the sealer easily; if I'm just repainting, I often leave that sealer coat. When you sand the finish off, it is normally visually obvious as you sand through the sealer and reach the unfinished wood surface.

The heat-gun method

The heat-gun method should always be your first point of call because on some occasions it works so well – the finish peels away like spreading butter and you're left with a clean, unscratched surface. However, most of the time this isn't the case. Instead, it will be the start of the process, with sanding to finish. The key is knowing when to stop using the heat-gun method and to swap.

It is important to wear heat-protection gloves because the surface of the guitar and the tools get hot. I once removed a finish from a Fender Telecaster that had been refinished sometime in the 1970s and it smelt pretty bad. Since then, I always wear a mask because if you don't know what the finish is you can't be sure that any fumes that come off are safe.

Make sure your gun isn't so hot that it burns the surface, causing blisters and discolouration. If there is a red glow on the paint from the gun, it's too hot. They key is to keep moving around a small area at a time, heating the surface and the scraper. Using a finger to bend the scraper helps and avoids scratching the surface.

Take the heat away and focus on the scraping.

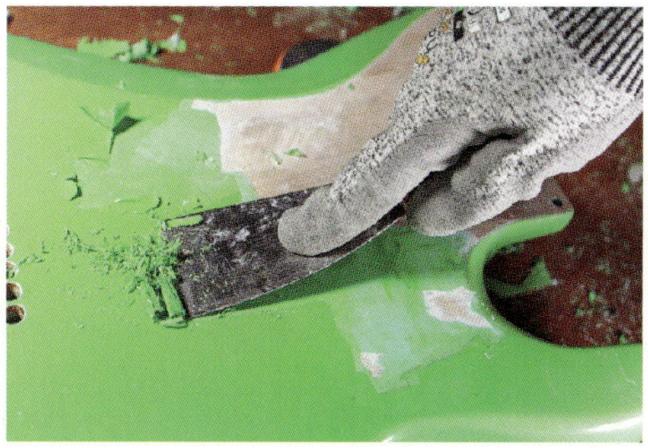

If you can get the scraper under the paint, you may be able to lift off larger areas.

Sometimes there may only be small flakes coming away.

If wood is chipping or flaking away, stop immediately so as to avoid marks in the wood.

Holding the scraper vertically may remove smaller stubborn pieces.

As well as the green finish, the sealer layer is coming away.

This guitar is a great example of when it's time to swap to sanding the finish away. Let me highlight a few things you should look out for.

Scraping has revealed an area of the guitar that was previous filled. The surface here is slightly recessed. The back will need a sand to get a smooth finish.

This join appeared to be getting larger with the heat. It may just look bigger from the paint being removed, but I didn't want to risk it.

Here you can see the green and the sealer layer clearly. The wood is chipping as it is revealed.

Some blistering is happening.

The top layers of paint are peeling off nicely, but lower ones aren't.

The wood has been burnt by the heat gun.

This is just some of the scrapings of finish removed from the guitar, evidence as to why a mask is needed.

Sanding off a finish

Some guitars have thin finishes, while others have thick ones. Some have multiple layers of different colours, while others have clear sealer or coloured primer. It's always a surprise. Sanding is messy and time-consuming, so I prefer to use bench-top machinery to work through the finish more quickly. However, you must be careful not to sand so much that the guitar starts to alter its shape. Subtle curved edges can be removed by the machines and need to be reshaped by hand. You will always need to finish by hand to ensure that all scratches are removed and the surfaces blend well from one edge to another.

It's important to know when to move from bench-top equipment to handheld powered tools, to doing it by hand, with each step being potentially less aggressive than the last.

Bench-top belt sanders are great for the flat surface of a guitar, but don't stay in one place too long or there will be an obvious mark.

An oscillating spindle sander is a great tool when it comes to stripping the edges of a guitar. You can buy handheld versions too.

Notice the cushioned pad on the random orbital sander that allows it to contour to the body shape.

I remove the pad for flat areas to ensure a solid, even backing.

After using mechanical sanding tools there will be a lot to finish by hand.

The belt sander has revealed the wood; the two colours indicate a sealer coat. Use the colour as a guide to get an even finish.

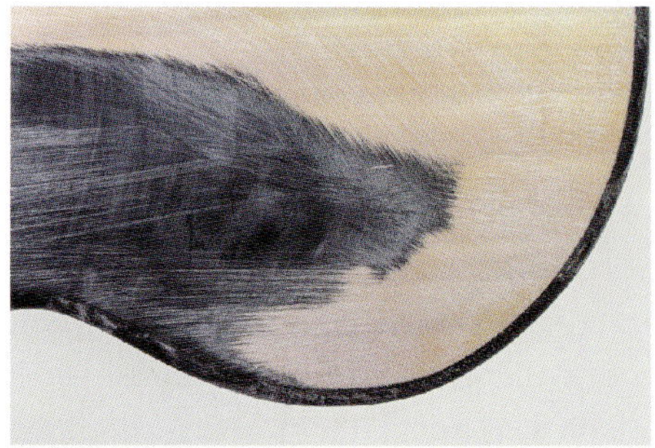

The white dust in scratches reveals that there is a clear sealer layer to be removed under the black.

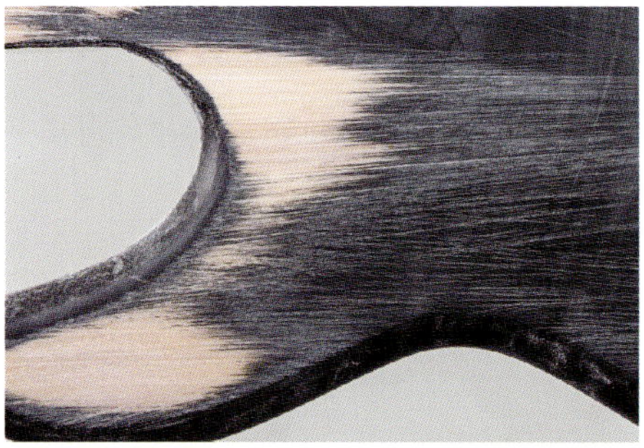

This close-up helps to show how the smooth transition from back to sides has been lost in the sanding process.

You can see how aggressive the scratches are from the belt sander. Moving to the handheld random orbital sander is the next step.

The oscillating sander has left marks along the edge of the guitar that need to be removed by hand.

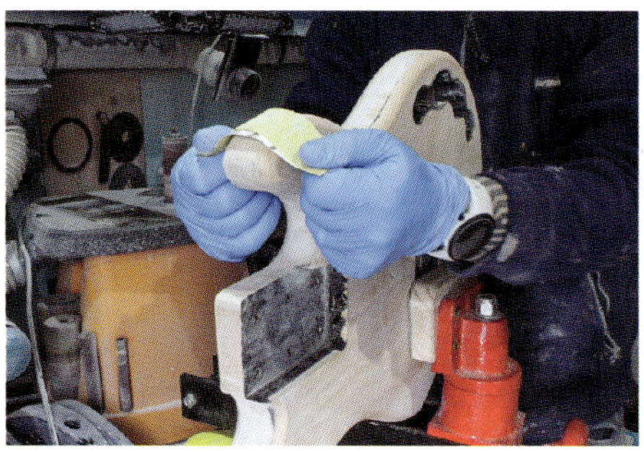

Start with 180-grit paper. Pull the paper over each side and move left and right perpendicular to the body length.

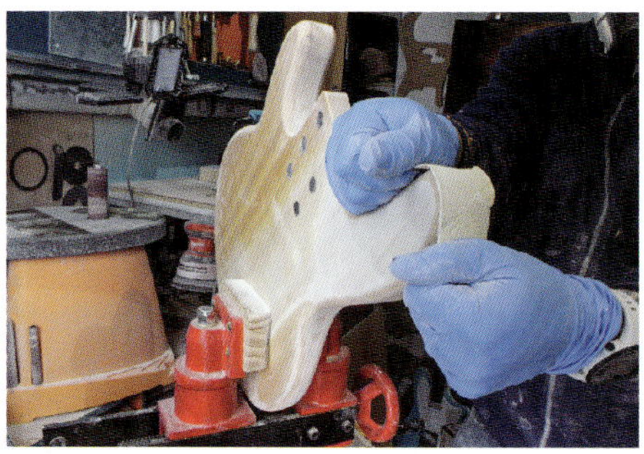

Pull the paper up and down to follow the curve horn.

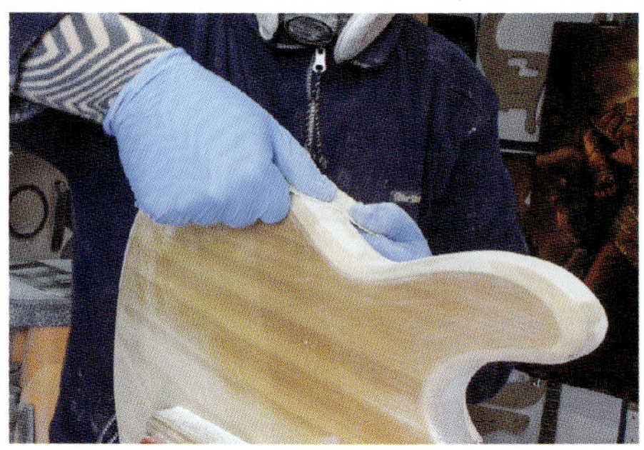

I prefer using my thumb to hold the paper flat whilst moving back and forth along the body. A small hard sanding block will work too.

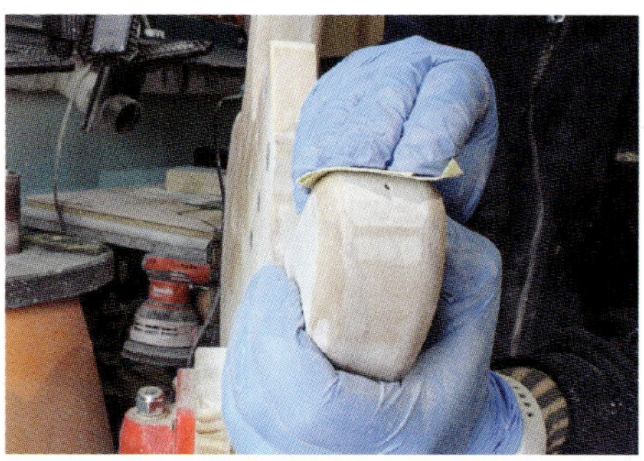

The advantage of using fingers is being able to form the paper around the contours.

With fingers apart, push the paper around the curve transition.

HEALTH AND SAFETY

* Sanding is a very dusty process. I have an extractor attached to all my powered sanders. It not only removes dust from the air, but can improve the efficiency of the machines. It's a great upgrade if you can add a shop vac to your set-up.
* Always follow the safety guidelines in the machines' manuals.
* Wear a mask with a P3 filter. Wood dust and the particles from the finishes are dangerous.

CHOICE OF PAPER GRADES

* At the end of this process, you are aiming for a smooth finish with no visible sanding marks. Check that all the edges are smooth and transition well from top to side to back, and that there is no unevenness caused by the machine sanders. A 400-grit finish is all you need to prep for the painting.
* To remove a finish, 180 grit on the electric sanders will do the job. Start with small areas for a short amount of time to see how much the machine is removing – some are more aggressive than others.
* Use a random orbital sander with 180, 220 and 320 grit on the front and back of the guitar to remove machine marks and do most of the prep work. Finish by hand with 400 grit on a hard-backed block.

FILLING HOLES

There may be some changes you plan to make to the guitar. If you're swapping the scratchplate, check now if the holes match the existing one; if not, you will need to fill them. If you're removing a tremolo system and adding a hard tail bridge, the old bridge cavity will need to be filled. This is the time to fill everything.

Hiding screw holes

The method shown in the photos is simple, but it hides the holes well. Make sure to finish with sandpaper to ensure a smooth surface.

Fill the holes with a cyanoacrylate glue. I prefer one with a medium viscosity, such as O3a. Then push a cocktail stick into the hole. Cut off the tapered end first.

When dry, cut the stick using nippers, a flush-cut saw, or a scalpel.

To ensure that the hole is fully sealed, drop on some more cyanoacrylate glue.

Work the glue into the hole, using the scalpel edge.

Filling cavities

This back cavity isn't required, so it needs to be filled. The best way is with wood so that it's solid. Luckily, the main part of the cavity is the same depth as the thickness of the plywood I'm using. If the plywood were too thick it could still plug the hole, then be sanded back, or the wood in the cavity could be layered up if it were too thin. Ideally, though, the plug should be as close to the hole size as possible.

This cavity passes through the body at one end. The best option is to plug the whole cavity at the depth of the larger area, then turn over and plug from the other side.

Tape over the cavity, then cut the shape out directly with a scalpel. You may need to double-layer the tape at right angles if it's thin.

Stick the cut-out on to the wood that the plug is being made from. Use the tape as a cutting and shaping guide.

Don't push it all the way in until you have added wood glue underneath.

Once the plug is glued in, fill the gaps with wood or car body filler.

Sand back once the glue is dry. The filler will probably be a much quicker set time.

In this case, I flipped the body and repeated on the other side. I needed a few pieces of ply to fill the depth of this hole.

Once sanded back, you can see that the wood only fills the centre of the cavity; the rounded ends are filled with filler.

MAKING HOLES

This is also the best time to make new holes and routs. Although it can be done once the guitar is painted, the advantage of routing now is that there's no risk of chipping paint. Additionally, the new finish can go over the edge of the rout, making a stronger edge finish for the future.

This cavity is for three single-coil pickups; I will be converting this to hold humbuckers so a swimming-pool cavity is needed (that is, one big rectangle).

The super glue and masking-tape trick works perfectly here. *See* the tip box for more details.

Remember when routing to remove wood in shallow passes, rather than all in one go. Follow your router safety guide.

Even with a dust extractor this is a messy process. Always wear a mask and goggles.

THE MASKING-TAPE TEMPLATE HOLD-DOWN TRICK

This simple trick makes it possible to hold a template down without drilling into the body, or using clamps that get in the way of the router. I use it for routing guides in situations like this and for holding scratchplate templates in place, as you'll see later in the book. Ensure that your router base is big enough so that you can run around the cavity without it falling in. Ideally, it should touch two sides of the guide at all times, but if you have a steady hand one side may do.

Take four straight edges of wood to use as guides for the router.

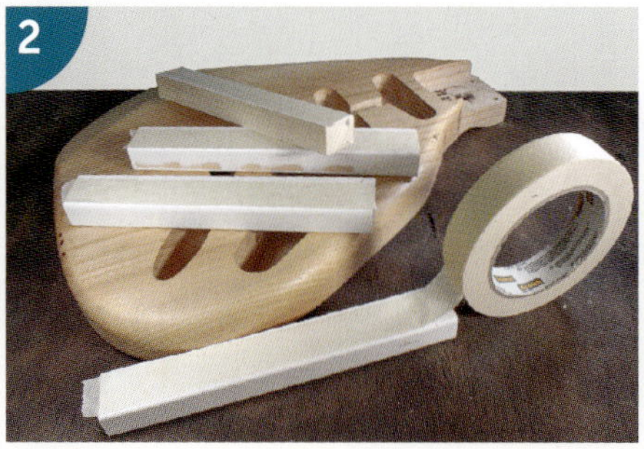

Apply masking tape along the base of the straight edge.

Put tape on the matching part of the guitar body.

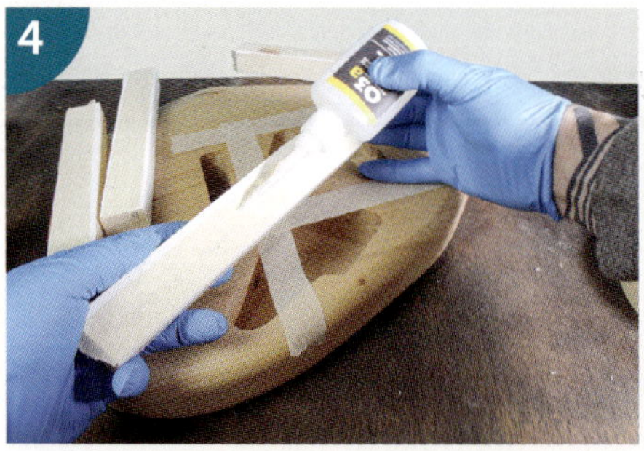

Run cyanoacrylate glue along the tape on the straight edge. I use medium or thick.

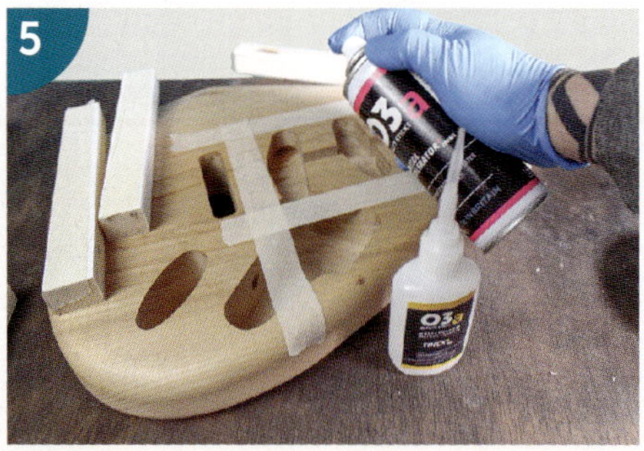

Spray the body with CA kicker and place the guide.

This pattern ensures a good rectangle whilst not having to cut all the pieces to size.

Once you have finished routing the guides pull away from the body, sometimes leaving the tape which can then be removed easily.

I have a 3D-printed guide that slides to the right size. I stick it down in the same way.

A scratchplate router template stuck down to a vinyl record using the same technique. Trim the visible tape before using the router.

BODY-FILLER COATING

I've never seen anyone else use this process, but I find it's a good way to seal any filled cavities to ensure that they won't be a problem at the painting stage. With certain finishes such as nitrocellulose, which lays very thinly with each coat, the edges of the plugged area can begin to show over time. Certain finishes can highlight the most minute change in the surface. Metallics, chameleon paints and crackle finishes are prime examples of this.

Using a good grain filler and primer as covered in future sections of the book can avoid these issues, but I often add the steps shown in the photos for added security.

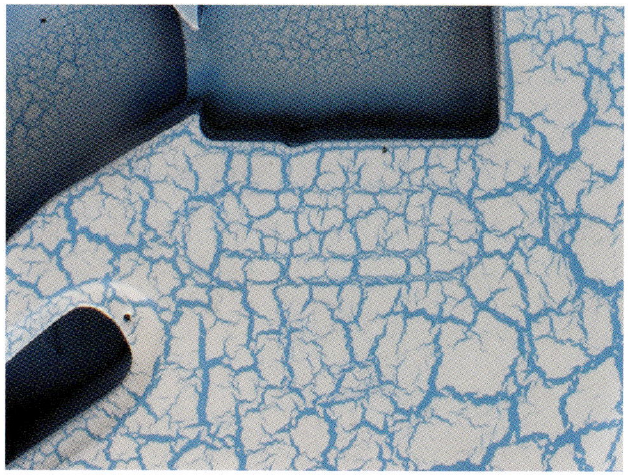

The crackle paint has highlighted the filled area from the top of the filled tremolo cavity.

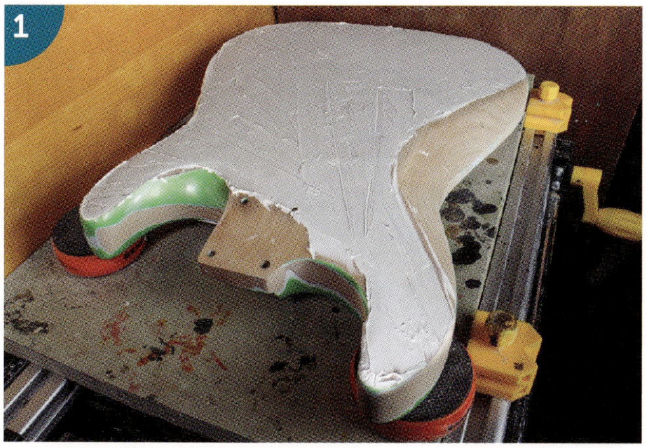

A two-part epoxy filler is spread over the surface just like icing a cake. Car body filler or wood filler work equally well – anything with a hard finish. I spread with a scraper and lollipop stick.

Sand back with a random orbital sander. Aim for as flat a finish as possible, but know that at the primer stage small issues will be highlighted and fixed. Use 240 then 320 grit.

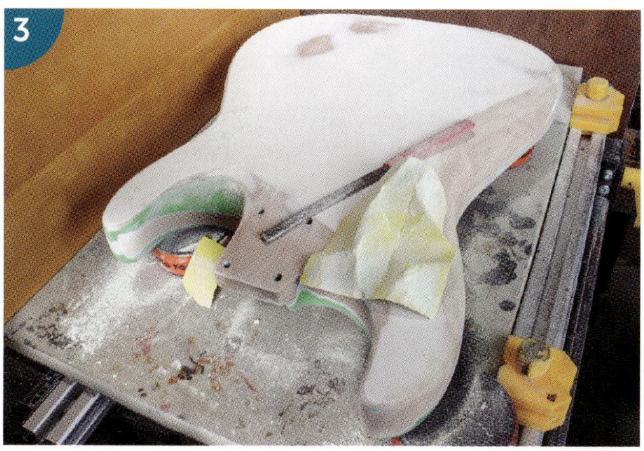

Sandpaper of 220 grit can be used on the edges. I also have a rasp for removing any large lumps of filler that have built up here, especially by the horns.

There will be areas where the filler fades into the wood underneath. When you add the primer, it will hide this transition and highlight any issues which can be fixed then.

CHANGING THE SHAPE OF A GUITAR

Changing the shape may seem like a daunting prospect, something that could ruin the guitar. But don't worry, it's only a bad design that can ruin it and that's a matter of personal taste anyway.

Les Paul's initial prototype for what eventually became the guitar that bears his name was essentially just a core strip. Made from a piece of 4 × 4 pine on which he attached a neck, bridge and pickups, it did not look much like a guitar. When playing it live, Les Paul discovered that people were distracted by its unorthodox shape, so he chopped the sides off an Epiphone hollow body and stuck them on as wings.

If you want a new shape without building a whole new body, you can cut up your guitar. The main thing to keep intact is the core middle strip of the guitar, running from the neck pocket to the back of the bridge and incorporating the pickups. You can simply cut the wings off and attach something new.

Cutting parts off

The advantage of cutting up an actual body as opposed to designing something on paper then cutting wood to match is being able to hold and feel the physical object to help decide on what works. Cut off small amounts at a time, although if you go too far you can stick them back on and use the body-filler method to hide the joins.

This Stratocaster style kit body from The Guitar Fabrik is an ideal experiment piece.

I have drawn on it in different colours with ideas for a new shape.

I picked a line and cut along it, removing smaller parts first.

It didn't feel quite right, so I cut off some more.

The edges needed some sanding and shaping, but the result is a unique customisation.

CASE STUDY: THE WILDHEARTS' SMILEY BONES

When I first started customising guitars, I decided to make one for the guitarist and genius behind one of my favourite bands, Ginger from The Wildhearts. The backstory behind the guitar is that it's a replica of one that was stolen from the set of a video for The Wildhearts' single, *I Wanna Go Where the People Go*. It was the twentieth anniversary of the release of that album so the perfect time for me to make one for Ginger. He loved it, but asked for a few changes so that he could play it live. I ended up making a second one for him and my original now hangs in my office.

I actually made the Smiley Bones body from scratch, but it inspired me to go on and customise a few guitars and basses.

I added an extra piece of wood to the bottom side of the neck to make the jaw balanced on both sides. This removes some access to the upper fretboard for the player.

This was originally a Les Paul style body. I cut it to fit the skull shape, filling the control and switch cavities and routing a new one.

You can see how close I have cut the body behind the bridge, the only difference to the guitar's function being how it hangs on the strap with less distance to the back where the strap pin is.

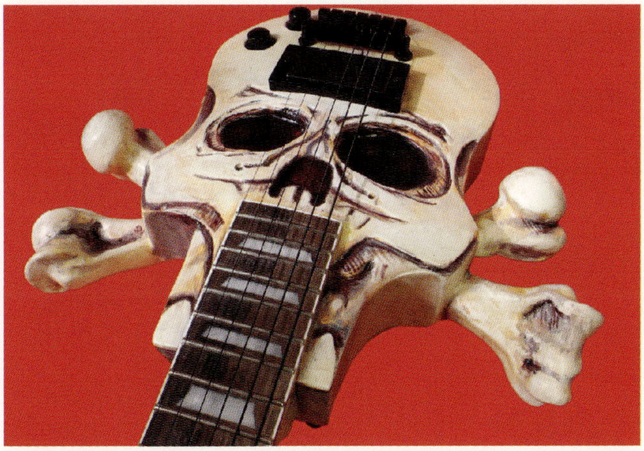

The bones are resin replicas I bought from a medical supply shop. They have metal rods linking them to the body.

CUTTING THROUGH THE BODY

There's no reason not cut through the body too. You'll see this guitar and others with holes in them later in the book under the section covering the use of epoxy resin.

Adding new wings

Attaching new wings to your guitar can be done either before the wings are shaped or afterwards. I prefer doing it before because it's easier and allows the shape to be marked

The sash clamps run under the body, allowing a level surface for all three parts to rest on. I have distributed all four clamps evenly across the length of the body.

Wings with shaped edges are hard to clamp in place. Clamps will have to be placed at angles, and be supported by with blocks.

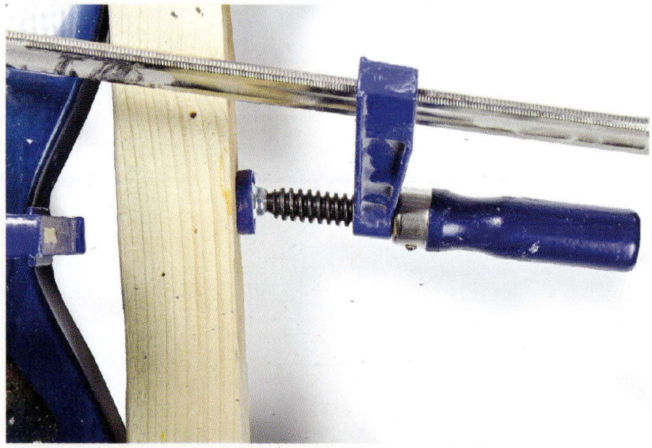

Screw clamps allow for an angle because the head swivels. Take care when tightening as they can pop out of place.

For the sash clamps a spacer is needed. This piece of wood will probably dent the body, but I will be sanding the finish off later and can hide the dent then.

directly on to the physical object. In one of the examples shown here I have done it afterwards simply because I am attaching the wings cut off the first guitar to a blank body strip on to which I will later rout the pickup and neck cavities.

Use a good covering of wood glue on one surface and clamp together as soon as possible. Tighten the clamps evenly and lightly until they are all on, then go back around and tighten them fully. Excess glue should be wiped off now with a wet cloth or paper towel.

Shaping new wings

Once the new wing wood has dried in place, it's ready to start shaping. There's no right or wrong way to do this, but I like first to find the centre line and then mark regular spacing out from it. This helps to ensure that everything runs parallel to the strings and the shape is even on both sides (should I want it to be). The neck pocket and the screw holes on either end of the bridge are perfect guides to mark the centre point at each and link up. I do all of this on masking tape.

After this stage I could simply draw on the body, just as I did with The Guitar Fabrik Stratocaster kit when discussing reshaping a body, or use templates.

MARKING IN MULTIPLE COLOURS

I like to take inspiration from all possible places. When I see an approach is new to me, my first thought is often 'How can I use that on a guitar?'. I have tattoos on both arms, an intricate mix of patterns that intertwine and connect. They were done by a tattoo artist called Tomas Tomas. He's moved to Japan now, so I have had to stop work on them. Part of his design process involved drawing directly on my arm with a Sharpie pen. His first rough design was in yellow, he'd then neaten in red, followed by dark blue to finalise it. Throughout this book you'll see me employing the same technique with pencils on the guitar. Different colours for different options and normally finalising the design with black.

The wood blank wings once the clamps have been removed. It is often easier to flatten the surface with a plane a router now before shaping the wings.

Using paper templates

The internet is full of templates for guitars of all sizes. They can be used as they are, manipulated before printing, printed out and drawn on, or even assembled incorrectly. In this example, I'm using a Gibson SG template, but intentionally misaligning the top and bottom.

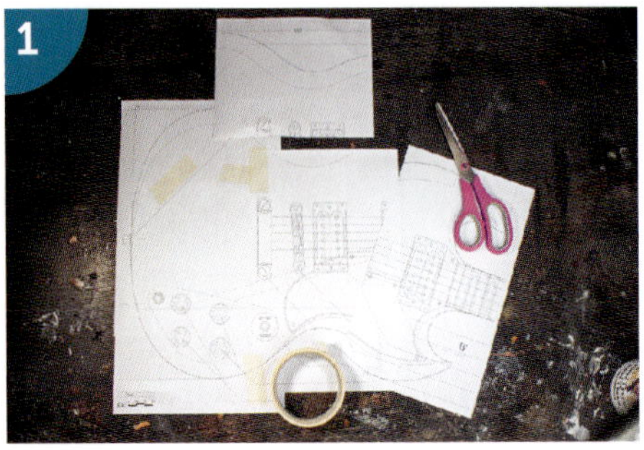

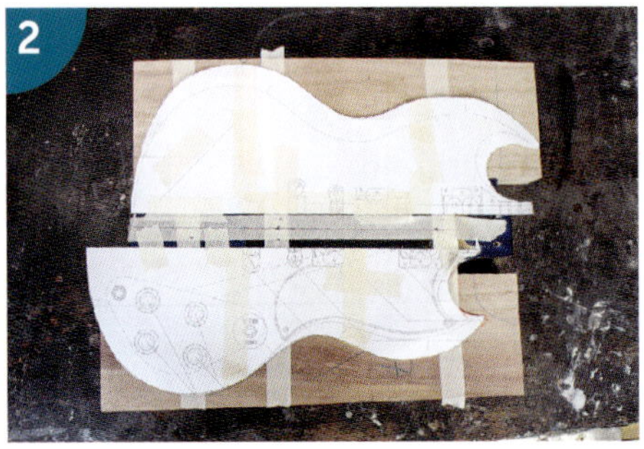

Using physical templates

A physical template is typically used for routing a guitar body. You can either buy them, or make them by sticking paper templates to acrylic or MDF and cutting them out. I usually draw around any guitar body that comes into my workshop to keep a record of it. Sometimes, I stick the body down to a sheet of MDF and use a router to cut an exact copy, including the cavities. Since this book focuses on customising guitars rather than making them from scratch, I won't delve into the details of this process. However, I hope this inspires you to record the shape of guitars you are working on and perhaps make copies of them.

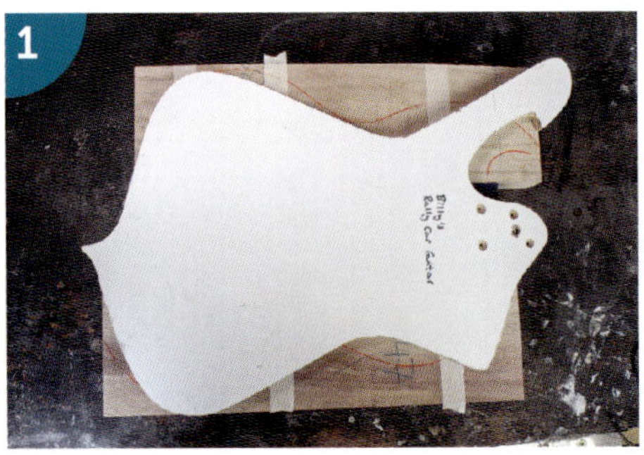

This template is from a guitar that features throughout the book. It's a slight variation on the Ibanez Iceman.

Once the template was marked in a blue, I could see how some lines would join to the red of the SG I marked with the paper template

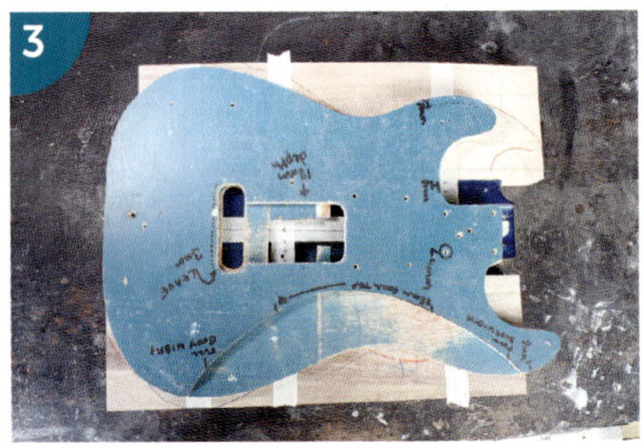

A Fender Stratocaster template is used to mark a third shape on the body.

Selecting between the three template outlines I highlighted a new line that mixed them up to create my own unique design

My new wings weren't quite big enough, so I cut a straight piece from the back …

… and glued on an offcut. When it's dry, I will be able to mark and cut it.

Routing with a template

You can stick a physical template down to the body using the masking-tape method, or screw in parts that will be hidden (such as the cavities that you will later rout, or areas under a scratchplate). Cut the new body and new wings close to the edge of the template, then use a template or trimmer router bit to finalise the shape.

You can buy ready-made templates, print them off on paper, transfer to MDF and then hand-cut your own, or 3D print them.

Control cavities

There will probably need to be a control cavity on the front or back of the new body shape. This can be done with a template and router (drill out as much material as possible first), or by hand.

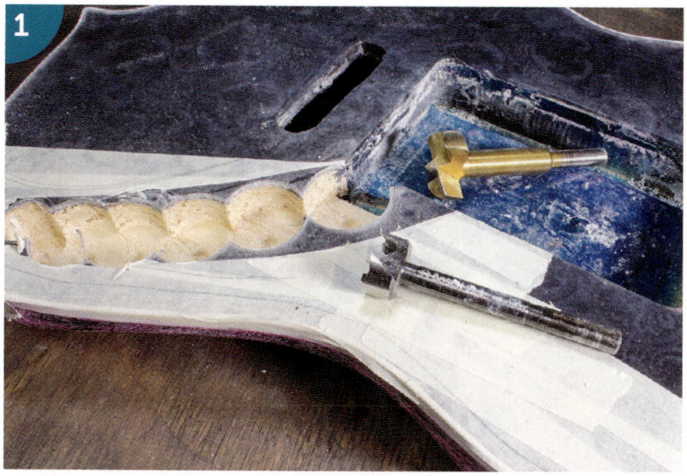

Once you have marked the shape, drill out the cavity to the right depth. Forstner bits are ideal.

Use a chisel to clear out the undrilled wood.

Neaten up the edge with chisels or a rotary tool with a sanding drum.

Dog-leg chisels and router planes are ideal for neatening the base.

Round-over bits for edges

Round-over bits are great for the edges of guitars. I use a ½in-shaft, four-flute one from Radian Tools. The radius of the curve is 12.7mm, which I really like. I rout the entire edge (except the neck pocket) with it, then at points like the inner horn use hand tools to make the round-over even bigger and give it a bit more shape. Of course, you can do this all by hand.

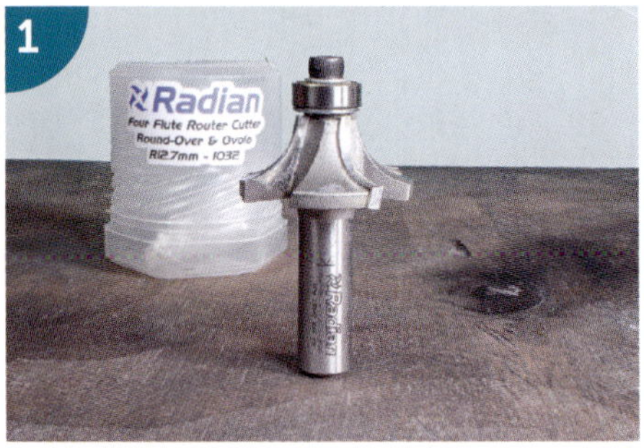

Round-over bits are shaped to add a curve to any corner edge.

I like this large round-over on my guitars.

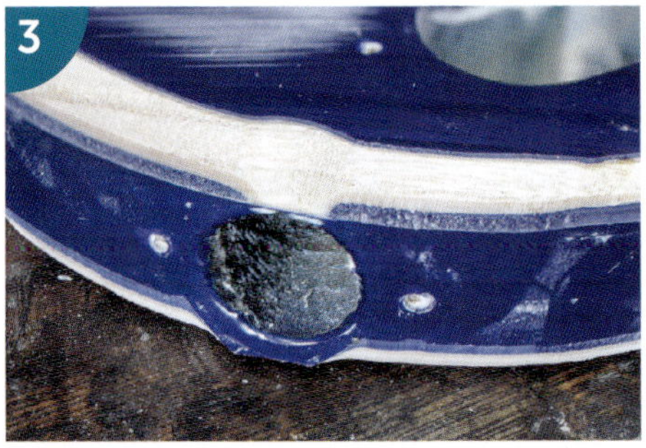

Look out for holes like this for the jack socket. They will interfere with the path of the bearing on the bit, causing dents like the one on the top edge, which will need filling.

The bearing runs along the edge of the body, ensuring that the cut is even all the way around the body.

The bearing will slip into the hole for the jack socket, causing the whole bit to move into the body. The damage could have been worse.

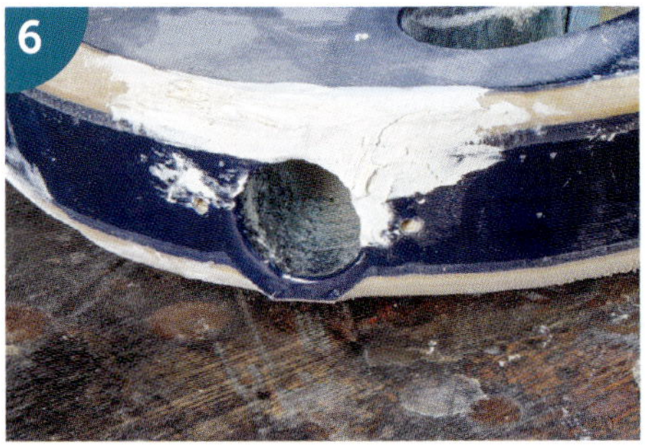

The dent in the body can be filled with wood filler or non-flexible car-body filler.

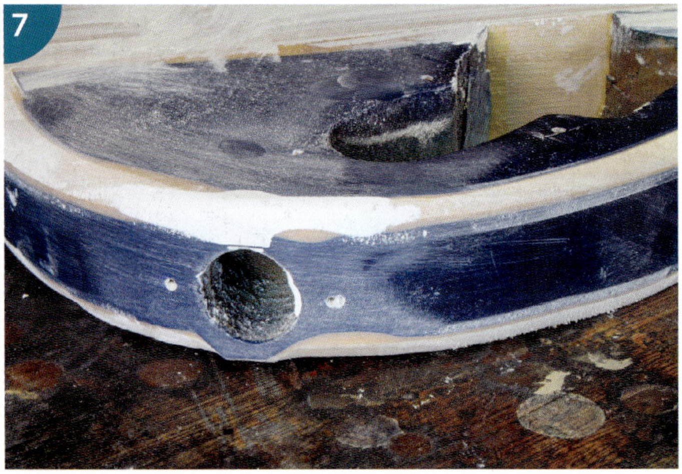

When sanded back, the dent is hidden. Any imperfections will show up at the primer stage.

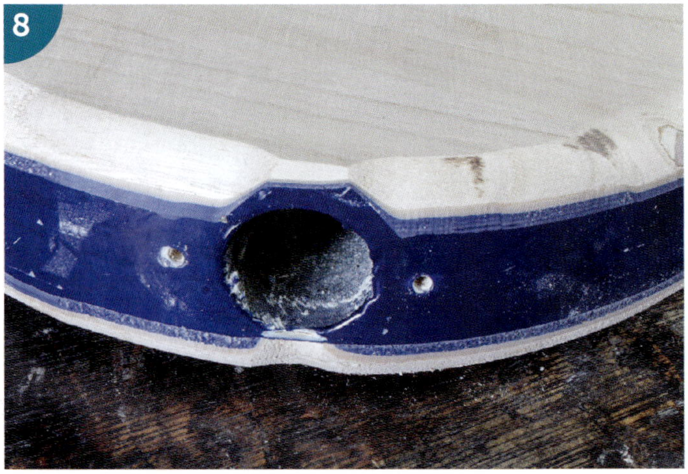

Here the guitar is flipped. I've stopped the bit just before the hole and can connect the two rounded edges on either side of the hole using sandpaper.

THE BENEFIT OF QUALITY ROUTER BITS

Whilst a bad luthier may blame their tools, you must have the right tool for the right job; equally, a sharp knife is a safe knife. There are many low-cost tools that do not perform their intended functions as well as the higher-quality versions. When I began making guitars and using routers, issues such as tear-out and wood burns were common. I had a hard time getting good results easily. Upgrading the tool bits resulted in noticeable improvements. Whilst my technique may have improved too, it made the use of routers more pleasurable and less scary.

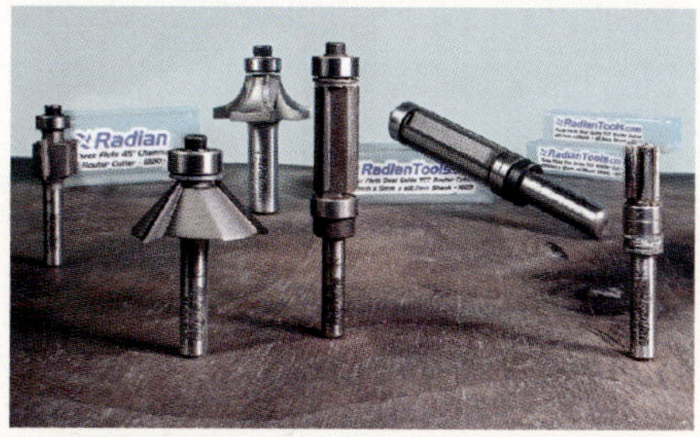

A selection of router bits, all from Radian Tools, my preferred manufacturer.

Comfort carves

Comfort carves on a guitar include forearm and belly carves. For example, Leo Fender added comfort-carve upgrades to the Stratocaster that did not appear on Telecasters. I like them in the horn areas too, but partly for the aesthetic.

Marking out the comfort carves on the back of the body. Marking them will help with seeing how they fit and as a guide for carving.

There are lines joining the edge of the comfort carve on the side and back of the guitar. Simply cut along these with a saw, then chisel the part out.

A wood carving disc for an angle grinder is effective at removing lots of wood in one go and for shaping.

Shinto rasps have a series of saw blades meshed together; they make easy work out of shaping and removing large areas. The Dragon rasps from StewMac are great for finer detail shaping.

Hand-sanding with 180 or 220 grit against a hard block works well on smaller areas, giving you a lot of control, but taking more time than a rasp or power tool.

My favourite use of the oscillating spindle sander is to shape the horn recess. It can be used for a body carve too. The process benefits from practice.

Adding a laminated top

If you are planning a finish that shows off the grain of the wood, you will definitely be sanding back the previous finish with your fingers crossed. When I sanded back the guitar in this example (bought on eBay), I discovered it was made from MDF, so no grain at all. It's very common for a body to be made from multiple parts of wood put together. These lines often disrupt the grain pattern, but even the new Player Series Fender guitars I've seen are made like this. For me, it simply means that when you look at the grain, you can see that the guitar is a cheaper model.

If you come across a guitar with a really cool wood-grain finish, the chances are it's had a drop top added. This is a sheet of wood around 5–10mm thick glued to the top of the guitar in the build process. For guitars with arched and curved tops like a Gibson Les Paul, the thickness of this top must be enough to allow for the carves. Often there are two pieces of wood cut from the same tree as adjacent strips, that fit next to each other with the join running along the centre line of the guitar. The resulting effect is a mirror image of the grain, often referred to as bookmatched. Some guitars will have a cheaper option, a thin veneer sheet glued across the top, while others may have a fake grain print applied in the finishing process.

I would not recommend adding a drop top to your guitar for customisation unless you are happy first to remove an amount of wood from the top surface equal to the thickness of the drop top. This can be done with a router and surfacing bit, in a planer thicknesser, or by hand with a plane and sanding. If you don't remove the wood, it will be necessary to add wood of the same thickness to the neck pocket to compensate. If you feel confident with a router, this shouldn't be too difficult. Drill through the drop top over the pickup cavities and use a flush trim bit to duplicate them in the top. Use the same bit to match the top to the edges of the guitar, looking out for the comfort carves, which could throw the bearing off, then drill control holes through from the back cavity access.

The easiest solution for customising a guitar to improve the wood grain is to add a veneer – exactly what I did for this MDF body using a teak veneer. You can buy veneer with much more interesting grain patterns, but this is what I needed for the desired result (an extreme relic guitar in my End of the Road series).

When prepping the surface of the veneer for the next stages, treat it exactly like preparing a wooden body finish, that is, a light sanding with 600 grit, using a flat hard-backed paper for the body and foam pads for the edge transitions.

1 Tape the veneer down with the grain facing up. This way, you can see how the grain will look by drawing around the guitar. Reposition and redraw if needed. Pencil lines can be erased.

2 Cover the guitar in wood glue. I use Titebond II because of its faster set time. Specific veneer glue is available

Spread the glue evenly all over the surface. (I was rushing to take this photo and could have done a better job!)

Place the veneer. Cutting it a bit bigger than needed allows for a bit of give.

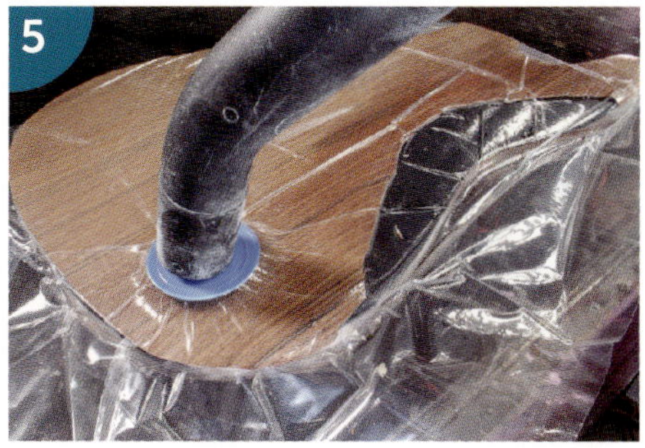

Use a large vacuum storage bag to clamp the veneer in place. With cheaper bags you may want to check every hour and use the vacuum again.

Always work one side at a time. Here's the other side. Doing them separately is easier, less messy and helps to avoid the veneer slipping.

Once the glue is set and the body is out of the bag, cut out the cavities.

Use thin cyanoacrylate glue along the edge join between the veneer and the body. Do the same for the edge of the cavities.

Any raised part of the veneer can be fixed with CA glue and pressure from a flat sheet of wood.

Where possibly clamp parts down whilst the glue dries.

Trim any small over hangs away once the glue is dry.

Sand the edges smooth with 220 grit.

Once the glue is dry, the edges can be sanded to create a smooth transition from the veneer to the body. This series of images show the guitar ready for the next stages of preparation for painting.

APPROACH WITH CARE

When sanding through a finish on a guitar in preparation for a custom refinish, there's a chance that the nice wood grain you can see will prove to be a thin veneer, or a thin drop top. This will be more common on a cheap guitar. Take care not to sand through this if you want to keep the grain pattern. If this is the case, the chances are that the sides will be a solid colour to hide the grain, or the pattern won't match up to the top. Try removing the finish from the edges first if you are uncertain.

INSPIRATION: TOBIAS CASPAR'S INCREDIBLE DROP TOPS

I love bookmarking inspiring guitar builds on Instagram. One day, while browsing through my collection of cool guitars, I noticed several luthiers showcasing similar stunning finishes. Intrigued by the seemingly complex and unique process, I wondered how they had independently achieved such cohesive looks. It turns out that they all sourced their drop tops from Tobias Caspar, a supplier of stabilised wood and resin drop tops. Looking over his website you'll discover a wide range of colours, woods, patterns and designs, all unmistakably marked by his unique style.

Tobias's proprietary process not only results in outstanding finishes, but means that by fortifying woods in resin that would normally be unsuitable for use in instruments, they can be machined and sanded like any regular timber.

BINDING

Binding is the strip that runs around the top edge of the guitar. It is made from plastic, wood or celluloid. It can also be found on the edge of some fretboards. As well as being decorative, it acts as a protective edge. I used to hate binding because I like the edges of guitars to have a smooth curve, which isn't possible when binding is installed. However, as I have customised more guitars, I have begun to appreciate the options it gives you, from adding a highlight, contrast or alternative colours to the scheme, to helping to divide two contrasting finishes or colours. Binding is easy to add to a guitar if the top and sides are perpendicular. As soon as there is a curved edge, the binding won't fit unless it is thick, or you fill behind it.

Creating the right edge for binding

You can create the right angle needed for the binding by sanding down the top surface of the guitar to remove the curve at the edge. Beware – the neck pocket's depth won't have changed, so the neck will now sit higher in relation to the top of the guitar. This will likely cause issues with the bridge alignment. If you remove wood from the neck pocket to compensate, do so in small amounts, attaching the neck and strings to check regularly that your action isn't too high.

Routing the binding channel

Binding comes in different thicknesses, so you will need a rebate bit for your router that recesses the channel (or rebates) to the right thickness. Most rebate or binding bits come with a selection of interchangeable bearings. Use a strip of binding long enough to wrap the whole guitar edge. Don't cut it until you have finished. Start gluing at one end (normally at the neck pocket) and glue it in sections, taping as you go.

Select the right bearing, then set the bit at the correct depth.

Always run on a test piece first to ensure a snug fit.

Work in sections, adding medium cyanoacrylate glue to the rebate. Tape the binding in place as you proceed.

Use the heat gun on the part of the binding that is about to be bent. There's no point heating up too far ahead. Note that on this guitar I'm not sticking the binding in place with the tape, but with CA glue with a kicker. Using tape is the best option.

ALTERNATIVE BINDINGS

Binding doesn't have to be a strip. On my Entomology guitars, I routed a binding channel then stuck spikes designed for clothing along it. The spikes have a screw thread on the base, so I spaced holes equally around the edge, filled them with epoxy glue and pushed the thread end in. Whilst the glue was drying, I used a similar method to holding the binding in place by wrapping masking tape from the top to the side of the guitar over the end of the spikes to hold them in place.

THE FINAL SAND BEFORE FINISHING

Before moving on to any finishing, sand the whole body with 600 grit. You'll need to work up in stages from where the guitar surface currently is. If it's been sanded back from having paint on it, you've probably used a 180 or 220 grit. Move forward in small increments, 180 to 220, to 280, to 320, to 400, then 600 to finish. Each time you move forward with a grade, check that you are removing the previous sanding marks. If you only sand in one direction, change 90 degrees each time you sand, as this can help with spotting sanding marks from the previous pass.

Once you've got to 600 grit, dampen the surface to raise the grain using a slightly wet cloth. When this dries, you'll probably see a slight fuzz where the grain has raised. Sand again with 600 grit to remove this. This stage is irrelevant if you are simply respraying your guitar, but still work the finish down to 600 grit.

Now you are ready for the next stages, working with the grain to achieve the finish you want.

nitorlack
CHESTNUT
AXE WAX
Shines Seals & Protects
Coffee
Guitar Wax
GLOSS

CHAPTER 3

FINISHING BASICS

Before starting to apply the finishes, you need to know what type of finish you want. Will it have the natural wood texture, show some of the open pores, or be a completely smooth finish? These choices are partly controlled now, before the finish is applied. The choice of gloss, satin or matt will come at the end stages.

GRAIN FILLING

Grain filling has two main roles – to fill the grain to eliminate it from the final texture, or to highlight the grain in the final finish. The choice of colour filler makes no difference if you apply a solid colour on top. If you want a finish to show off the grain, such as a translucent colour, stain or simply a clear coat, it can make a difference. Use the one that best matches your wood for a subtle grain finish, or that contrasts to highlight the grain.

Applying grain filler

Start by ensuring that the body is sanded up to 400 grit. Any machine marks and so on must be removed. This is the final stage of sanding.

Grain filler is thinner than wood filler; it's designed to fill smaller pores, whereas wood filler is for bigger dents and holes. There are different types of grain filler available, but you'll probably find that you will need to water it down. I use the filler from Nitorlack which works well on a ratio of one part water to two parts filler. Essentially you want a custard like viscosity.

CASE STUDY: TO FILL, OR NOT FILL?

The kit guitar from The Guitar Fabrik has a spalted maple top. You can see a difference in texture between the blue side and the multicoloured central stripe. The outer has had the grain lightly filled to give a subtle open grain finish, whereas the stripe has been untouched to emphasise the texture. The light filling is achieved by one application of filler; many deeper-pored woods will need a second coat once the first has dried and been sanded. Some clear coats of wipe-on water-based finish from Nitorlack have been added to create the sheen, but not enough to fill the pores and texture.

IS THIS STEP NEEDED FOR A FLAT FINISH?

If you're just after a flat finish, you may think that it can be achieved with good sanding, but often the finishing process will highlight the grain texture, as the different densities of the wood respond differently to your choice of finish.

I will be showing you how to seal, prime, paint, then topcoat the guitar, all of which will help to fill the pores and can potentially negate the need to fill the grain now. However, it is normally the case that by skipping the grain-filling stage you will end up needing more primer layers and spending more time.

Apply the filler using a cloth or piece of hessian. I find that the hessian helps to distribute the filler slightly better. Go with the grain, then against it. Leave to dry; you can see the colour change as the water evaporates. After ten minutes, scrape as much off the surface as possible at a low angle, being careful not to scratch the surface. It's then ready to sand.

As you can see in photos 7 and 8, I have used the Nitorlack black, natural and mahogany. After sanding, differences are subtle on the unfinished wood. Often the changes will be more pronounced once the finish has been applied. Wetting the surface will mimic what it will look like with a wax or varnish on. Use some denatured alcohol or my meths-vinegar mix, as it evaporates quickly and doesn't sink into the wood.

1 Decant some of the filler into a separate container that can be sealed for later use.

2 Add water, starting with a less than recommended. Mix thoroughly until the paste is even.

3 I like a consistency like custard. It's easier to add more water than more filler to your mix.

4 The weave of a hessian rag helps load it up with filler for application.

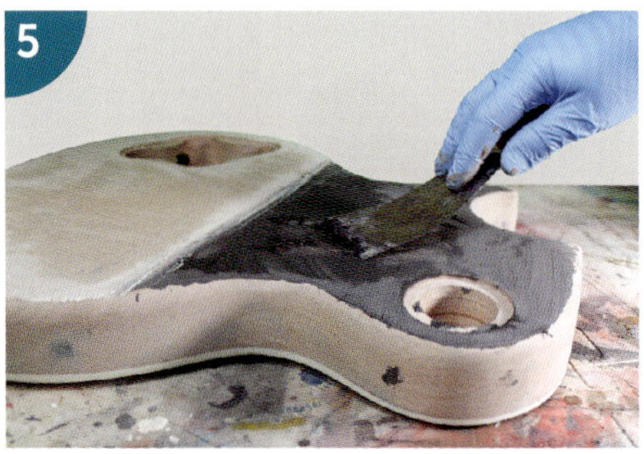

5 Here you can see the colour change in some of the filler where it has dried out.

6 Apply pressure to the middle of the scraper to box it as I push at a low angle to remove filler from the surface.

The surface is still covered in filler after scraping, but the big clumps have been removed.

Sanding the remaining filler away with 400 grit reveals a subtle difference in the grain colour. Here the untouched left side is slightly lighter. The surface of the filled side is smoother.

EMPHASISING THE DIFFERENCE

In order to exaggerate the difference between the inside and outside of the black lines on the spalted maple guitar kit from The Guitar Fabrik, I decided to fill the grain on the outside with Nitorlack's black filler. Not only will this help to give a different texture to the finish, but also the black will emphasise the quilted wood effect.

The Nitrolack natural filler, applied to the right side only, appears to have made the wood seem much lighter.

By wetting the wood surface, you can see no difference in the wood finish. However, close inspection does reveal that the grain is mainly filled. At this stage, I would apply the filler a second time to ensure that the grain is fully filled.

WHAT COLOUR FILLER TO USE

Assuming that you don't plan to hide the grain with a solid, non-translucent colour, the filler's colour can impact the finish. Companies like Nitorlack make transparent filler so as to maintain an authentic look whilst achieving a flat finish. The subtle colours of the grain will show through. You can also buy epoxy-resin grain fillers; using standard resin isn't ideal as it will potentially be too viscous. Here are some tips:

* Use a filler with a colour like the main wood if you want a faint grain pattern.
* For a natural grain pattern that stands out use a darker filler. The grain will now have an even colour all over.
* If you're staining over the top or using a translucent spray colour, filling with black will emphasise the grain the most.
* For something wilder, you can take a light filler and add colour to it. Nitorlack's standard fillers can be tinted by their stains for more interesting finishes. Experiment with your fillers and dyes to check their compatibility before committing to the guitar.

SANDING SEALERS

Sanding sealer can be used to fill the pores instead of a grain filler. It also provides a great base for whichever process you decide to use next, helping to ensure an even finish. If you've stained the wood, it can help to prevent bleed-through to topcoats. Sanding sealers have a sanding agent in them, mixed with a compatible thinner or solvent. There are shellac-, acrylic- and cellulose-based sanding sealers. I have often used the acrylic as a base for an acrylic or polyurethane finish. I recommend sticking to a cellulose sealer for nitrocellulose finishes. Shellac is ideal before a wax finish. Companies such as Chestnut Products make a range of sanding sealers and recommend which is best for the product you opt to use next.

Whichever you choose, the principle is the same – the sanding sealer fills the open pores and creates a smoother surface for your finish. This means potentially less finish is needed, saving money, but also helping to prevent the finish becoming too thick. Often, the thicker the finish, the more prone it will be to chipping.

Shellac is traditionally used in furniture making before French polishing because it fills the grain and seals the wood, preventing the polish from soaking in unevenly across the surface. It is available in flake form, which is scraped off trees where it has been secreted by female lac bugs in India and Thailand. These flakes are ready to dissolve in solvents such as ethanol, methanol or isopropyl alcohol, but I prefer to buy mine pre-mixed from Chestnut Products.

All sealers need sanding afterwards. The sanding agent will be left on the surface, causing a slightly textured finish. It acts as a lubricant when sanding.

Applying sanding sealer

In principle, the application of all the types of sanding sealer is similar. Some come in spray cans or are spray-gun ready, which can be an advantage for coating the entire body in one go. I cover how to use spray cans and guns later in the book. Alternatively, they can be applied by brush or cloth. I recommend using a cloth over a brush, as it's a bit easier on a guitar-sized piece of wood. A foam brush is better than a bristle brush. Cellulose sanding sealer dries quicker, so you will need to work faster.

REPLACE THE LID!

In the photos, while I'm applying the sanding sealer, I have left the lid off the bottle ready to recharge my cloth with more sealer when needed. Terry from Chestnut Products recommends you put the lid back on to avoid accidents. Sound advice which I have regretted not following a number of times.

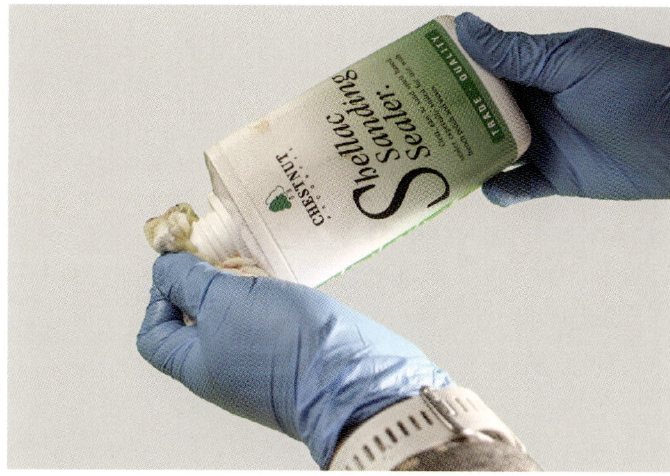

Hold your cloth over the end of the bottle; tip both to soak the cloth.

Apply evenly over the surface, keeping a wet edge of sealer as you move.

Once dry, the surface will need sanding with 600 grit.

USING SEALER BEFORE OR AFTER STAINS AND DYES?

A dilemma I had when writing this book was deciding the order in which to put certain processes. Having the sanding sealer straight after the grain filler made sense, as it is after all a potential alternative. However, as the test piece shows, you shouldn't apply it before using stain.

This wood has been treated in four ways. From left to right: filler only; sealer and filler; sealer only; and untreated wood. Scarlet Nitoraqua, a water-based stain from Nitorlack, has been wiped onto the top half with a cloth. As you can see, the stain won't penetrate the wood where the sealer is – the wipe-on marks from the stain application are visible.

The red is equally vivid on the two sections of the wood not treated with sealer. The left side looks a bit more vivid where the grain has been filled with Nitrolack's natural filler, hiding some of the darker grain colour. Therefore, if you are staining or dyeing the wood, delay the sealer until afterwards.

Stains and dyes

In this book, the terms 'stains' and 'dyes' will be used interchangeably, but there is a difference. Stains sit on the wood surface and dyes penetrate into the wood. In general, I don't favour one over the other; instead, I have preferred brands where I find the colours suit my work better.

Solvent vs water-based

In general, I prefer water-based stains, so that I don't have to wear a mask. They are also safer to use and easier to

A selection of dyes from my workshop.

clean up. The solvent-based dyes pick up the colour of a previously applied dye much more readily, which allows for a difference in the mixing of colours if aiming for a burst finish (there's a chapter about that later). They also offer a longer working time before drying to help in the process.

My preferred brand of stains and dyes is Nitorlack. Their products provide a good example of some of the differences between solvent- and water-based options. Their solvent-based stains, the Nitortints, are concentrates designed to be dissolved in water, solvent or alcohol. They can be used diluted in a spray gun, or mixed with Nitorlack's finishing varnish products (including water-based). Although they recommend diluting at a 3–10% mix, when applying by hand I usually use these products undiluted for a really intense colour. Diluting them would mean more value for money, though, or multiple layers could be used to increase the intensity of colour. Nitoraqua water-based stains are designed for hand application, can be diluted with water, or applied in multiple layers to intensify the colour.

I find the choice is often just down to which colour you want and what base your preferred supplier makes it in. Check with the manufacturer how the stain can be used if you want to do more than just apply it by hand.

Powder dyes and stains

These pigments are made to dissolve in water or alcohol (denatured alcohol or methanol). You can control the strength by how much you dilute them. Each company will advise on the best way to mix and dilute. When I first started using dyes, I bought a set of Keda Dye powder stains. They were great because having powders saved room in my small workshop and I could mix the colours.

Applying stains and dyes

Whilst each individual manufacturer may have a different suggested technique for application, I prefer to work by hand, using a cotton cloth. I use old cut-up baby muslins, worn-out tee-shirts or lint-free car rags. Waste not, want not!

Prepare the surface with a 320-grit sandpaper. Then wet the surface and let it dry. This helps to raise any grain, which can now be removed with a 400-grit sandpaper. Use a hard, flat pad for the body and foam-backed one for edges. It's important to raise grain now and sand, otherwise it may raise with the dye and result in an uneven colour if sanded afterwards. How you hold the cloth is important, as shown in the photos.

Keda Dyes before mixing and diluting.

Once the stain is dry, you may want to apply one or more additional coats. Lightly sand with 800 grit between each coat to remove any slightly raised grain. The final colour of the stain will be emphasised by the topcoats. You can emulate this by wetting the surface lightly with water or denatured alcohol, but do it in a non-precious area such as under the scratchplate. I advise staining the neck pocket, pickup and control cavities if you want to test anything.

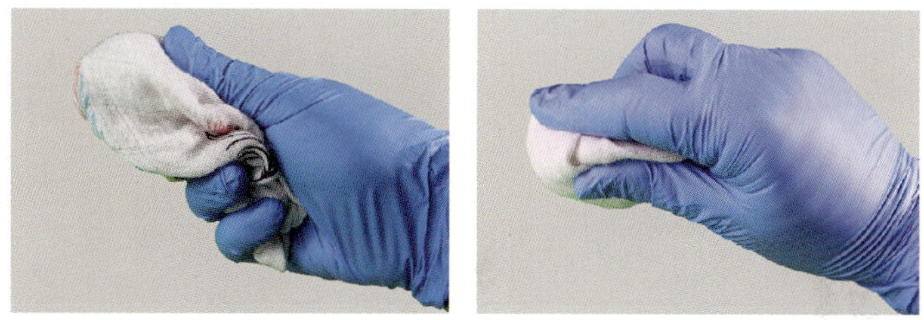

Bunch up the cloth slightly to make a padded surface. I use my finger as a backing guide for when I wipe the stains on to the guitar. You need just enough cloth to fill your hand.

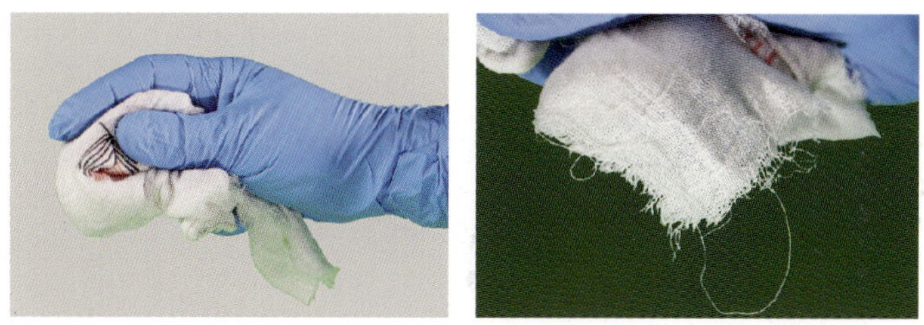

Make sure that no part of the cloth is hanging down. If you've cut it yourself, check for stray threads. If these catch in the dye when spreading it can result in uneven coverage.

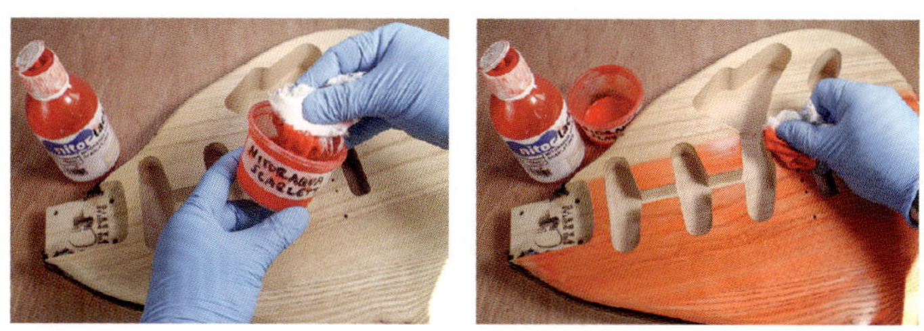

Dip the cloth in the dye (or apply straight from the bottle), then spread in even strokes along the length of the body, overlapping each stroke.

Using stains to emphasise the grain

Dyes and stains can be used to emphasise the grain. By staining the whole body then sanding back the surface with a hard-backed 600 grit, the stain can be removed from some areas of the wood and not others. The wood grain is generally more absorbent than the main wood, allowing the stain to seep in further; it won't be removed by sanding just the surface.

If you dye a highly textured wood, then flat sand with a hard-backed paper, the dipped areas will also retain the stain. If you do this on a guitar that has already had grain filler applied, the surface will be smoother, so you may think it will be harder to accentuate the grain with this look. However, often the stain will absorb better in the filler, so a combination may bring out the grain even more. If you have an area you can test on, such as under a scratchplate, have a go first – you can always sand back if you're not happy.

Later in the book, I have a section demonstrating the ceruse technique, also called liming, which is a method for achieving an even more exaggerated grain fill.

1

The guitar before any stain is added.

2

The body is covered in Nitorlack's Nitoraqua black stain.

3

Once the stain is dry it is sanded back to emphasize the grain. I could have sanded further but want this dirty rustic look.

4

Colour stains have now been added. This is the guitar to which I added a veneer earlier in the book. I'm going for a rustic and battered look. It will later have a relic treatment.

EXAGGERATING THE GRAIN

To further exaggerate the grain on The Guitar Fabrik Les Paul, I applied Nitoraqua Black stain with a cloth and brush to the areas to which I had already added the black filler.

1 The brush was helpful to get a neat edge.

2 Once sanded back with 400 grit, you can see how the filler has been darkened further.

3 After four coats of Nitortint Teal, the colour difference between the treated and untreated wood is obvious.

Marks in the stain

The staining process can often highlight some problems that occurred in the preparation of the body that wouldn't be a problem were you spraying a finish on top. Small marks and patches appear where the stain doesn't seem to have taken so well to the wood. The cause of this is usually glue on the wood, or some contaminate left via a fingerprint. It's normally easy to deal with if you are using one solid colour, simply by sanding away an area and reapplying the stain.

If the body is lightly stained, or has a pattern like a burst (covered later in the book), note that this technique may not work, as the patch you re-stain could still stand out. The only solution then is to sand back the entire body until the marks are removed, then reapply the stain.

1 The staining process has revealed glue marks stopping the stain from taking to the wood.

2 It's best to sand back to the same grit as the body was before staining, 400 or 600.

3 The faded edges of the area will help the new stain to blend in.

4 When applying the new stain, do a final pass over the whole body.

Stain marks on binding

When staining a body that has binding, the binding could be masked off to avoid stain getting on to it, although I usually just stain over it, then scrape back.

If you scrape too aggressively, you may end up stuttering along the edge, preventing it from being smooth. Go slowly and repeat over an area if all the stain is removed in one pass. A light 600-grit paper folded up may be needed to smooth off some areas of the binding; be careful not to sand the body.

The stain covers the top edge of the binding and has spilt over the sides slightly.

Lay a utility knife blade flat on the guitar, tip touching the edge. Mark the width of the binding using masking tape.

The tip of the blade will be used for scraping.

Fold the tape over, but leave a piece hanging down as a guide.

The completed tool, masked off and ready to use. Make sure that no blade is visible except the tip.

The blade is used for scraping. The tape hanging down is a guide to stop you moving over the binding edge.

Work slowly around the body, scraping in short sections at a time. The left side has been scraped here.

Make a new tool with a larger tip to match the side width of the binding and repeat.

CRACKS IN THE BINDING

Little cracks in the binding may allow stain to seep in deeper and need further scraping back. If the binding was new and applied properly, there shouldn't be any cracks, but if the guitar is second hand make sure you check for them first. Also, if you've scraped the binding before staining and been too aggressive, you may have caused some.

If you are at all worried, seal any cracks you can see with thin cyanoacrylate glue. The CA glue can be scraped back once the stain is applied. Masking binding is also an option; there is a section on binding later in the book which includes how to do this.

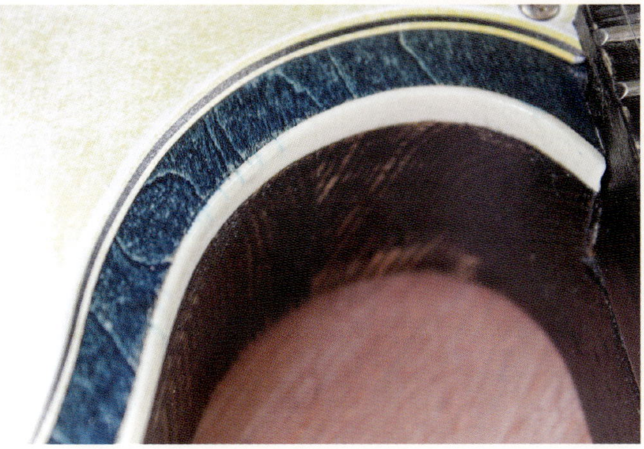

Finishing over stains

Your stained finish can have any topcoat put on it; however, I would advise against wiping on a topcoat of wax if you have created a patterned or burst finish. If you have used a solvent-based dye and are applying a solvent-based topcoat by wiping on, you can easily remove some of the colour. If using a wipe-on topcoat, first use a spray sanding sealer. I often use the Chestnut Products acrylic sanding sealer, as it comes in a spray can ready to go.

A wipe-on finish was applied over this stained surface and the cloth held in one place for too long. You can see that the stain has been partly removed in the middle.

WAXES AND OILS

The main difference between these two types of finish is that wax sits on the surface, whereas oils penetrate the wood. Each type of oil and wax will have a slightly different appearance and feel. The main ones used on guitars will be covered now because it's a common option to apply them over bare wood to accentuate the natural finish. Sometimes they can be used in the finishing process on top of a paint or lacquer finish, which will be covered in the finishing section of the book. Waxes and oils will not be as durable or protective as a hard paint or lacquer finish and will require recoating in time. However, they are more suited for enhancing the appearance and feel of the wood. For that reason, some players prefer a neck with an oiled or waxed finished.

You can use either an oil or a wax to finish, or combine them, with the oil layer first. As with all products, there is a huge range of manufacturers, brands and suppliers, and I recommend trying a variety over time to find the ones you prefer.

Types of oils

As oils are penetrating, they are often also described as nourishing. This is why fretboards are treated with oils to prevent them drying out and cracking. Oils can enhance the natural look of the wood. Dampening dry wood will give you a preview of what the oiled finish will look like. Some manufacturers may describe their oils as adding a slight colour to the finish too. Different oils offer different levels of protection, sheen and ease of application.

Tung oil is a hard-wearing oil with no solvent in it to assist with drying, so it will require longer wait times between coats; 24 hours is normally enough, depending on conditions. It normally has a subtle golden tint to it. It dries with a satin finish, but a glossier look can be achieved with multiple thin coats.

Linseed oil comes either raw or boiled. The boiled version has been heated and treated with chemicals to speed up the drying time. It has a harder finish than tung oil and is glossier.

Tru-Oil is a commonly used finish on gunstocks and is popular for guitars. It contains a mix of oils, including linseed, and is known for its ability to build to a glossy finish.

Danish oil is a blend of oils, such as tung or linseed oil, with added resin, solvents or driers to speed up drying time. Four hours is typical between coats. It has a stain finish and will need a wax topcoat to achieve a glossy finish. Some manufacturers use the description finishing oil instead of Danish oil.

Hard wax oil is a blend of oils and waxes that gives a tough, hard-wearing finish. It comes in a range of sheens and requires fewer coats than the other oils.

Applying Oils

In general, the process for applying all oils is the same, but the number of coats required will vary. Refer to the manufacturer's guidelines. Typically, you can expect three to five coats of tung, linseed or Danish oil, with two to three normally being sufficient for hard wax oil.

Use a clean cloth to apply the oil generously in the direction of the grain. I prefer cleaned, used tee-shirts or cut-up baby muslins. Washed old cloths are less likely to leave behind lint, but don't use fabric softener in the wash (it may react with some oils). You can also buy lint-free cloths for this purpose. Allow for the oil to be absorbed, but not to get sticky before wiping off. The manufacturer will have a recommended time of between ten minutes to an hour.

Each coat needs time to dry fully before applying the next, sanding first with 400 grit. Some oils, like Tru-Oil, benefit from increasing the grit each time between coats to help achieve a glossy finish. For five coats, start at 400 grit after the first one, then 600 grit, followed by 800 grit then 1000 grit, before the final one.

A burnishing cream can be used once the oil is fully dried to help increase the gloss finish. Alternatively, use a super-fine polishing compound if it's designed for a final finish, as others will be too abrasive. It can be applied with a cloth, or using extra-fine (0000) wire wool, rubbed in the direction of the grain. Allow the cream to dry for a few moments; it should start to haze, then can be buffed off with a clean cloth. You can also buff it mechanically; I cover this process later in the paint and lacquer finishing section, where I'll also discuss the difference in polishing compounds. In order to achieve an even, satin finish, the fine wire wool can be used on its own with no burnishing cream.

Decanted oil being applied to a neck with a clean cloth.

⚠ SPONTANEOUS COMBUSTION

Some oils generate heat during the oxidisation process that occurs when they are drying. The heat generated in a pile of used rags can reach a temperature that could ignite the rags. It's therefore always recommended to leave rags flat to dry after the process and not screw them up into a bin until they have.

Types of waxes

A wax finish is designed to protect your instrument by creating a durable shield over the surface. Some waxes will need just one coat, whilst others can layer up. They can be buffed to a gloss. When they get damaged or dirty you can clean, light sand, and apply a new coat.

Carnauba wax is a natural wax made from the leaves of the Carnauba palm tree. It's sometimes called Brazil Wax or Palm Wax. It leaves a hard finish that can easily be buffed to a gloss finish.

Beeswax is also a natural wax, but softer than Carnauba. It can be used on guitars, though I would advise the use of Carnauba. However, some companies such as Chestnut Products make a wax that mixes both to create a blend that is easy to use.

Microcrystalline wax is derived from the petroleum refining process and has a very fine crystal structure, resulting in a dense and hard-wearing coating. A popular brand for luthiers is Renaissance Wax, which was developed in the British Museum Research Laboratory.

Coloured waxes are a great way of changing your finish without the mess of paints and stains. You can apply them just as you would any other stain to make a solid colour. Later in the book I explain liming, for which using coloured waxes is an ideal way to highlight grain. Some coloured waxes contain stain, which penetrates the wood, whilst others contain pigment, which sits on the surface in the wax. You may want to add a clear wax over the top for extra shine and protection, depending on the manufacturer's guidelines.

As a further note, whilst you can buy waxes specifically for guitars, you can also use woodworking waxes.

Applying waxes

Applying waxes is easy, but always check the manufacturer's suggested method and wait times between coats. Often, you'll just need a single coat. Building up layers can result in a softer finish for some waxes, but a glossier one for others. You can use a wax over an oil finish for an extra layer of protection; just ensure that the oil is fully cured. Applying wax over a sanding sealer can help to achieve a smoother finish. Some manufacturers may recommend this for their products, giving the wax a sealed base for better adhesion.

Ensure that the bare wood surface of the guitar is good to go – sanded to 320 grit is common for wax applications. Don't forget to dampen the surface to raise the grain, then sand again. If a stain or dye has been used, you won't need to sand. Always test the wax in a small area first in case the solvents in it start to lift the stain (in which case a sealer is advised). If you are applying wax over an oil finish, either lightly rub the surface with fine wire wool (0000) in the direction of the grain, or lightly sand with 600 grit.

Apply the wax with a cloth, rubbing with the grain. Most waxes will suggest a liberal application, a short wait of up to 30 minutes for the wax to haze slightly, then buff back with the cloth. Some waxes will be suitable for buffing with a mechanical polishing wheel. If you are applying extra layers, don't fully buff to shine. Instead, lightly rub down the surface with a fine abrasive; 600 grit does the job, using a foam-backed one for sides and a hard one for the flat surfaces.

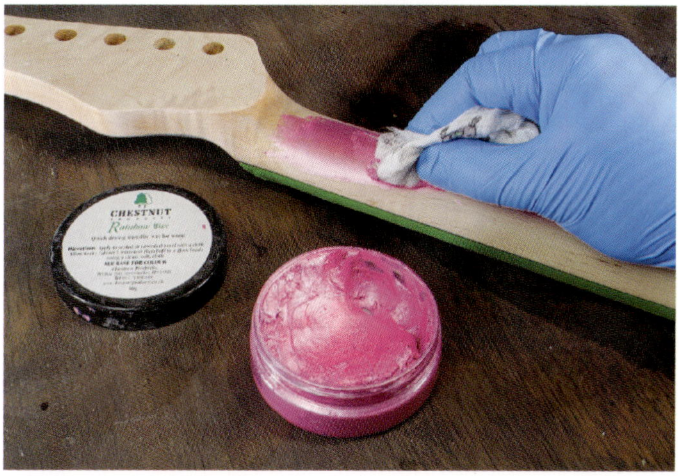

Applying a metallic pink Rainbow Wax from Chestnut Productions to a neck.

FRETBOARD WAXES

There are several companies that make waxes for use on a guitar fretboard. Monty's make one called Instrument Food, designed to reinvigorate and protect bare wood fretboards, and one called Montypresso, which they label as a relic wax because it contains a stain that darkens the wood. Axe Wax has a Naked Balm for use on new bare wood fretboards, a range of scented waxes, clear waxes and stain waxes in various colours. Potentially all of these can be used on a neck or body too. Monty's do sell larger tins of their products, but you can get at least one body out of a standard tin.

A selection of waxes made specifically for use on a guitar body and fretboard.

INSPIRATION: FRANKLYN GUITARS COLOURED FINISHES

I met Chris from Franklyn Guitars online via The Guitar Builders Collective – he set up the original forum for it. I'd seen his guitars on social media, but it wasn't until we both exhibited at the British Boutique Guitar Festival in 2022 that I saw them in person and was blown away by their finishes. What I had mistaken for bright, solid, sprayed-on paint finishes were in fact coloured wood wax finishes from Osmo. It was how the open pore of the grain retained a very natural look whilst having such a vivid colour that struck me most. Chris says these are real crowd pleasers at guitar shows, people being more likely to pick up and play the coloured instruments over the natural wood finishes. He even colour-waxed some that were originally intended to be left natural as a result.

PAINTS, VARNISHES AND LACQUERS

There are plenty of options when it comes to products with which to finish your guitar. At different stages of the finishing process you may make different selections, mixing and matching the types to suit what you are making. However, not everything is compatible in every order of application, so let me start with a basic overview of the types of finish available to use on guitars, before talking about how to apply them and the difference in technique for each.

Nitrocellulose lacquer finish

Many believe that nitrocellulose lacquer is the best guitar finish because Leo Fender used it on his early guitars during the Fender Golden Age up to the mid-1960s. However, Fender chose it in the same way he did many of the materials used in the guitars; it was inexpensive and readily available. It also had the benefit of being an established automotive finish already in mass production with a wealth of knowledge and experience around how to use it.

Sometimes referred to simply as nitro or lacquer, it had some properties that made it distinct from other finishes. It applied very thinly, yellowed over time and was prone to cracking (sometimes called checking). Many people will associate the classic vintage sound of old instruments to this finish. In fact, there is a section later in the book aimed at giving a guitar the relic look, a deliberate faded or changed colour with finish cracks and a worn appearance. Nitrocellulose lacquer also gave a soft finish that was easy to mark.

However, modern nitrocellulose is made in a different way, partly due to the toxic qualities of nitrocellulose and partly to make the finish more durable. Companies such as Nitorlack, which specialises in making guitar finishes, produce different types of nitrocellulose lacquers. They have a modern formula, a Golden Age one that is made to crack and wear like a traditional nitrocellulose, and a special Relic lacquer that can achieve the relic effect very quickly.

Nitrocellulose dries via evaporation and even the modern formulas take time to do this, so it's not a good choice for a quick finish. This is no doubt one of the main reasons factory lines would have moved on to other finishes that allowed them to speed up production times. Some suppliers won't sell nitrocellulose direct to the public because of its health and safety implications if not used in a safe environment with protection. I'll cover that later.

Acrylic finishes

Fender also used acrylic lacquer at the same time as the nitrocellulose. It's less prone to cracking and had more colours available. It was the standard paint used in the automotive industry at the time. We don't always associate it with the vintage guitars because it was often coated in a layer of clear nitrocellulose to finish. Looking back at a 1950s guitar where the colour seems to have yellowed, we may actually be seeing a yellowed clear topcoat over acrylic lacquer.

In this book I'm going to use both acrylic spray cans designed for artists and some designed for home automotive repair. These are water-based, cheap, readily available and come in a massive range of colours. They dry via evaporation, which can happen quickly, and go on in thicker layers than the nitrocellulose.

Polyurethane and polyester finishes

Both of these are often referred to as poly finishes and are the most common in the modern guitar industry. Some poly finishes are single component, but many require the addition of a hardener. The latter reaches its final hardness via a chemical reaction and does not need to evaporate in the same way acrylic and nitrocellulose do. This means that the finish can be applied a bit more thickly, and in fact it naturally does lay thickly, helping to fill pores and leave a smoother surface. A two-part finish like this is sometimes referred to as 2-Pack, 2Pac or 2K. Although it's mainly used in spray guns, there are some brands, such as SprayMax that I will cover later, which offer the same technology in a spray can.

Water-based varnish

Water-based products are becoming more popular as a finish for guitars, partly because they are safer to use and more environmentally friendly. They are often easy to apply and add additional layers to, as well as being easy to clean up afterwards. The finish is normally softer than a polyurethane finish, more like a nitrocellulose, and therefore more susceptible to marks from bumps and knocks.

IS IT A PAINT, A LACQUER OR A VARNISH?

I've noticed people describe various finishes in different manners. For me, the key aspects are whether the finish is nitrocellulose, polyurethane or acrylic. Essentially, we can say:

* **Lacquer** is a solvent-based finish.
* **Paint** is pigment added to a water- or oil-based liquid.
* **Varnish** is clear and often resin and drying-oil based.

COMPATIBILITY OF DIFFERENT FINISHES

Nitrocellulose is the only spanner in the works here. The thinners in the nitrocellulose can react with other finishes that are applied on top, causing poor adhesion or lifting off. This may not happen all over, but in wrinkles or patches. It's best to use only nitrocellulose on nitrocellulose. However, nitrocellulose can be put on top of other finishes.

In theory, all the other finishes are fine to go on top of each other in any order. However, if you are planning on mixing any finish type, or even the same type but different brands, it is best to carry out a test first.

Methods of application

Spray cans

Spray cans are potentially the way you are going to start if doing this for the first time. The nozzles of a spray can make a huge difference to the spray pattern the can leaves. I prefer a wide pattern, allowing more coverage in one pass.

Some nozzles and their spray patterns

The Nitorlack can's nozzle can be adjusted to change the direction of the spray pattern.

It's best to have the spray cans at room temperature before spraying. I sometimes put them in a bucket of warm (not boiling) water for an hour beforehand if they have been kept in cold conditions.

MAINTAINING CANS

Once you have finished with a can for the day, hold it upside down and spray until no more paint comes out. This will clear the nozzle ready for the next use.

Some nozzles on specialised cans made for the guitar finishing and automotive industries have nozzles designed to replicate the spray pattern of a spray gun. By twisting the nozzle, you can adjust the orientation of the spray pattern.

If you are spraying from two cans with the same style of nozzle, varied results can still be achieved. Sprays designed for guitars and manufactured by a guitar finishing company have the end goal of a smooth finish. I use Montan Gold cans a lot because of their cost, colour range and availability. However, they are designed for graffiti artists, therefore the finish tends to be more speckled and bumpier and needs some extra work once sprayed.

Spray cans must be shaken before being used to ensure that all the components are fully mixed. Often, they contain a small metal ball inside called a pea that helps with the mixing. Sometimes you won't initially hear the ball when you start shaking the can, as the contents will have settled, but as the insides mix, you will hear the distinctive rattle that leads to the nickname 'rattle cans'. Two minutes is normally enough, but always check the manufacturer's recommendations.

2K spray cans

Some cans hold a 2K (or two-part) finish in them. The two liquids are held in separate inner compartments until released. Don't get this confused with 2X, which normally means twice the coverage.

Once the two parts are mixed, there is a limited time in which to spray before the components have completed their chemical reaction inside the can and are no longer sprayable. This pot life is normally 24 to 48 hours. I tend to spray the first coat one afternoon. Sand the following morning, then spray the second coat. If a third coat is needed, I repeat the sand and spray on the second morning. There's more on the process of applying finishes later in this chapter.

SprayMax is my go-to 2K in a can finish. Shake it for two minutes to start.

Remove the red button from the lid.

The button fits on underneath the can.

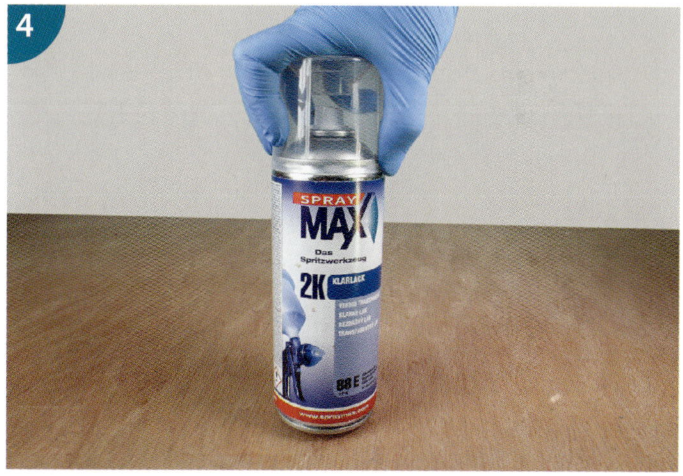

Press the can down hard until you hear a click, then shake for a further two minutes.

Airbrush

Airbrushes have their place in the guitar finishing world, but I wouldn't recommend it for finishing a whole guitar. They can be good for burst finishes, for spraying through stencils for headstock logos, or any other fine work. They stand out if you're using the guitar as a canvas for an artwork where the airbrush can be a unique tool in the right hands. Whole books have been written on the art of using an airbrush, so I won't cover it here.

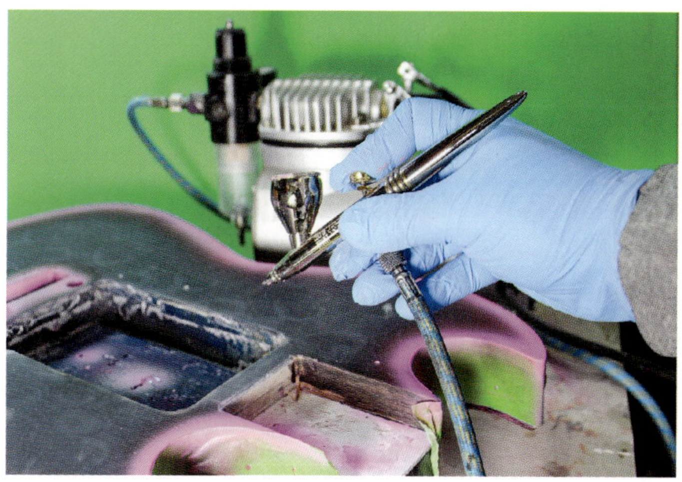

An airbrush being used for a fine fade on the edges of the Model 666.

INSPIRATION: ARY GUITARS' AIRBRUSHED ARTWORK

Airbrushing is an art from in its own right; a whole new set of tools to use and techniques to learn. Ali Yucel from ARY Guitars is a great example of how these methods can be transferred to guitars. I first met Ali when we collaborated on a build for Cancer Research UK (like a lot of small builders, he sells instruments for charity fundraising). He painted this Stratocaster style guitar with a finish inspired by an RAF plane. Ali says, 'I based it on a particular Spitfire, using the original colours and markings. It was used for training in World War II, and restored about a decade ago, and it was used in the 2017 movie *Dunkirk*.'

Some of the steps in Ali's process.

The guitar Ali sent me to work on.

A selection of ARY Guitars.

Spray gun

Easily the best option for spraying a guitar is a spray gun, but they aren't cheap as you will need extra equipment such as an air compressor and cleaning tools.

All guns are different, although they will have similar controls. Always check the guide for your gun for specifics. Some finishes you use will be in two parts. Mix them outside of the gun cup, then pour them in.

A spray pressure, set at the compressor in most cases, should be around 20–25psi. A combination of gun and product may require something different, for example 35psi may work better for a thicker topcoat or sealer, but 15psi for a thinner finish such as when adding a burst. You will need to test with your own system and product choice before spraying the guitar. Start with a lower pressure and work up. A common problem is the orange peel-like texture. That often happens with too little pressure.

If your gun is sputtering, the finish may be too thick and require thinning. Polyurethane and cellulose products normally have their own thinners. Some manufacturers have specific thinners for their two-part products. Nitorlack has one thinner for all of its different products. Water-based finishes can be thinned with water. Always thin very gradually and test. You may need to balance this with the pressure. In some cases, thinning will help with a more even and consistent finish.

A selection of spray guns and equipment. The small gun is often called a touch-up gun.

There will be an air cap where spray comes through; this can usually be rotated to adjust the direction of the spray pattern.

Many will have a spray adjuster that changes the quantity of air flowing out of the cap and therefore changes the shape of the spray pattern/fan.

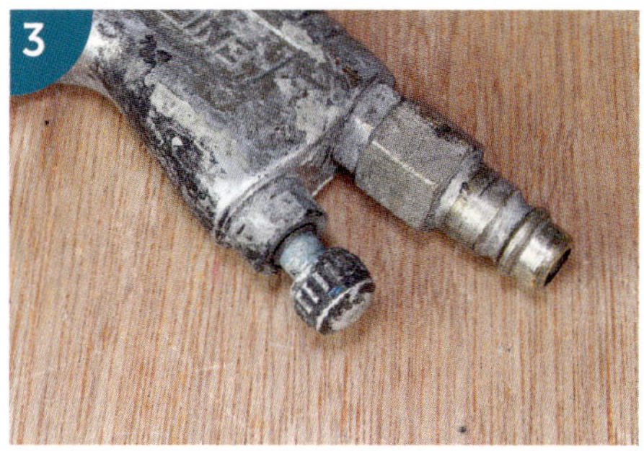

There will be an airflow adjuster that is adjusted for the material you are spraying – lower for thinner materials and higher for thicker.

The needle adjuster restricts the amount of fluid coming from the gun. Adjust this to help prevent too much paint being sprayed.

The cup holds the paint. It is above for gravity-feed guns, which is what you need for most finishes. A cup below is called a suction-feed gun.

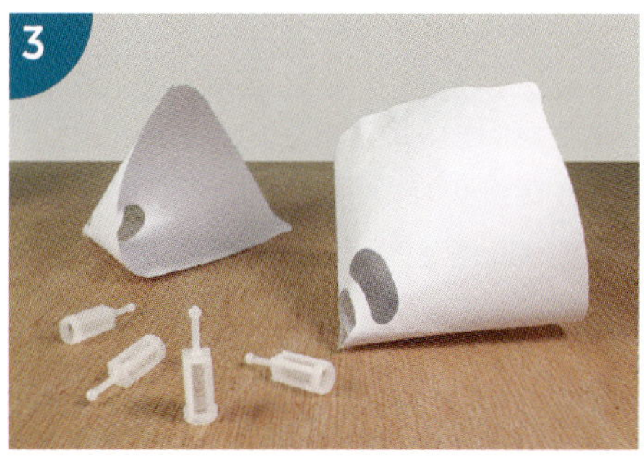

When pouring the finish into the gun, use a filter to ensure that no small contaminants are in the paint. Some guns have disposable internal filters too.

CLEANING A GUN

You must clean your gun when finished. The relevant thinners are ideal for this. Take the gun apart to clean all the small parts, use small brushes and cleaning needles to check that no holes or passages are blocked. If you don't clean the gun, it will be hard to clean in the future and will begin to operate badly. I use an ultrasonic cleaner to occasionally treat all the parts in addition to the daily clean.

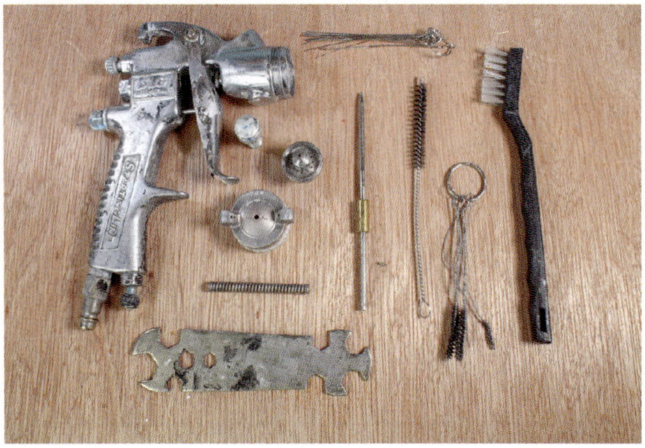

Spraying

Spray booths and safety equipment

Paints and lacquers contain VOCs (Volatile Organic Compounds). Although water-based ones may be marked as safe, I still don't like the idea of breathing in the fumes. Buy a good mask with the relevant filters. Filters have different ratings and ABEK-1 is the type of filter that covers the widest range of products you may encounter when finishing guitars. I add a P3 filter over the top so that I can use the same mask when sanding. Some chemicals in the sprays can be absorbed through the skin, so wearing long sleeves and gloves is essential, and a full-face mask is best.

Always spray in a well-ventilated area. If you build a spray booth with an extractor fan, use a fan that is explosion proof, or at least separates the motor from the air stream. Volatile substances being pulled through an extractor and passing over the motor could be flammable.

I've seen quite a few people convert hydroponics tents or Ikea tent wardrobes into a spray booths. Simply hang the guitar inside, spray standing outside, then zip up to prevent dust getting in. An added extractor is great. You can also just spray outside, but wind and dust can be an issue.

Spraying conditions

Ideally, spraying should be done at room temperature, with a relative humidity of 40–60%. I often heat my spray booth for several hours before spraying to achieve this temperature during colder months. Be careful if you leave a heater on whilst spraying, or turning one on whilst there is spray vapour in the air; many heaters will create a spark when switching on. I have an enclosed electric oil heater. All plug sockets in my spray booth are enclosed and water- and vapour-sealed too. If the humidity is too high, I often find it lowers once I've heated the space, or had the extractor on for a short time.

A selection of safety equipment. I've glued an old pair of glasses into my facemask.

A cheap thermometer and hygrometer (humidity meter) is a useful addition to any spray area.

If you spray outside, be sure to denib for lumps and lightly sand between coats of nitrocellulose to remove any extra dust that may have settled. You will be sanding between all other finishes anyway.

Spraying jigs

There are specialist jigs you can buy that attach to a work bench, or are held by a bench clamp, which allow you to twist and spin the guitar body whilst painting. Here are some simple alternatives.

I made this jig with a Lazy Susan bearing screwed on top of a piece of 2×4. It allows me to spin the guitar body to work on edges and spray one facing-up surface. Spray at an angle when spraying downwards to avoid drips.

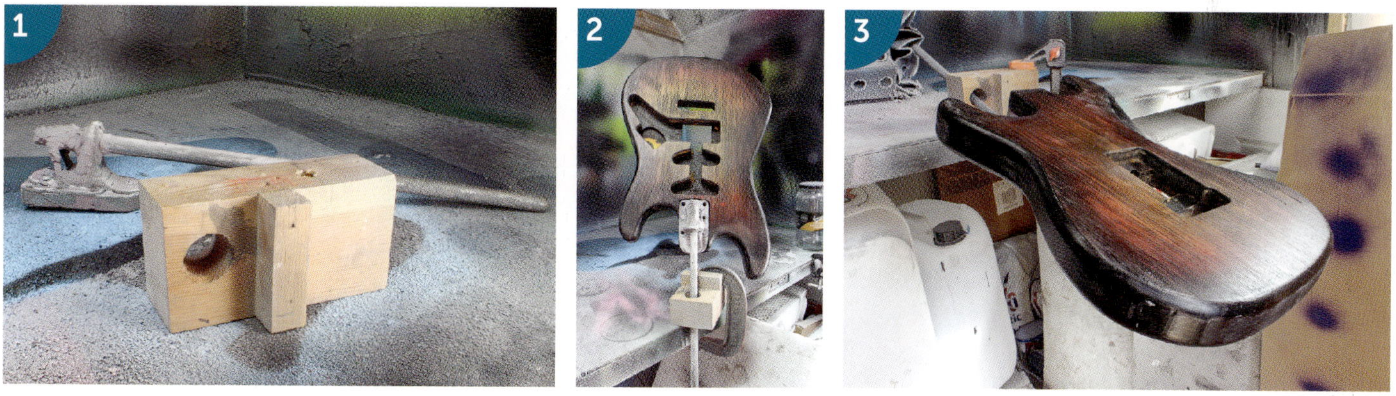

This piece of wood with a hole in it can be clamped in place, with the other piece (made from odds and ends) screwed into the guitar neck pocket. Combined, they allow me to rotate and spray all sides of the guitar.

Hooks are great for both holding whilst spraying (I often need to steady the body by holding the lowest hook) and for drying.

Spraying technique

A good technique is essential for achieving a great finish and the approach for spraying a guitar is the same as for using a spray can or a spray gun.

Always start the spray away from the body, then move on to the body. This helps to avoid any sudden bursts or build-up of paint as it is released from the can. Finish the spray off the body for the same reason.

Move at a steady speed. If you observe paint beginning to drip, you are too close or too slow. If the surface looks thin and powdery, you are too far away or moving too fast. It's normally best to allow a drip to dry, then deal with it. Trying to wipe a drip off can often make it worse and harder to fix once dry.

The process in the five photos below counts as one coat of whatever you are applying. Leave it to dry for the recommended flash time, normally ten to fifteen minutes, then repeat. You should aim to do three coats in one sitting. Leave to dry for 24 hours before applying more coats.

Those are the basics for spraying. The number of sessions you spray at each stage will vary and the type of paint will dictate how much sanding, if any, must take place between them. Now you know the type of paint you will be using and how to apply it, it is time to explain the full process of painting a guitar.

Make sure that you are observing the spray pattern produced from the gun or can. If your nozzle or air cap produces an oval pattern, ensure that as you move the gun the widest strip of paint is being sprayed. Adjust accordingly.

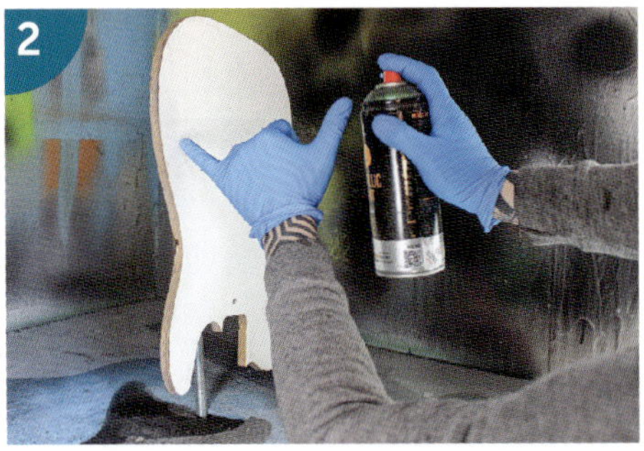

Spray from around 20cm away (one handspan).

Move from one side to the other in a straight line.

Move back, creating an overlapping straight line.

Once the whole body is covered, repeat the process at 90 degrees.

SPRAY ORIENTATION

Remember that when you change spray direction by 90 degrees, you will need to adjust the gun or can so that the spray pattern turns too. You can physically turn the can 90 degrees to match, or if you have a nozzle that can be changed adjust it each time. Spray guns can have their air cap rotated.

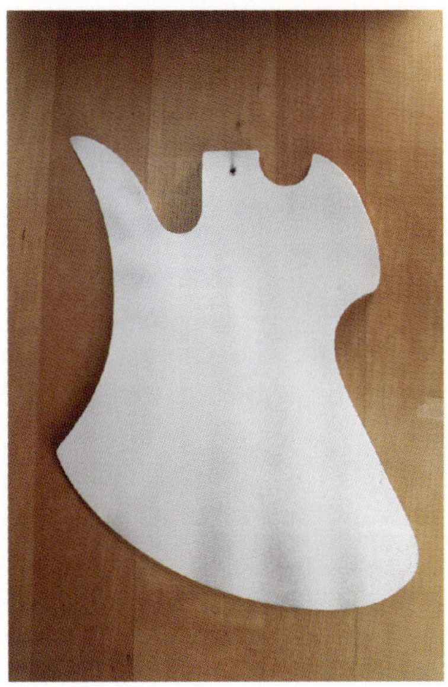

Here, you can see the streaks where each pass hasn't overlapped the last. This can be hidden by the second pass at 90 degrees and by applying three coats in one session. A better spray technique will result in an even finish with each coat.

PAINTING A GUITAR

Preparing the surface

The guitar body will need to be ready to take the paint, meaning that all the shaping and filling of holes, dents and dings should have happened. Sand the body up to 400 grit, as this will give the paint a surface to key into. If the body was previously sanded with a coarser grade, work your way up in small increments – 80 grit to 120 grit, to 180 grit, to 220 grit, to 280 grit, to 320 grit, ending on 400 grit. There is no need to sand if you are spraying stains, as the surface will already have been sanded to the correct grade.

Always remove all dust with a tack cloth (a sticky rag designed for this purpose). If you are using a spray gun, you can also spray clean air over the surface just before spraying the paints. I usually also wipe the surface over with my cleaning solution, or an alternative such as denatured alcohol, let it evaporate, then go over it again with the tack cloth.

Masking

It's best to avoid getting paint on the neck pocket edges, as paint here can prevent the neck from fitting back in. Mask the edges only with tape. The base of the pocket may have paint on it. If you don't mask, you can always sand back at the end to help achieve a good fit. I do this if I'm painting the neck itself, as its width will change with the paint and it won't fit the pocket anyway.

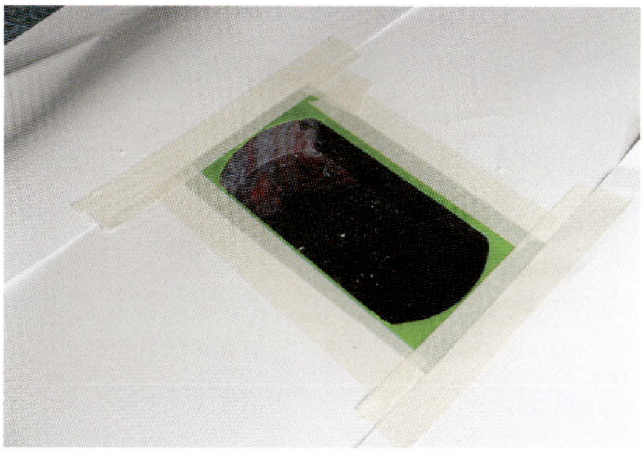

Whilst I'm mentioning masking, if you want to spray a small area such as inside a cavity, I often mask neatly around the edge with tape, then stick paper to that masking tape. The paper covers the whole guitar and saves using lots of masking tape.

The binding should be masked. Later in the book is a section on masking for advanced painting techniques.

REMOVING BINDING MASKS

When you remove the tape after spraying primer and colour, and before applying the topcoats, you will likely find an uneven edge. This is partly caused by paint not coming away when the mask is removed; it's still attached to the rest of the paint, but not directly to the body. It can be removed by scraping with a blade as in the photo, or neatly cut off with a scalpel.

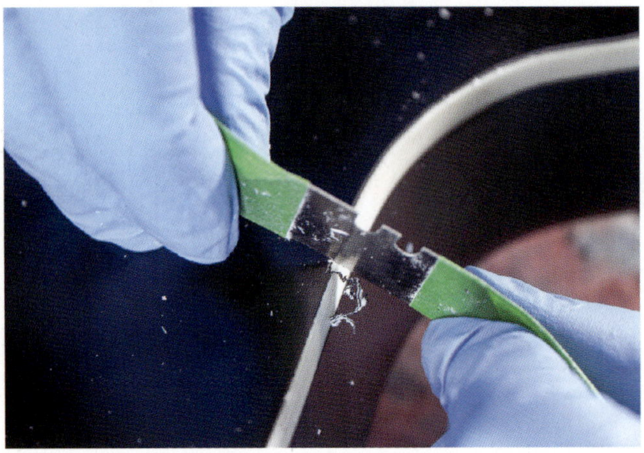

PRIMER COATS

Primers come as water-based, acrylic, nitrocellulose or polyurethane. I always advise sticking to the same type as you intend to use on further layers, but the normal caveat is there; any can go on top of each other except nitrocellulose, which can only have nitrocellulose on top. Always test if you are mixing types and manufacturers.

A primer coat is a lot like the sanding sealer coat. Some companies don't make sealers, just primers. If the primer is clear, it can be used in place of the clear sealer as it helps to create a uniform surface by sealing in pores and small dents. Primer coats serve other purposes too. Often, they are coloured, creating a solid base for the colour you wish to apply on top. As some colours are translucent, particularly lighter colours such as yellows, a white or grey base can help the colour pop. Sometimes a manufacturer will recommend which base colour should be used. Primers can also help with adhesion for the main colours and topcoats. In practice, whenever a manufacturer offers a primer in their range I recommend using it.

Primers should be applied using the normal spray technique, with three coats in one session. I advise two sessions for most primers, sanding with 400 grit in-between. I can get five coats of a standard body out of one 400ml can of Hycote Grey Primer, which is normally enough. However,

My favourite acrylic primer in a can is Hycote (there is a wide range of colours and variations; I've tested most of them and find them pretty much all as good as each other).

the primer coats often highlight issues that were not noticeable before. If you are using a clear primer, it is harder to notice any small imperfections. Shining a lamp or torch over the surface will help to highlight any issues.

You will need to repeat the process of a spraying session (three coats), followed by 400-grit sanding once it has dried, until the surface is smooth. Then finish with 600 grit. It is essential that you do not proceed until you have a smooth finish with an even primer colour, as future coats are unlikely to lay as thickly as primers and won't fill imperfections as successfully.

PRIMER BEFORE TOPCOAT

I also use a clear primer coat over some of the more advanced techniques covered in this book, such as gilding and acrylic pouring. It helps to seal in the previous layer and to achieve a flat surface when the technique has left a textured layer. It makes the application of a smooth topcoat much easier.

Imperfections and unfilled gaps in the wood have been highlighted by the first primer coat.

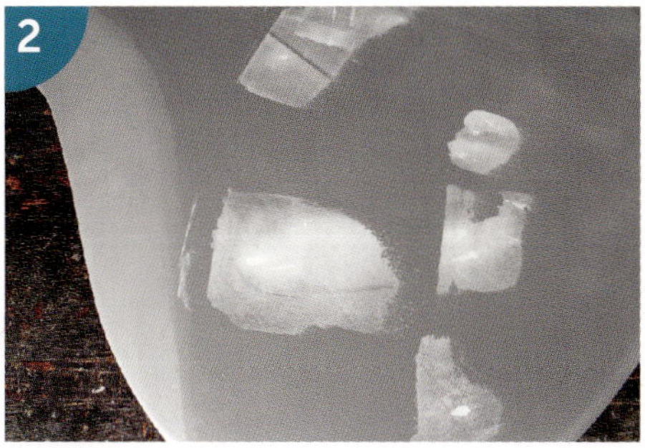

A two-part hard body filler or wood filler should be used to fill them.

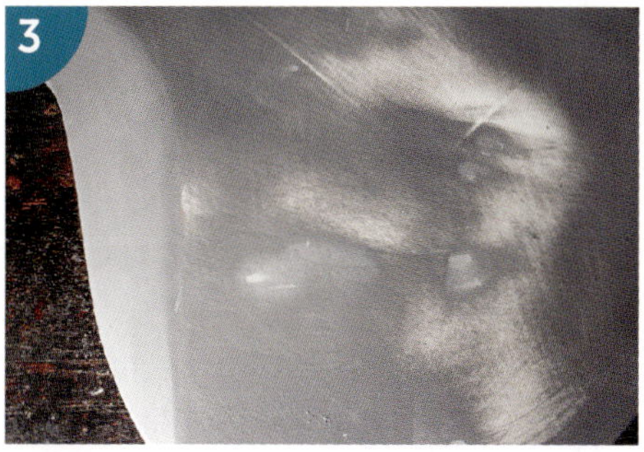

Once sanded back, the body is ready for the next primer coat session.

Covering large areas with the same process is sometimes needed. When sanded back the edge transitions are smooth and all the dents and dings underneath are concealed.

COLOUR COATS AND ADVANCED TECHNIQUES

Once the primer stage is complete, you can move on to the colour. Not all colours are equal. Some will leave an even solid colour after one session of spraying (three coats), but some will need more sessions. This is also the stage where you may want to try out some of the advanced paint techniques covered later in the book, then come back for the topcoats.

Sanding between sessions

It is essential to treat the surface between spray sessions by sanding back to create a key for the next coat. Remember that although you have sprayed three coats in one session, the thickness of the paint will depend on the product. Polyurethane will lay much more thickly than nitrocellulose. Nitrocellulose will not need to be sanded for bonding purposes, as any additional layer will 'melt' into the previous one; it will only need to be sanded if there are lumps (a process called 'denibbing'). Sand with 600-grit hard-backed on flat areas and foam on curves.

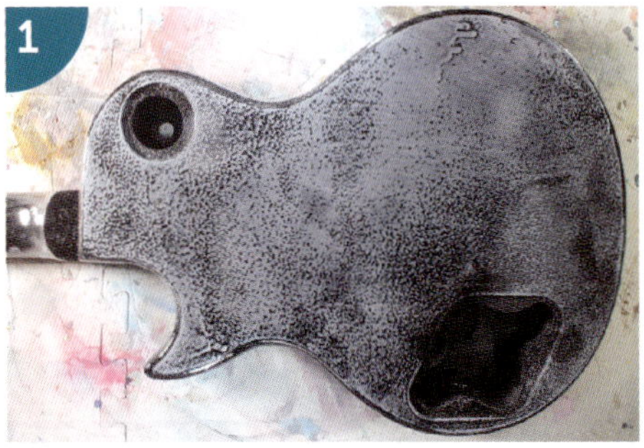

A light sand of this black surface reveals that the paint has dried in a textured fashion. This is normal when spraying, even with good technique.

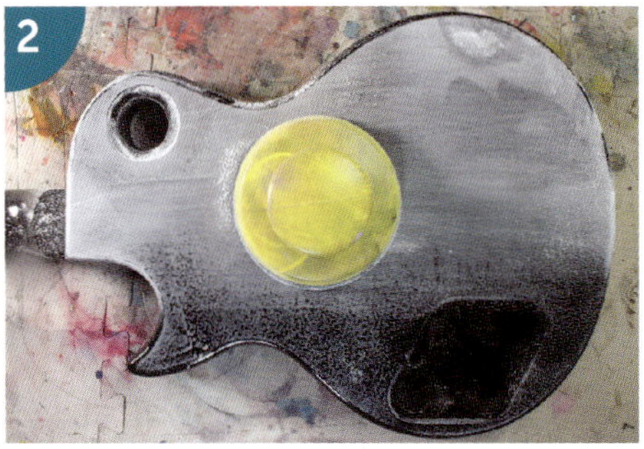

Keep sanding until the surface is even all over. The top part here is ready for the next spray session.

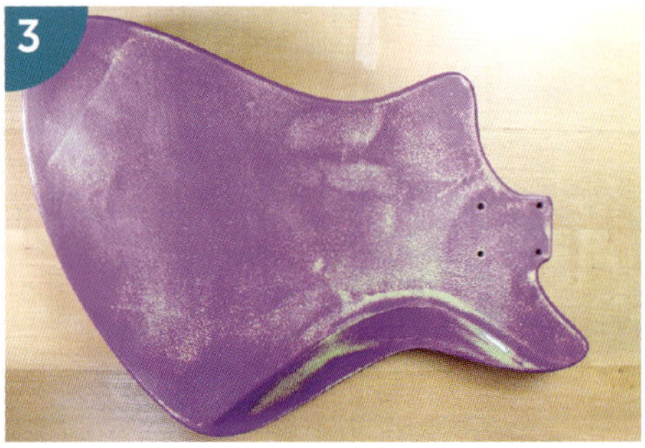

This body had two coats of colour applied in one session. The use of two colours reveals how sanding smooth sands through to the previous layer in some areas. If one colour was used for all coats, the surface would appear even.

TAKE CARE NOT TO SAND THROUGH THE LAYERS

Problem areas that you might sand through include any hard edges like the neck pocket and curved edges along the whole circumference where the paint will naturally lay more thinly.

If you are worried that you might sand through, stop sanding and apply the next spray session of three coats. Once that is dry, continue sanding with the benefit of the safety of a thicker layer. Ideally, though, you should aim to have the colour on and sanded flat in two sessions, three maximum. Thicker finishes are often more fragile and prone to chipping.

Dealing with paint problems

There is a range of problems that can occur, and often the same visual symptom may have been caused by different reasons. This section will cover the more common issues and how to solve them once the paint is dry. Always remember to sand with 600 grit all over after dealing with the issue and before spraying the next session of coats.

Blushing in nitrocellulose finishes happens with high humidity or low temperatures. It leaves a milky white patch in the finish; sometimes the edges can look a bit like an oil spill with a rainbow of colours reflected on the surface. To fix it, apply heat gently and evenly using a heat gun before the patch dries. You can also use a blusher remover spray. Sometimes, applying the next coat in proper conditions hides the blush. Otherwise, sanding might be needed. A retarder can also be added to the spray-gun mix.

The paint has separated, a bit like the crackle finish described later. This is normally the paint not adhering to the layer below. Lightly sand through this, then reapply.

Unwanted texture from the grain is visible. You can use filler, just as you would with the primer coat, or apply a sealer coat next session, sand, then continue with the colour in the session after that.

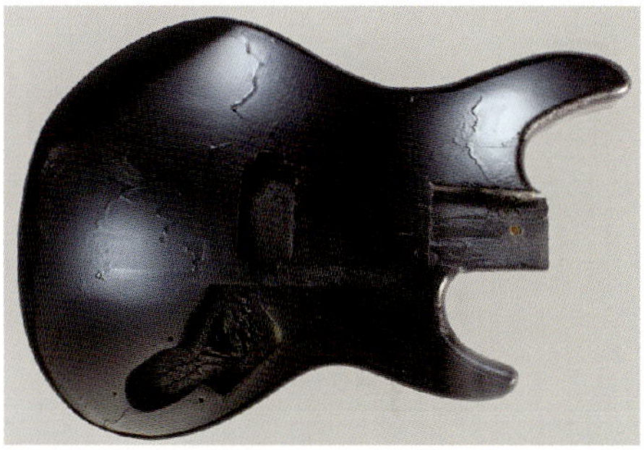

The paint will probably be thick all over and you will have drying issues if you try to fix big drips like these. The best course of action is to sand back with a more aggressive grade of paper, then start again from an earlier stage in the painting process.

Medium-sized drips can be gently scraped back in small layers until flat with the surface. Mask off a blade so that the cutting edge is the width of the drip.

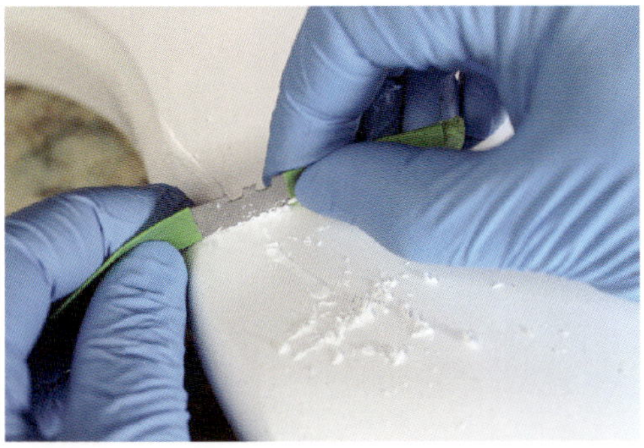

Small drips can be sanded back, but if you focus on one area too much there is a risk of sanding through. Using a larger pad and sanding an area is often best. Go slowly and use 600 grit.

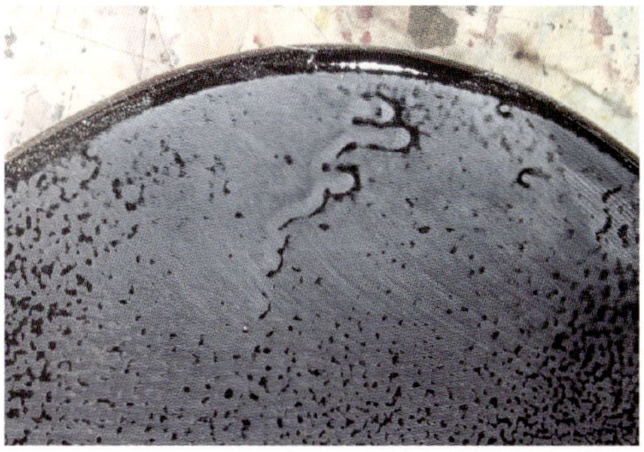

An orange peel-like surface isn't a big problem and can be sanded smooth. It's normally caused by poor spraying techniques, such as moving too fast, being too far away, the gun pressure being too low, or having the wrong viscosity for the paint.

This result often implies incompatibility between two products, the most recent one applied pulling up the one underneath as it shrinks and dries. Sand back smooth to 600 grit and use a sealer coat between the two products, or switch product.

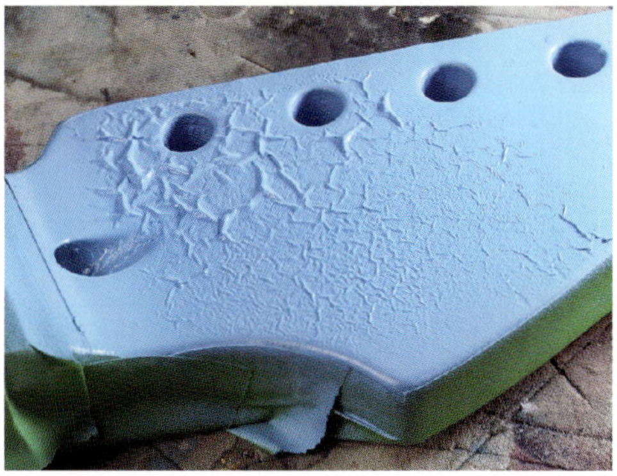

HAPPY ACCIDENTS

The blue I used on this guitar didn't react very well with the primer. When I sanded the raised paint back, I liked the cracked appearance. I have since deliberately used this paint on a few guitars to achieve that look.

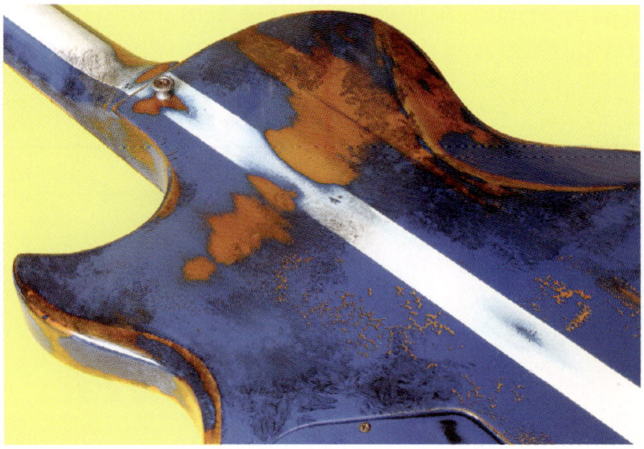

You can see the texture of the paint around the volume control hole on this body.

A clogged sanding pad.

Wet-sanding the finish.

Montana Gold art sprays and orange peel

As you will see throughout the book, I like Montana Gold art spray cans. They are acrylic-based, come in a range of colours, are readily available and a pain to spray! They aren't designed for guitars and like many art cans they leave an orange peel-like effect.

What should be an easy process of sanding flat is made harder by this type of paint. My preferred sanding material is Abranet, but, like many other papers, the Montana Gold clogs it up. Instead, this finish has to be wet-sanded. I use 600 grit. I try my best only to do one spray session of Montana Gold colour, but, if I have sanded through at any point, I always wait a few days before applying the second session of spray. Applying this paint too thickly can result in a very long drying time, so better to take a bit more time now than a lot in the future.

CASE STUDY: A 3D PRINTED BODY FROM PRIMER TO TOPCOAT

Read this even if you aren't using a 3D print!

Unlike the other case studies in this book, this 3D-printed example isn't just a finished guitar; it's a step-by-step guide to achieving a perfectly flat finish on a 3D print ready for the topcoat application. A 3D print has layer lines that are essentially an exaggerated version of sanding marks and dents, so the process for filling them can be followed for any guitar in a bad shape.

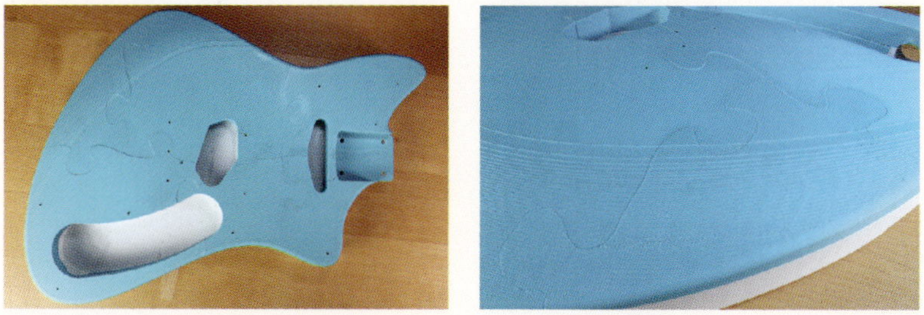

A 3D-printed guitar body showing the printing lines. It's the Teleora from Tasmaniak Guitars.

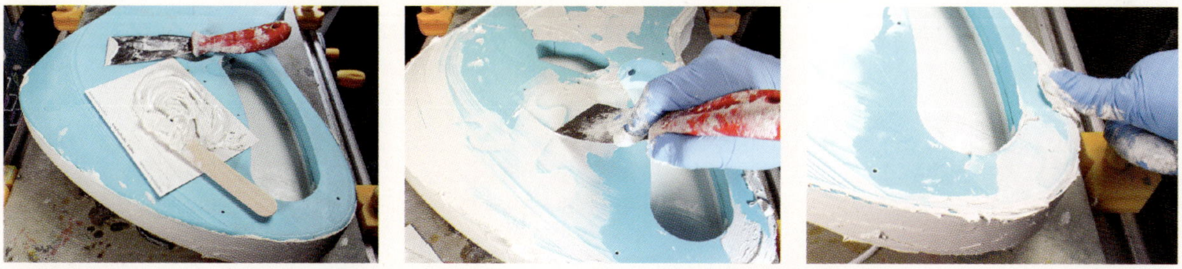

Using a hard two-part car body filler, coat the sides and the top with a spreader. Use your fingers for the edges.

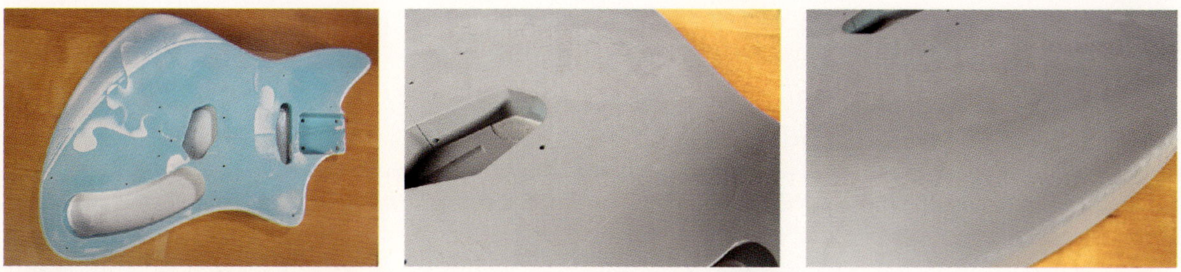

The filler was sanded and the first session of primer sprayed. It revealed that the print lines are still visible.

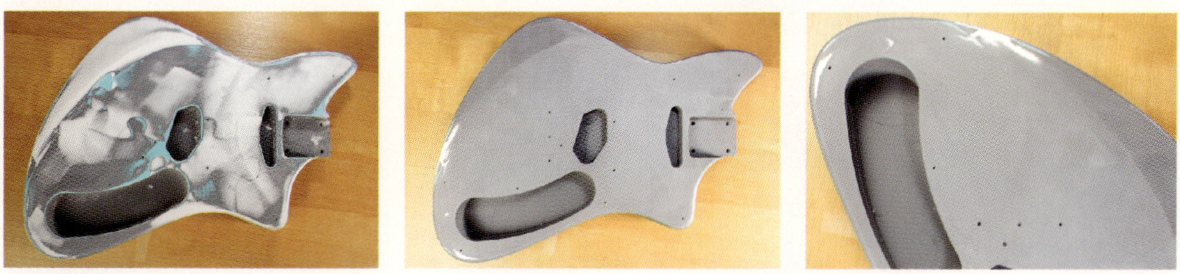

More body filler, another session of primer sprayed and sanded back, revealing just slight imperfections.

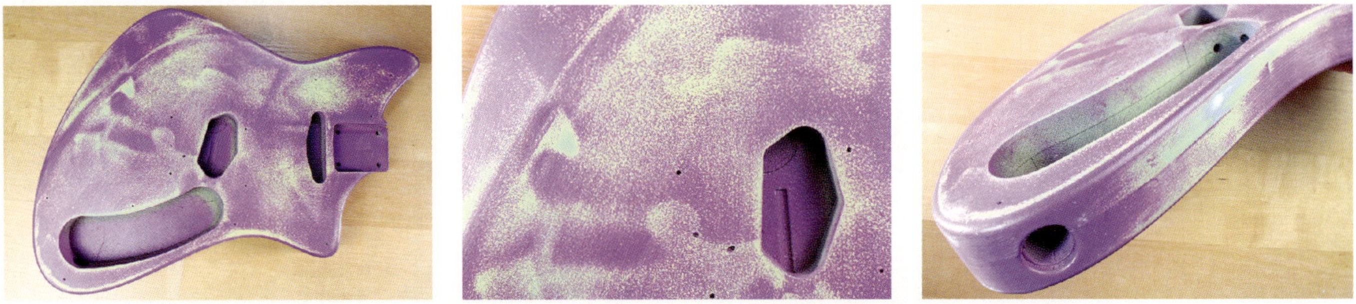

I sprayed two colours instead of of two coats of the same colour of primer, then sanded. They reveal how the top layer has been sanded through to achieve a flat surface.

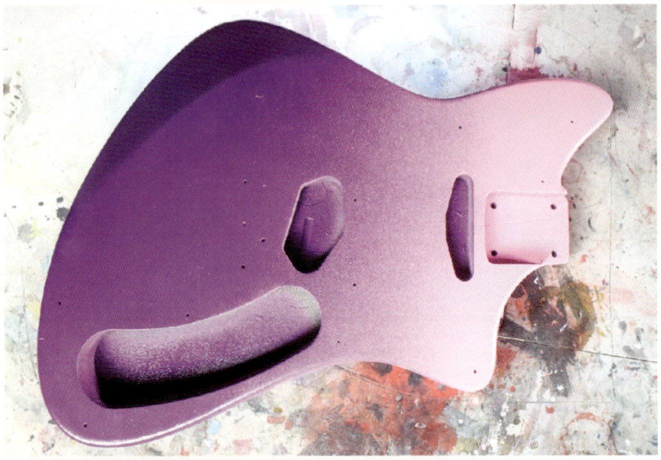

The guitar next had the fade finish applied using Montana Gold colours.

The finished Spatter Teleora.

TAKING ADVANTAGE OF THE SURFACE

On The Guitar Builders Collective Chat podcast we often talk about the beauty of a 3D print, how the material and process are part of the overall design. I, however, do like any excuse to spray some paint on to something, so for this version of the Teleora I used no filler or primer and applied two sessions of Nitorlack's white polyurethane and one session of a green Montana Gold. The final colour coat was lightly sanded back with 600 grit to reveal the layer lines and joins of each individual part. I like its unique look and will be experimenting more with this technique on future builds.

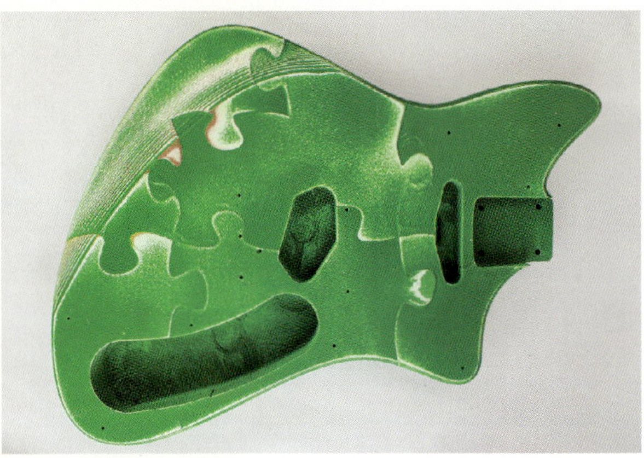

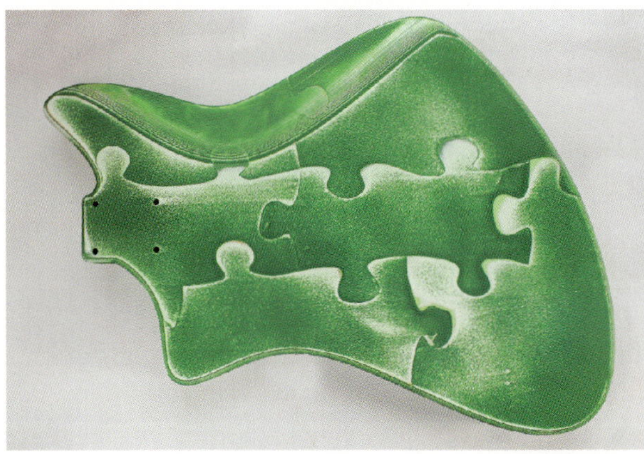

TOPCOATS

Some paints come in a matt or gloss finish, intended to be the colour coat and the topcoat. You can take these straight on to the next stage of buffing on polishing and skip applying a topcoat. If you do that I would advise making sure you have carried out three spray sessions (five for nitrocellulose which settles thinly). However, most finishes will need a clear topcoat applied, and all will benefit from one. I think a clear coating over the top of a colour results in a richer and deeper finish.

As with all stages you can find topcoats in any product type. You may have a preferred finish based on how easy it is to spray or finish, or how thickly it settles. One additional consideration is that this final coat is the surface that the players will feel. Whilst polyurethane makes for a lovely thick clear, I personally prefer the feeling of nitrocellulose. Nitrocellulose settles thinly so will require more sessions of topcoats.

As a guide, I usually apply two sessions of most topcoats, and three of nitrocellulose. If working with cans, a whole can of SprayMax 2K, or a Nitorlack clear will be sufficient. If it's your first time doing this, you can play it safe and add an extra session because it's easy to be overzealous in the next polishing and buffing stage. Always stick to three coats in one session following flash times between them. Wait a day then sand with 600 grit hard backed on flat areas and foam backed on curved. Carry out the next session then repeat. Whilst you normally only need to sand nitrocellulose if there are lumps, a light sand between the topcoat sessions is beneficial for achieving a really smooth finish.

GLOSS, SATIN OR MATT TOPCOAT?

Topcoats normally come in gloss, satin or matt. However, as I'll cover in the section on polishing below, you can achieve any finish with any topcoat. I often find the matt and satin ones are great out of the can, provided that you have sanded flat between spray sessions at all stages of the process They need no treatment once the final topcoat has been applied. Using these finishes straight from the can saves the need to sand and buff to a matt or satin finish later

I have always ended up sanding the gloss finishes during the polishing process to achieve an even higher gloss than from the can or gun. As you're going to sand it anyway, it really doesn't matter which topcoat finish you apply – the same gloss end result can be achieved from all of them with the same amount of time and work.

Applying a topcoat over a textured or raised finish

Some of the advanced techniques, such as the spatter finish, result in a textured surface. You may like this and wish to keep it, in which case simply apply a topcoat and don't sand flat. If you want to achieve a flat surface, there are a few things to consider. As you put topcoats on, the whole surface will become thicker, both the low points and the high points. Sand back the highest topcoat layers between the spray sessions until the lowest (which isn't being sanded) is level with the highest. At this point, all will be flat. This means more sessions of topcoats.

Despite having layers of topcoat applied, the black is raised enough that when flat-sanded the clear is completely removed and the black is now being sanded.

In this example, it doesn't matter that the highest topcoat has been sanded through and the black has been sanded into, because the black is solid all the way through. For a hand-painted finish, where the paint applied by brushstroke is higher, sanding through can ruin the image or design. Extra care and time must be taken with such finishes. This spatter finish needed five sessions of clear before I could get it completely smooth.

Wipe-on products

Companies like Nitorlack make products specifically for application by wiping on, but you may be able to wipe on other products too. With experimentation, you may find that some other products designed for use in a spray gun can be applied by hand.

Wipe-on finishes are applied in much the same way as oils and waxes, with a cloth (sometimes a sponge brush is recommended for certain products, such as acrylic ones). Once a coat has been applied, let it dry, sand with 600 grit, then apply the next coat. Each product will have a guide drying time between coats and a recommended number of coats.

POLISHING AND BUFFING

At this stage, you will have a guitar body with a flat surface sanded to 600 grit and the finish of your choice, either a flat colour or one of the more advanced techniques from later in the book, and clear topcoats applied. You are now ready to complete your guitar with polish and buff for the desired finish. A matt or satin finish don't follow the same process all the way to the end, but I will also show you how to bring a gloss finish back to a matt one.

Polishing to a gloss finish

The gloss finish is achieved by progressively sanding the surface with a finer grit to remove all imperfections and be left with a super-flat finish. This is then taken further with a wax or polish to leave a mirror-like surface that evenly reflects light all over. Start with 600 grit, then move through to 3000 in stages. The exact grades available will depend on the product you use, but following this progression as closely as possible works well: 600 grit to 800 grit, to 1000 grit, to 1200 grit, to 1500 grit, to 2000 grit, to 3000 grit. It makes no difference if the topcoat you applied was described as a matt, satin or gloss finish; all can be sanded to a gloss finish.

Wet-sanding method

When wet-sanding, sand as you would with normal paper, changing direction 90 degrees between grades in order to confirm that the previous marks have been sanded out. One method is to have a bowl of water to dip the paper in, so that it's damp, not dripping. Change the water between grades and wipe the surface dry to ensure there are no stray grits or bits. The best option for wetting is to use a spray bottle, such as the misting ones that hairdressers use. Use hard-backed paper on flat areas and foam-backed for edges and curves.

Dry-sanding with Buflex

To avoid the mess of wet-sanding, you can use Abranet to start, then switch to Buflex from Eagle Abrasives, which comes in finer grades. Work up to 3000 grit. I much prefer this method; it's quicker and less messy. Remember to vacuum the dust regularly that is collecting in the sheets as you work.

This body was finished with Nitoraqua matt clear, a water-based topcoat from Nitorlack. The right half has been sanded to a flat finish using Buflex.

Using polishing compounds

The method I recommend for polishing to a gloss finish is only to work up to 1000 grit with paper, then switch to a polishing compound. Polishing compounds are abrasive liquids, essentially liquid sandpaper. You can use a guitar-specific one such as those from Axe Wax or Nitorlack, or an automotive one. Either way, just use a fine polishing compound, as the medium ones will probably be a step back from what you have achieved reaching the 1000 grit.

It can be applied by hand with a cloth, but using a foam pad on a variable speed drill or random orbital sander is best. Pads come in different textures and hardnesses. Harder pads are for heavy- and medium-cut compounds and softer ones for lighter cut and polish. The surface texture of the pad won't make any difference. Cone pads are good for hard to reach spaces, such as in-between the

Polishing compounds and buffing sponge pads.

Working evenly over the body with a figure of eight motion.

horns and neck pocket. More expensive pads made for the automative industry feel much better quality and normally last a lot longer than cheaper versions.

Avoid going too fast or staying in one place, as this may cause a friction burn. Splashing a bit of water on the pad can help. Move in a figure of eight pattern over the surface of the guitar body. Once you have worked over the body a few times, stop, let the compound haze over, then buff off with a clean rag. Repeat this process until you are happy with the gloss finish.

Finishing with waxes

If you've achieved a great shine from the polishing stage, you may choose to complete the job with a finishing wax, which may make the surface feel smoother. There are several guitar-specific brands of wax made for finishing over paint. I use Axe Wax's G2, mainly because I use their whole system and I like to buy from other British manufacturers. I used to use Turtle Wax, which, like many automotive waxes and polishes, is great on guitars.

I prefer to use a liquid wax, applied with a cloth, left for a few minutes, then buffed up with a clean cloth. Harder waxes can leave a residue in screw holes. The choice of wax that is right for your guitar may be dependent upon availability and smell. Some are highly scented, which can be a turn-off (after a customer complained I stopped using scented finishes even though I like them, particularly the Axe Wax Candy).

The waxes (and oils) covered earlier in the book can also be used as a final finish, either after the topcoats are applied or after the polishing stage. Microcrystalline wax and Carnauba can be applied and buffed just as they are applied on to the bare wood surface, using a cloth. Different brands will recommend specific wait times between applying the wax and buffing it off. Normally, one coat is all that is needed over a topcoat sanded to 600 grit.

Creating a matt or satin finish

A matt finish refers to a flat surface with little or no reflection. Satin sits between matt and gloss. You can often achieve these finishes when applying a matt or satin topcoat as long as you have sanded well with 600 grit between coats to ensure a flat surface for the last spray session. Normally, I don't do anything to the final coat applied from a can or gun. Sometimes I find a light rub by hand with a finishing wax can help the surface to appear richer. Test this first in a hidden area.

If you are unhappy with the flatness of the finish from the gun or can, or are converting a gloss finish, start by sanding at 600 grit and stopping at 800 or 1000 grit. If 1000 seems a bit too shiny, go back over with 800 grit. Again, a light rub of finishing wax can help even everything out.

For a satin finish, keep sanding through grits until you are happy with the level of gloss. I have found stopping at 1000 grit and applying a medium-cut polishing compound like Axe Wax's Mass X achieves the results I like in a satin finish. Sometimes I will make two or three passes with the compound, buffing with a cloth in-between, until I am satisfied.

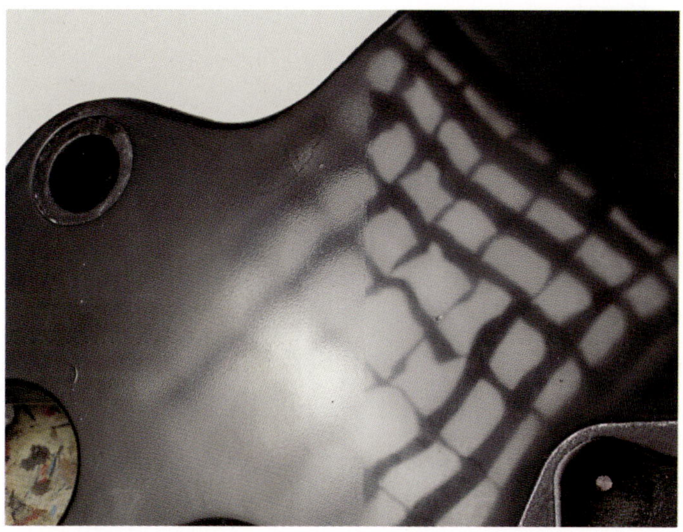

Here you can see the side that has been polished, first with four passes of Axe Wax's fine compound polish, then one pass with their G2 liquid wax.

CHAPTER 4

ADVANCED PAINTING TECHNIQUES

Now that the basics have been covered and before the main creative stages of finishing are explored, it is time to discuss design. Some people will already know exactly what they want; others will be here for inspiration on techniques and processes. I hope that many of you will be wanting to make something unique, to find your own style and design, and create something no one else has. There are so many approaches to design that whole books have been written about them; instead, I want to discuss how to harness your creativity and give a few examples of my design approach … then I'll get back to the actual finishing techniques.

This is the pen and ink sketch of an idea that I sent to Mikey Demus from Skindred; a guitar made using the logo from their album *Kill the Power*. He loved it, but they were recording a new album, *Volume*, so he asked me to design a guitar featuring that logo.

DESIGNING YOUR CUSTOM GUITAR FINISH

Top tips for creativity

Creativity comes to different people in different ways. What inspires one person can put another off. To put it simply, everyone is different and so is what they like. However, I have found that there are some simple strategies that can help anyone with their individual creative design process.

My original sketch for the Skull & Crossbones series of guitars and one of the finished ones.

Documenting the process

I started teaching art in 2001 and have taught thousands of people in various settings, including schools, universities, hospitals, community centres, art galleries and museums. I've used mediums like drawing, paint, sculpture, collage, photography, film, animation and computers. My top tip is to photograph and document your process at all stages. This provides future inspiration and serves as a learning tool to review the process and iterations of the work. Think of your creation as a tree branching in different directions. Sometimes a choice will lead in one direction to a certain outcome, or it may branch out again, or lead to a dead end. With good documentation, you can always repeat the process and branch off at different points.

One of things I like the most about the documentation process is sharing it. This isn't for everyone, but I have found that the feedback I have had on social media often leads to new ideas, or a renewed enthusiasm when my creativity is running dry. Sometimes social media can hinder, though, especially if you're creating something unique. There's a surprising amount of people out there who get very upset with anything that isn't a 1960s style Telecaster and want to tell you so using quite harsh language. If you can ignore those naysayers and find an audience that chimes with your work, social media can be a creative hotbed.

Sketchbooks and collections

When I was at university studying art and then in my first years of teaching, keeping a sketchbook of ideas was pushed as an essential part of being an artist. Nowadays, I think about sketchbooks in a slightly different way – they don't have to be a physical thing that you can hold in your hand. There are plenty of ways to collect images, notes and writings together, such as bookmarking on social media and on browsers, or a digital album of photos and screenshots; anything that allows you to look back on a collection of things will work.

This book is about customising guitars, so obviously you'll want to be recording, storing, or somehow remembering cool guitars you've seen. But inspiration for paint jobs can come from anywhere. My Instagram feed is almost exclusively guitars, guitar builders, sci-fi illustrators and artists. On YouTube, my subscriptions include channels of miniature painting, terrain building for wargames, prop builders, luthiers and musicians. For me, inspiration can come from finding out about a new tool or process, listening to some great music, or seeing another artist's work. I highly recommend curating a social-media account solely for inspiration; perhaps a new account where you only follow things that spark creativity, where you can follow and unfollow whoever or whatever you want, and where you can spend some time when looking for new ideas.

Personally, I have a mix of digital and physical collections, including books on film set and prop design, saved posts on Facebook and Instagram, and a few folders on my phone of screenshots from websites I've been inspired by, and, of course, sketchbooks. Trying asking yourself, 'Could it work on a guitar?' whenever something catches your attention – an object in a museum, food packaging in the supermarket, flaky paint on a wall, a pattern on clothing, special effects in a film, oil spilt on the road, a flower, an animal, anything …

Mood boards

Most of the customisations I do are for clients, many of whom have approached me because they like my work and have a vague idea of something they want but can't do it themselves. This is one of the aspects of the design process that I most enjoy, working with someone to help them realise their 'vision'. Step one is always a mood board.

A mood board is essentially a collection of images that help me put together a design. I can look back on it throughout the design process and then the build to check that I'm still meeting the brief or original idea. However, I always expect the board to change and develop as the design evolves; it's not a static thing. I like to record how a design changes. I used to work with an artist called Daniel Lehan who liked the concept of a detective board, linking ideas together with string until you solve the case. Here are the questions I ask of my clients, and indeed myself, to get a design started:

* Are there any guitar shapes or models to work from?
* What colours or general mood?
* Is there a theme or image to use as a starting point?
* Any other imagery of similar things, but not guitars.

Then I ask them to email me some images that I can put in a folder for reference. In the past, clients have sent me photos of a rally car as inspiration for the final colours and paint work, a collection of posters and adverts for Zombie films, TV shows and computer games, four or five images of relic guitars showing the amount of relic work they want done, a colour chart from a paint company, artwork or lyrics from their own band's album to use. My favourite was a collection of images of skulls, animal skin and supernatural-looking occult objects.

Iterations of design

Scientists call them experiments, artists say sketches, designers use the term iterations. Essentially, everyone is agreeing that whatever they are working on needs to be developed or tested first. Sometimes I do this by hand, in drawing form, sometimes I paint directly on to a guitar, strip it and start again, but most often I create layouts on a computer.

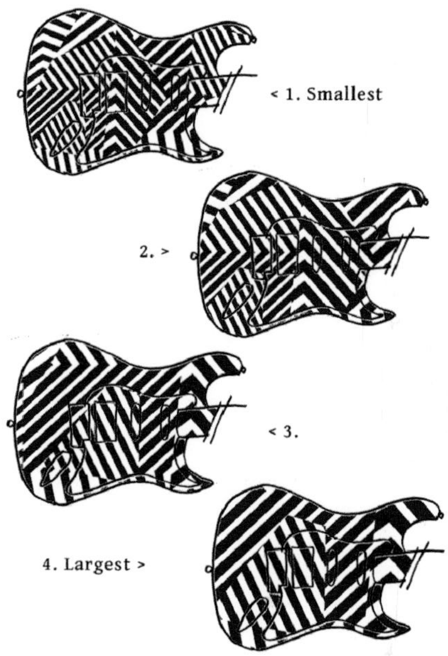

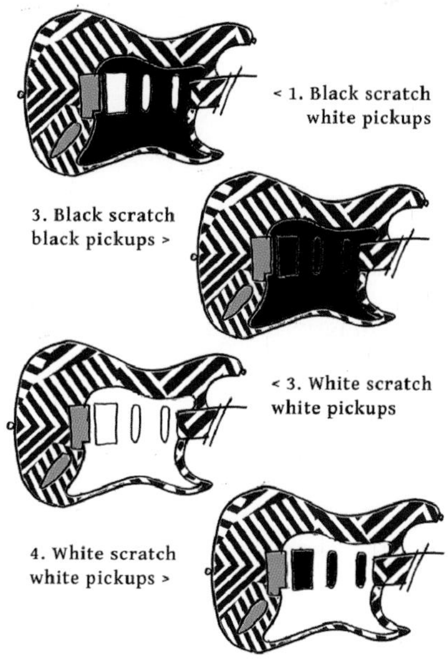

I try to give clients limited options at a time. First, four options on size of pattern, then four scratchplate options based on the first choice.

Happy accidents

Throughout my career in teaching, I've encouraged people to embrace mistakes and turn them into an opportunity for creativity and learning. Not knowing what the outcome of something will be can help in exploring a process and learning to control it. In the artworld, we often talk about 'happy accidents', when a mistake or unintended action leads to an unexpected, surprising and favourable outcome. Although made famous by television painter Bob Ross, the concept has been around for a long time; was the apple that landed on Newton's head a 'happy accident'?

If you have an idea for a design but are unsure of it, give it a try on paper. The worst outcome is realising that the concept doesn't work, which helps to inform you of elements to avoid, reinforce what does work, or highlights what is missing. I remember when I was the bass player in a band called Age of Pilots, I used to often suggest rearranging the song structures, much to the annoyance of my bandmates. Most of the time it didn't improve the song, or even made it the worse, but sometimes it took the song to a whole new level – we would never have found that with trial and error.

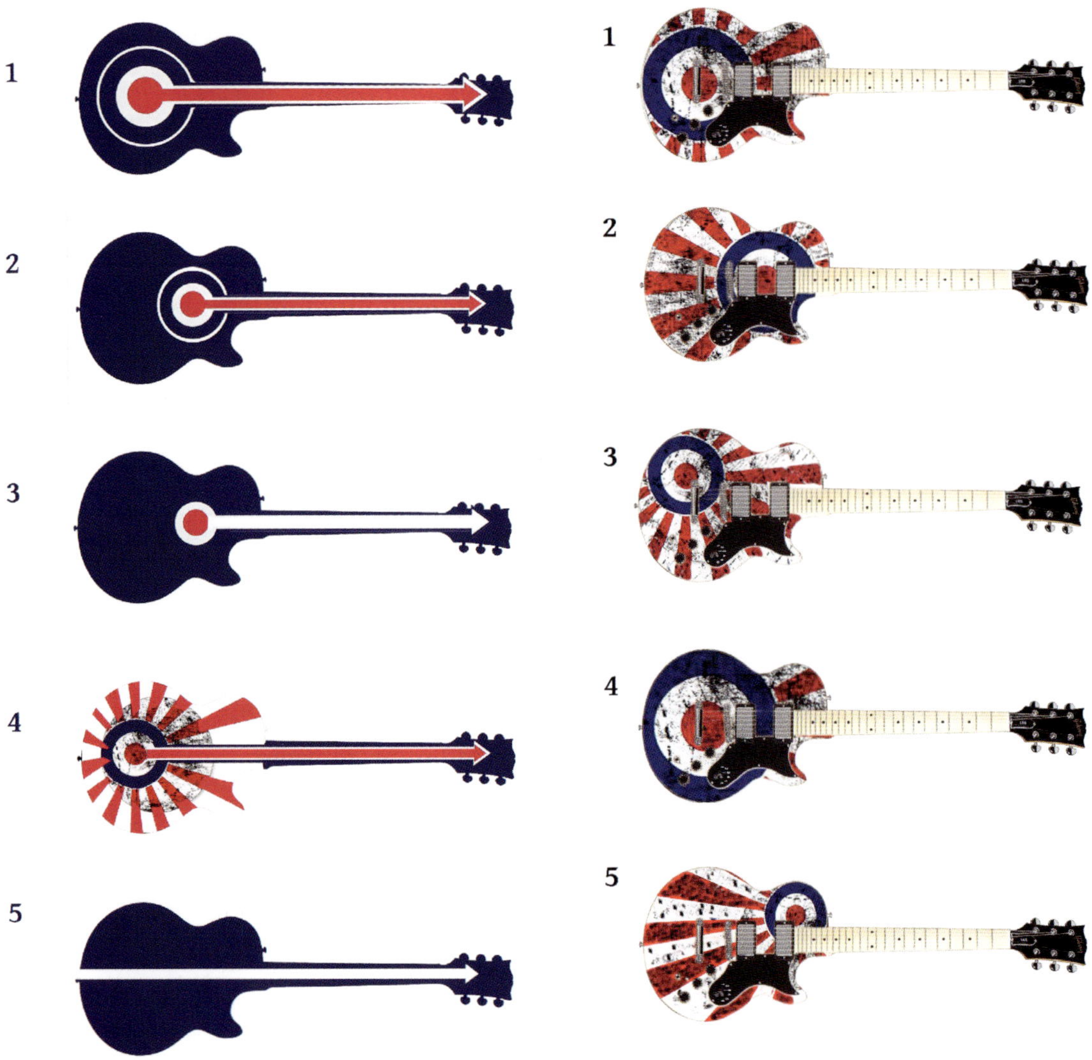

Design options for a client. The finished guitar didn't change much from option 1 (front) and option 5 (back), but often elements of different designs merge for the final work.

'TAKING A LINE FOR A WALK'

Paul Klee was a painter and leading proponent of the Bauhaus art and design movement. He wrote, 'a dot is a line that went for a walk' and set in place an activity that creatives have been using ever since. Placing your pen on the page and starting a drawing with no end goal is a technique often used as a form of meditation, to help find a starting point for design, or to relieve a creative block. Normally you would do it in response to music or poetry. Try drawing some random guitar shapes whilst listening to Metallica for a new metal design, or some Prince for a curvy funky shape, for example.

In your mind, on paper, or digital?

There's no wrong way to design. For this book a lot of the finishes were simply described in words on sticky notes stuck on to photos of the original guitars, or scribbled drawings on the edge of the printouts stuck in a notebook; the visual representation existing only in my mind. Many of these I changed on the fly when a new idea hit me, or I realised I hadn't covered a certain technique for the book yet.

When I first started customising guitars, I would draw around the original body and sketch at life-size. I would stick bits of paper and tracing paper over the top, or cut and move elements if I wanted to change the actual body shape. In the section on changing the body shape, I made my decisions by drawing on the guitar body itself. That's normally how I design custom scratchplates too. There's something about working at life scale that I like.

I do, however, find that computer work is essential for my process when experimenting with colour and design iterations, as I can create many variations quickly. I think it also looks smarter for presenting to my clients.

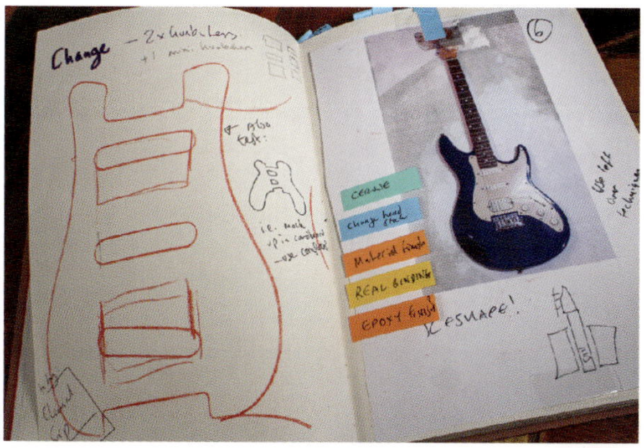

Notes on the design of some of the guitars that feature in the book. My original plans changed for almost all of the eleven I planned.

The first Mad Axe guitar I made was a kit guitar that I chopped up, added parts to, then painted. The whole design happened first on a life-sized drawing. I also like this final photo of the guitar superimposed on to a background inspired by the film that I drew inspiration from, *Mad Max: Fury Road*.

Annotation, sticky notes and lists

I annotate my drawings, both the hand-drawn and computer-made ones. I love marginalia in other people's books, but I can't bring myself to write in my own, so my collection of books on guitars, artists books and sci-fi illustration collections are all full of sticky notes. I also have notebooks full of lists. For me, this is often a great way to remember what I was thinking when I was first inspired by something and often triggers those ideas again when I come across the notes in the future.

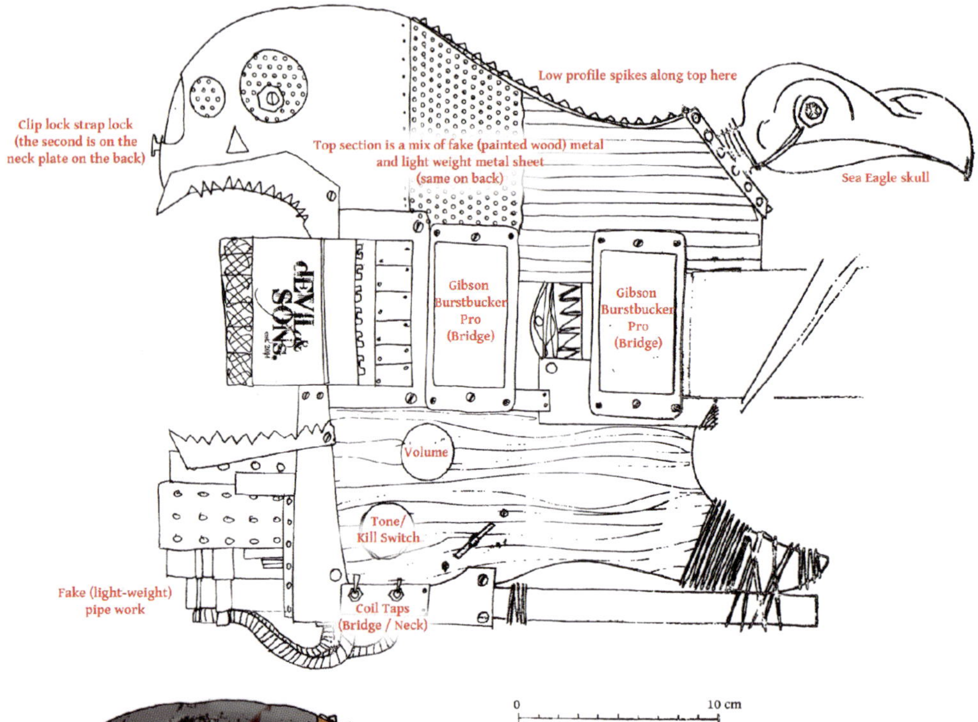

This black and white line drawing is a photo of my drawing for the second Mad Axe guitar. I took my original drawing (seen on the previous page) and stuck some paper over bits for quick alterations. Having it on the computer allowed me to send my client an annotated version confirming parts, plus a version in colour.

INSPIRATION: JAMIE HEWSON'S FABRIC-TOP GUITAR

Jamie Hewson, known as fatpotanga on social media, is a guitar builder I met through The Guitar Builders Collective, an online community that inspired me to start The Guitar Builders Collective Chat podcast, a place where builders from around the world support, advise and inspire each other. Jamie was a guest and I was particularly interested in his design process and unique layered guitars with fabric tops.

Jamie starts with a digital version of the guitar design and a scaled copy of the fabric. This allows for perfect positioning of the fabric before committing to cutting and gluing it in place. While this can be done with the physical material on the body, the computer rendering ensures optimal placement of all components and hardware, making the best use of the fabric.

Jamie's computer rendering of the guitar.

Stages of the making. There's a section on fabric tops later in the book.

The completed guitar.

SOME BASICS TO AVOID

This may sound obvious, but although I keep referring to the guitar body as a canvas, it's still a guitar. This means that it's going to have guitar parts screwed back into it. Nothing ruins a great artwork on a guitar body like an unfortunately positioned knob, or interferes with a cool headstock logo like a string tree. Plan your designs with the hardware in mind. Jamie's computer-based designs on Photoshop always have the hardware, including pickups and strings, as a layer that I can drop in and out to see how everything interacts with the design.

BURST FINISHES

There are a number of different methods by which to produce burst finishes, as well as several styles of burst. The choice of technique may come down to the equipment you have, but I recommend trying multiple approaches if possible. You'll see demonstrations in this book on simple guitar-shaped templates cut from plywood. It's a cheap way to experiment and practise, and help with visualising how your colour combinations will work. Even if you know which method you want to use, you should still read the others as there are elements that can easily feed from one technique into another.

Using stains and dyes

When using stains and dyes to create a burst finish, it's normally best to work whilst they are fresh and wet. Spirit stains may lift some of the previous dry colour out when overlaying a new one, mixing the colours together as you work (although you can use this to your advantage). With water-based stains, it will be harder to blend colours together if one is completely dry. I covered the differences between stains and dyes earlier in the book. As a rule of thumb, start with the lightest colour, but, as with all types of art, creativity and rule-breaking are encouraged, so you may end up with an unexpected and more interesting result.

Two-tone burst

It's possible that this approach will be slightly different depending on the brands of stain you use. In this example, I'm using Nitorlack's Nitoraqua stains undiluted. They are strong and mix well, so not many coats are required. With some brands or dilutions, more coats of the black may be needed.

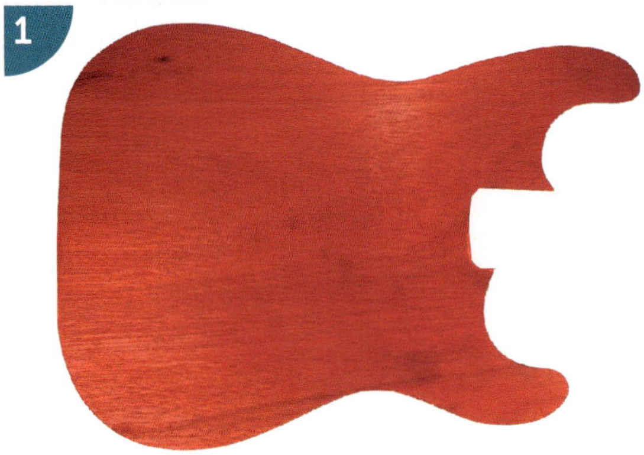

Apply the lightest colour, in this example red, to the entire body using the stain application techniques previously covered.

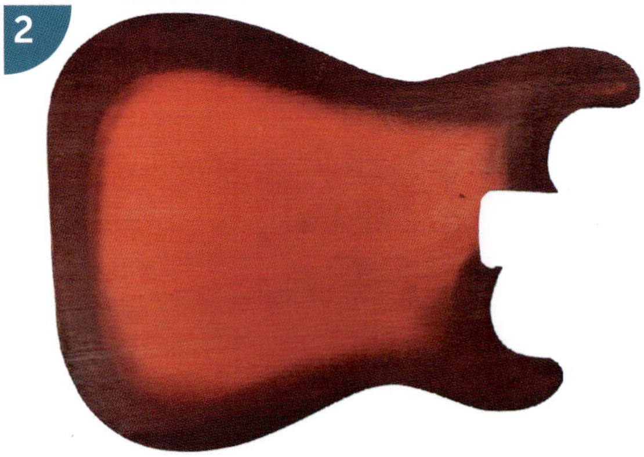

Using a cloth, apply a black border around the edge of the guitar. This single pass won't leave a solid black finish.

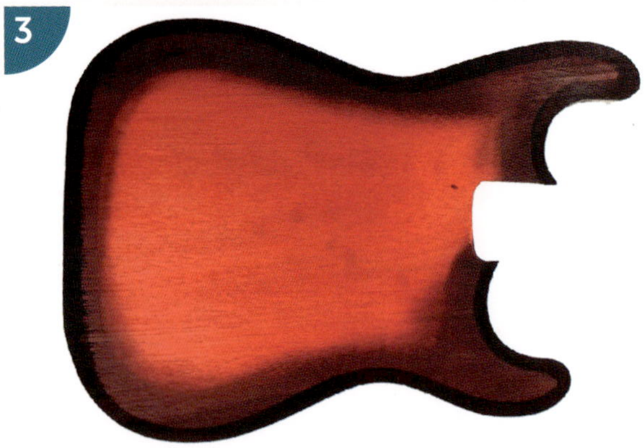

Repeat a second pass of a thinner width with the same cloth and more stain around the edge.

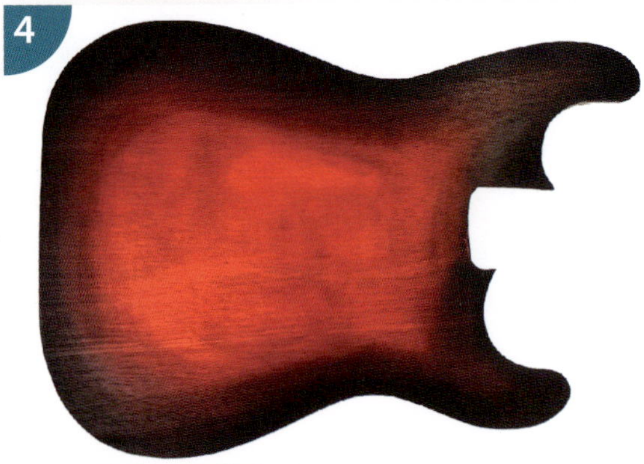

Using a new clean cloth, run around the edge to begin to blend the black coats into each other. Spread slightly into the body but leave the centre so that no black darkens the red.

Using spirit dyes

This example is essentially the same as the red and black finish, except I am using the Nitortint series from Nitorlack. These are spirit-based stains and as a result I needed just one coat of the darker colour (green) finding it to be enough because of the way it pulled up and blended with the first lighter yellow coat.

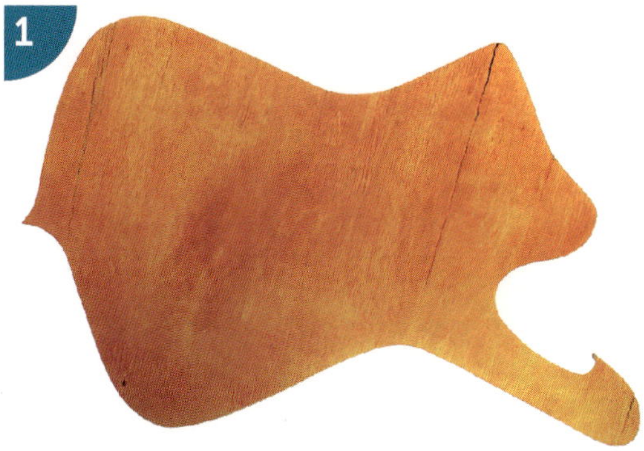

The lightest colour is applied over the whole body.

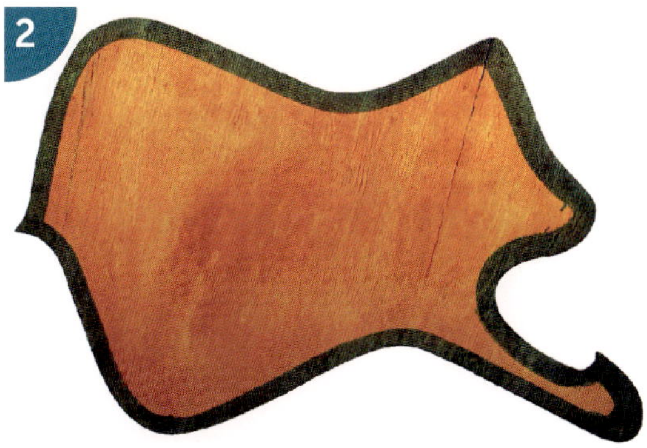

An edge is marked with the darkest colour, start thinner than you need.

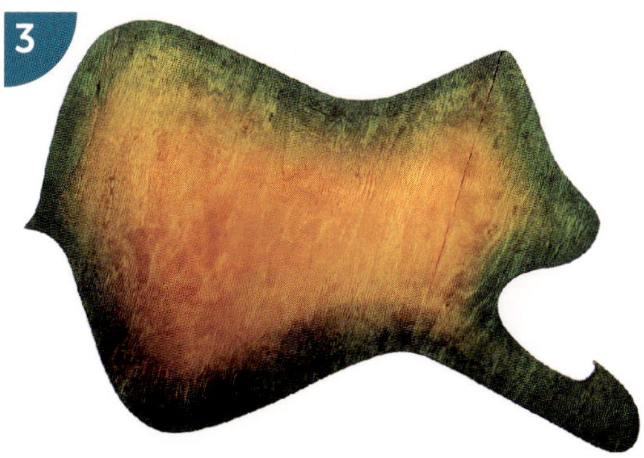

Blend the edge into the main body using a dry clean cloth but add more dye if needed.

Reverse burst

When creating a reverse burst, still start with the lighter colour and apply the darker colour straight afterwards, leaving enough border to blend. It's a matter of taste, but looking back on this example I think there could have been more space for the blending to take place around the edge.

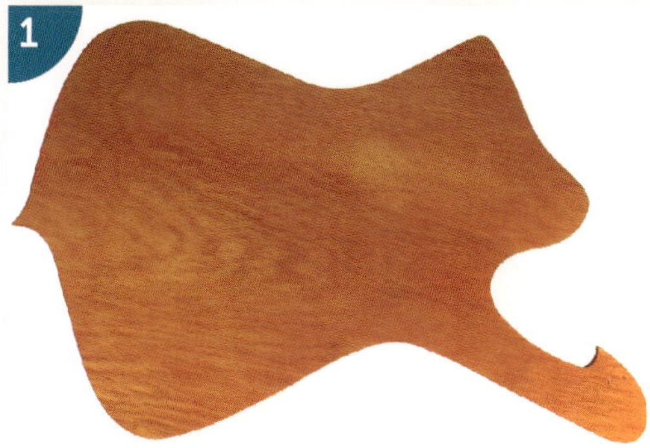

The lightest colour is applied over the whole body.

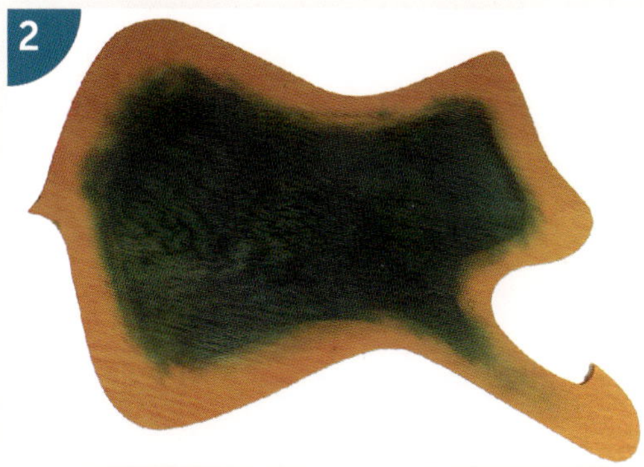

Fill the middle with the darkest colour leaving a band around the edge.

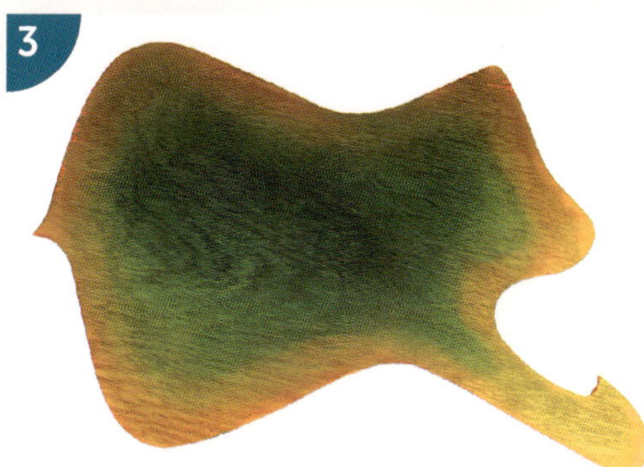

Blend the edge using a dry clean cloth but add more dye if needed.

Three-tone burst

To approach a three-tone burst, you can picture it as two two-tone bursts; blending the darkest colour into the middle colour, then the middle colour into the lightest colour. It is best to use a clean cloth for each to ensure that the darkest colour doesn't spread over all three colours. Notice that I didn't cover the entire body in the lightest colour first, which could have been an option potentially affecting the final finished colours.

Start with the lightest colour in the middle.

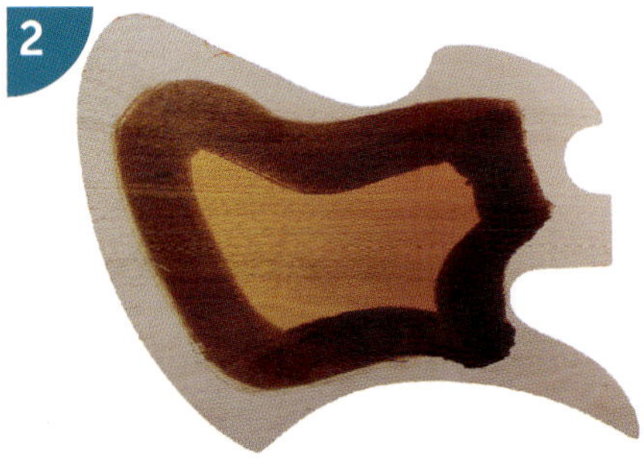

Add a band of the middle shade.

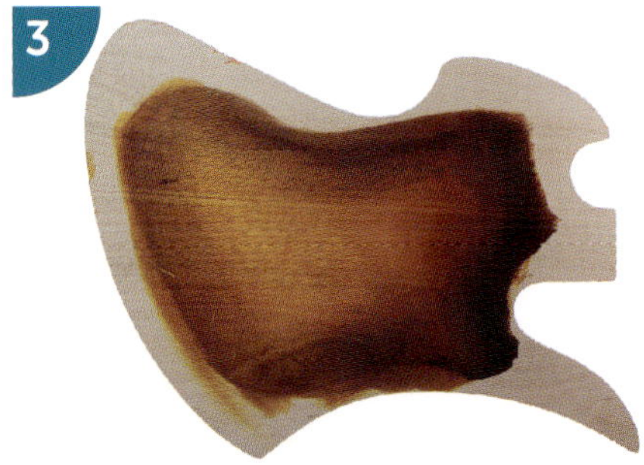

Blend these together with a dry cloth but add more dye if needed.

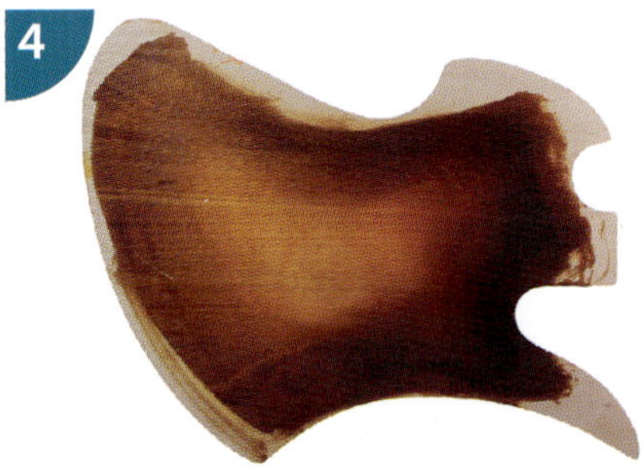

Add another band of the middle colour nearly to the edge.

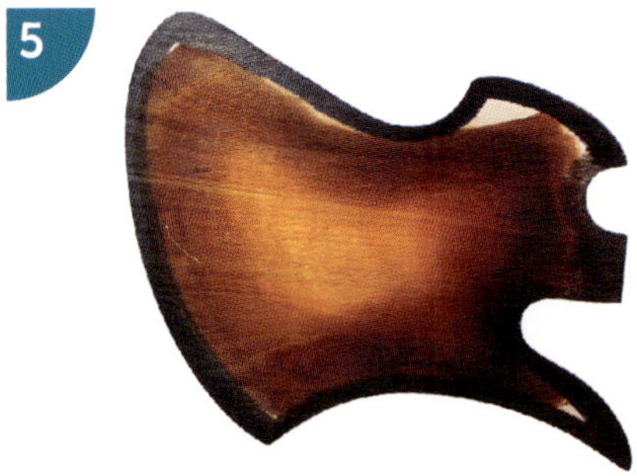

Use the darkest colour to follow the very edge.

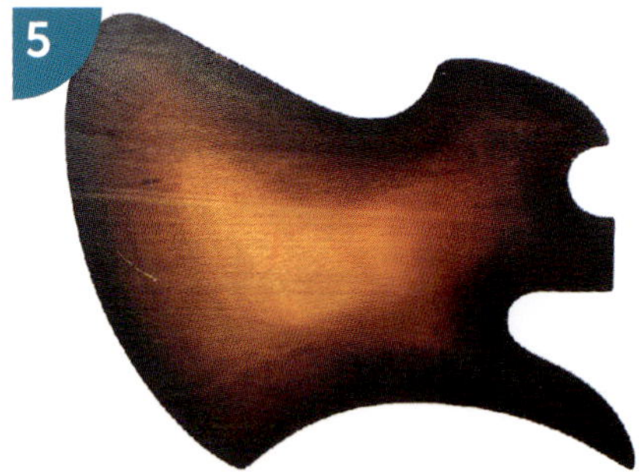

Use the darkest colour to follow the very edge.

TESTING HOW THE DYES INTERACT

I recommend testing the colours you've chosen for the burst on a scrap of wood first. In this example, the whole piece was first stained red, then black added whilst the red was fresh, exactly as I would if applying the stains to the guitar body. Once it was dry, I put another coat of red over the left side of the piece, which has helped to create a richer dark red. I really like this blend, although it means there isn't a solid black at the edge.

For the three-tone burst example in this chapter I could also have tested what the final finish would look like if I had covered the whole body in the lightest colour first.

Using sprays

The process for using spray cans, spray guns and airbrushes is to spray the main colour over the whole body, let it dry, sand with 600 grit, then spray the outer colour. It's far easier to spray a border than the inner part of the body because you can start the spray off the body and not risk the heavy paint spills. See the section on using spray cans and spray guns for technique advice. It's important to have a test piece if you haven't done this before, so that you can experiment with fade-outs, helping one colour transition to another. Normally I point the centre of the spray next to the guitar body, so that only the edge of the spray pattern falls on the body. The edge of the spray pattern is often fainter and thinner. You can also try increasing the distance between the guitar and the spray nozzle (which will also increase the area covered by the spray), although too far away and the paint may not settle correctly.

Aim to achieve the finished pattern in one session of three spray passes with the flash time between them. As it is likely that the paint is being sprayed thinly you may get away with five passes, but I would avoid any more. You can return 24 hours later to continue, remembering to sand lightly if the paint type needs it. Ensure that when you do sand (which will be necessary before applying topcoats unless using nitrocellulose), it is lightly with 800 grit to avoid removing some of the burst pattern.

Your choice of can, gun or brush may depend on what you have available, or may simply be what you are more confident using. An airbrush may be easiest for the beginner, as it gives more control over creating a smaller border and fading out due to the airbrush having a smaller spray area and amount of paint being sprayed. Using spray cans can give varied results depending on the make and the nozzle type; sprays made specifically for guitars will give a more consistent and even pattern that helps with the fade more than art or automotive spray cans.

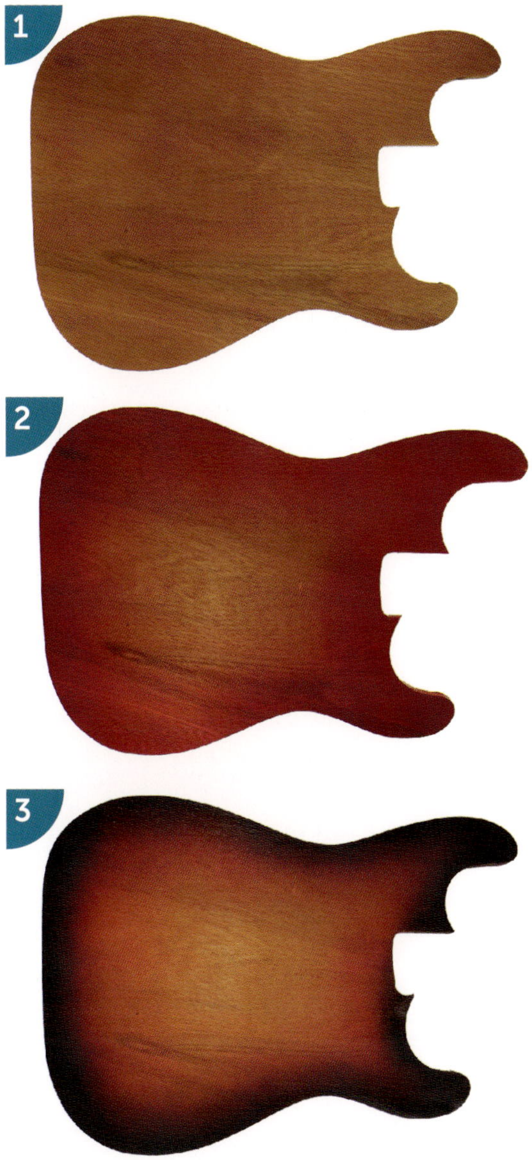

A three-tone pattern applied with Nitorlack's Nitortint spray cans. The advantage of sprays like these is that they are translucent, allowing for easier blending as the previous colours come through.

Using a template

Using a template can be a great way to ensure an even border around the edge of a guitar. The size of the template (therefore the area visible to be sprayed) is a matter of personal choice. I recommend testing your template, even on a scrap of paper, so that you get the spray angle and distance correct. Place a piece of masking tape folded in half underneath the template to stop it moving during the spraying process. You will need to lift the template between each pass to judge if you have sprayed enough.

Corrugated card such as that from a box is ideal for this template, which needs to be 3–5mm thick.

Once you have drawn around the guitar body, draw an inner line for the edge of the spray border. I've made some marks 4cm in all around the body, then connected them with a line.

Cut out the template and place it on the body ready to spray.

Angle the spray so that you are spraying out from the centre of the template. Expect to need more than one pass, observing the normal flash times.

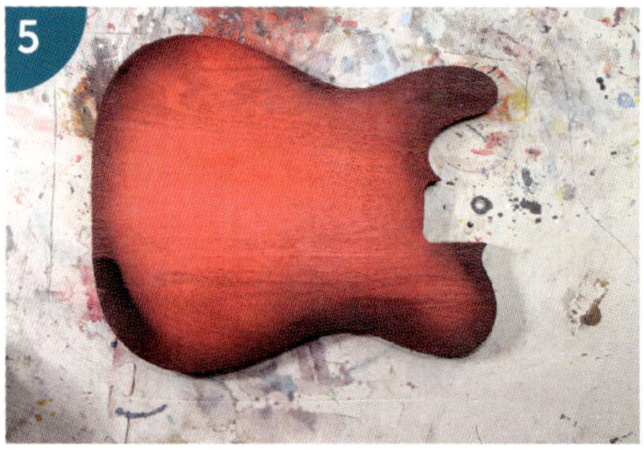

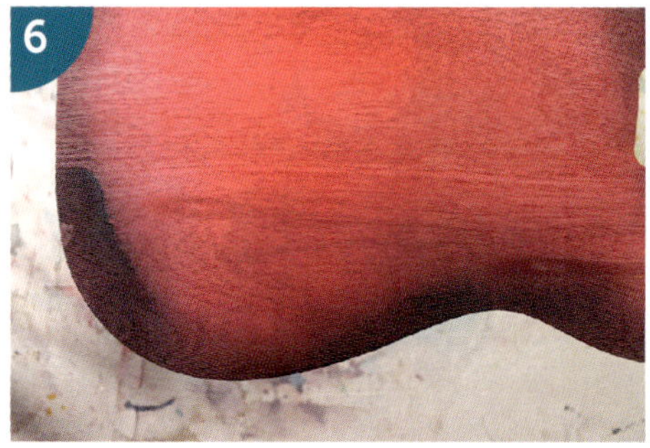

The first pass reveals that the burst is not dark enough. You can also see that the spray was started over the body, leaving a more defined and darker patch. You should always start the spray off the body.

The second pass reveals that the border isn't even. The best way to fix this is to rotate the body (with template) for the next spray. This problem has been caused by my physical position when spraying.

After the third spray pass, the burst looks how I want it.

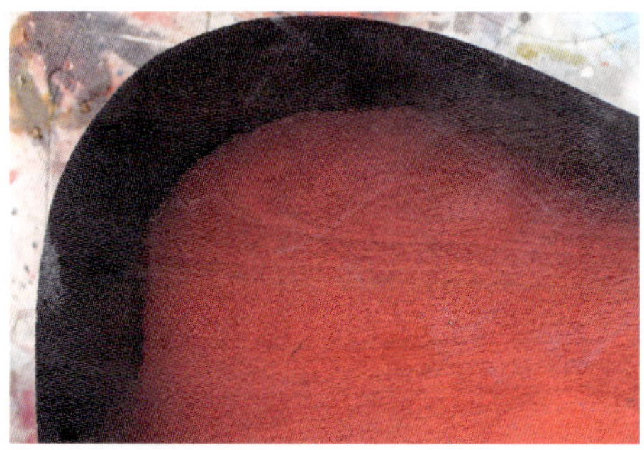

Here you can see a section where the spray was angled perpendicular to the template, spraying down and causing a harsher line. This was the result of trying to do the entire border in one pass. Having the body on a spinning platform, or physically lifting and rotating the body with the template, will help to avoid this.

Testing how the sprays interact

This photo shows a three-tone burst with yellow, then red, then black. The top section has then been sprayed over in red, the bottom in yellow, and the back end left. The red coating mutes the yellow, makes the transition into the black smoother than just using the red and black, and gives the black a slight red tint. Here, the number of red coats can easily change the look of the guitar quite dramatically. The yellow on top dulls the red slightly leaving a yellow tint to the black.

Finishing bursts

After doing a burst, I like to give it a light sand with a 600-grit soft pad, trying not to remove any of the burst effect. Then I apply a sealer or clear primer in one session of three coats, which gives a good surface to flat-sand without risking removing the burst pattern. The body will then be ready for topcoats.

Using art sprays

As previously mentioned, I love using Montana Gold sprays because of their range of colours, but like many art or automotive spray cans they won't work as well for creating a burst pattern. You can experiment with their range of nozzles, spray patterns and paints, but expect to have a finish that is more flecked. A smooth transition from one colour to the next is not always obtainable with this type of can. I do like to embrace this limitation, though, and often use it as part of the design. Also note that Montana Gold paints can be tricky to sand, plus there's a chance that they may have gone on quite thickly with a burst, so I often wait three or more days before using a sealer.

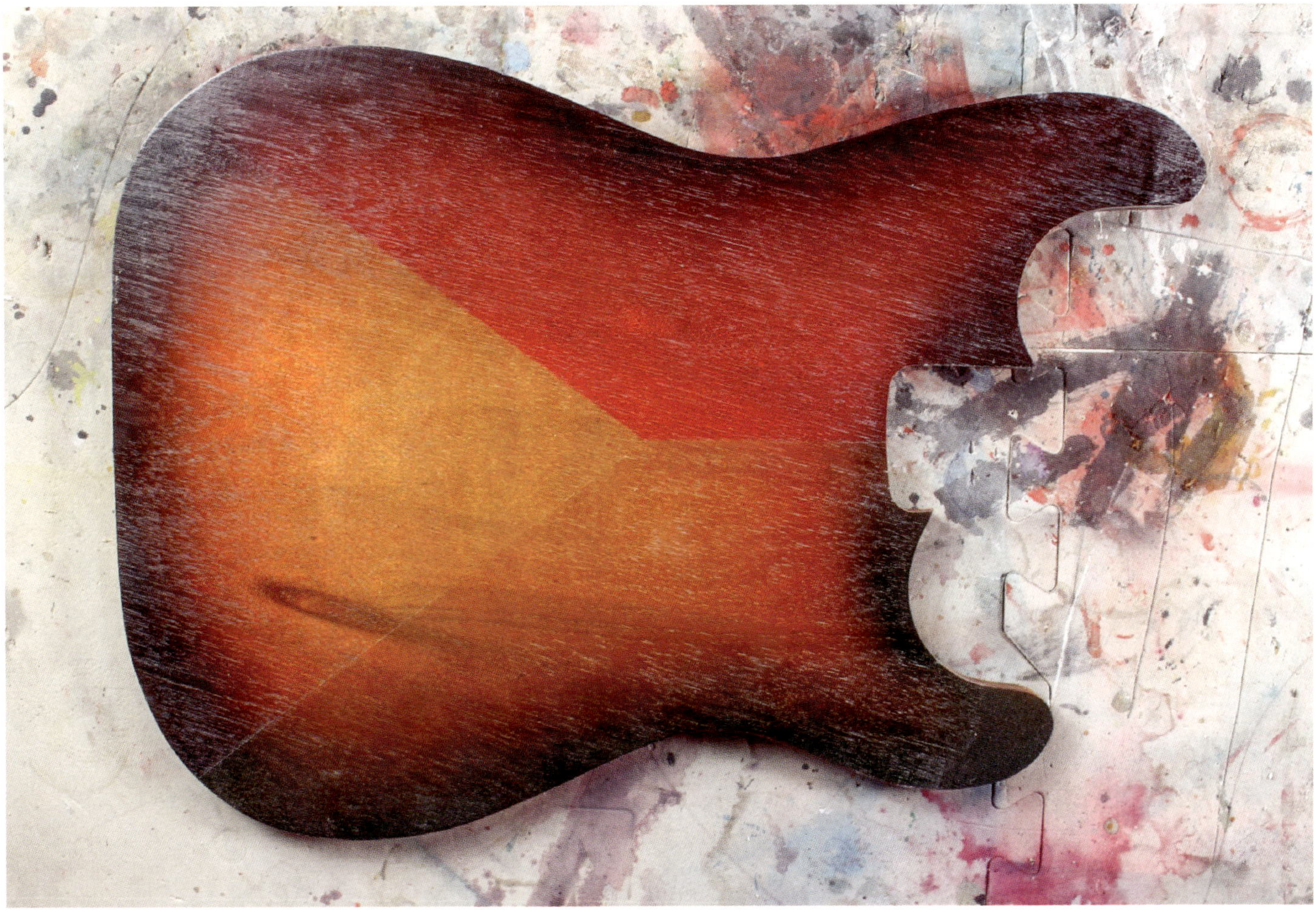

A body demonstrating how translucent sprays interact.

This bass was sprayed using two Montana Gold colours. The more obvious spray-pattern transition is evident.

I even sprayed the neck and fretboard on this guitar. There's a chapter on painting the necks later in the book.

Once the bass was finished, it become clear that the quality of spray was part of the design.

INSPIRATION: LT CUSTOM GUITARS

Lewis from LT Custom Guitars uses a range of very cool finishes on his guitars, from bright metallic colours to flip paint, but it's his take on the burst that I want to share here. These are his Pioneer and Pioneer bass models, each made to order with a custom finish. The 'fade burst' finishes gradually transition from one colour to another. Lewis says: 'As a musician myself, I have an appreciation for all styles of music and I'm constantly searching for new ways to combine perfect tone and aesthetic design into my instruments.'

INSPIRATION: HILDITCH HANDMADE GUITARS

One thing I love about the finishes Mark at Hilditch Handmade Guitars produces is the variety. Each of the four guitars I've chosen here showcases a unique aspect of a burst finish to consider as inspirations for your own designs.

We're so used to seeing the burst edges in a darker colour that this white burst seems unusual. Combined with the natural wood, it creates an ethereal, ghostly finish.

This burst is combined with a bold stencilled pattern, resulting in the sharp edges of the red contrasting with and complementing the fuzzy fade of the black.

Here I find the black edge really helps to accentuate the texture and pattern in the wood. It's a great example of two techniques combined to enhance each other.

The body of this guitar has a sharp physical contour that the fade follows, accentuating it and helping add depth to the body. I love the red binding to complement the main body.

MASKING

Masking is important not just for screening off areas of a guitar that you need to keep pristine and free from any new finish, but also for creating interesting patterns and designs. Often there are multiple ways to achieve the same outcome and I recommend experimenting with different approaches each time, or on a test subject. The more you do, the easier it will be to decide which technique best suits your way of working.

Before masking off areas, the surface must be prepared. Grain filler and primer will have been added and the surface will have been sanded ready. It may be the case that you want a textured grain finish and therefore haven't used filler, or that you want the grain to show through a translucent spray and haven't primed, or you may have already sprayed colour over the whole body. Whatever the situation, the new paint being sprayed has to bond with the previous and therefore the surface must be ready, so lightly sand the base colour with 600 grit.

Many of these techniques will use masking tape. There are various painting-specific masking tapes available on the market, some designed to have a low tack, others to work over gloss or satin finishes. I use Frogtape green (multi-surface) and orange (satin and gloss). Test the tape first on an area that isn't going to be seen, such as under a pickguard, or on the lower side. Put the tape on, leave it a day, then remove. If any paint comes away with the tape, it could be that the previous layers haven't bonded properly with each other, or that the tape is too strong. If it's leaving a tacky mark, it could be coming from the tape itself, or a reaction to the tape. When using nitrocellulose, I avoid masking an area until I am confident that the surface has cured, which means leaving it a month after the last coat, and I don't leave the masking on for more than a day.

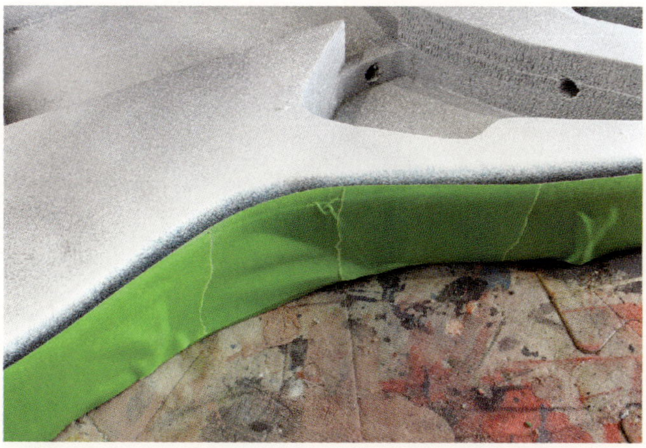

On the example guitar you can see that four pieces of overlapping tape have been used to keep the line neat as the body bends. The very ends of the tape don't always meet at the same height, but somewhere along the length they touch and create a smooth transition from one piece to the next.

Masking off one side

In my opinion, guitars with a design on the top and plain colours on the back and sides look really good. We're used to seeing factory guitars with a standard wood-grain side and back but with a quilted maple or gold top; the plain body can help to accentuate the feature top. I often find myself playing with the techniques I use and inverting or changing colours on each side of the guitar. In this book, you'll see example guitars where the front and back show different-coloured crackle finishes, alternative methods for creating spatter finishes and complementary techniques such as gold leaf and acrylic pouring-on. These are not just to demonstrate a range of techniques, but because they make the guitars look unique and also work for each individual design.

Use the straight edge of the masking tape to run around the edge of the guitar. You will have to do it in multiple strips of tape, as the tape will naturally slant up or down as you follow the bends and contours of the body. Here I have used the depth of the neck pocket to determine the positioning of the line.

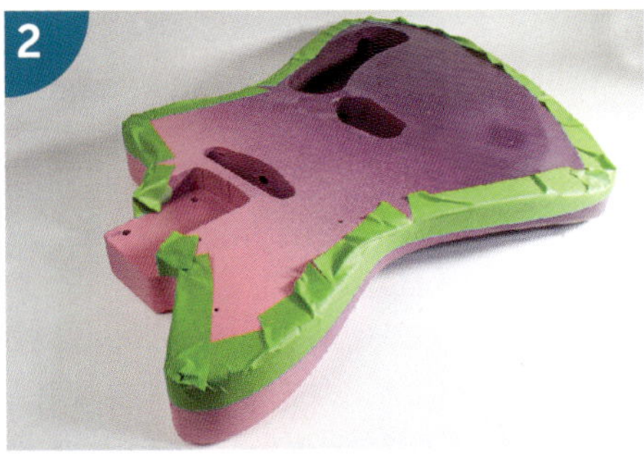

When folding the tape over and on to the top surface, make some slits in the tape. Make sure to use extra pieces to cover them and prevent any risk of paint seeping through later.

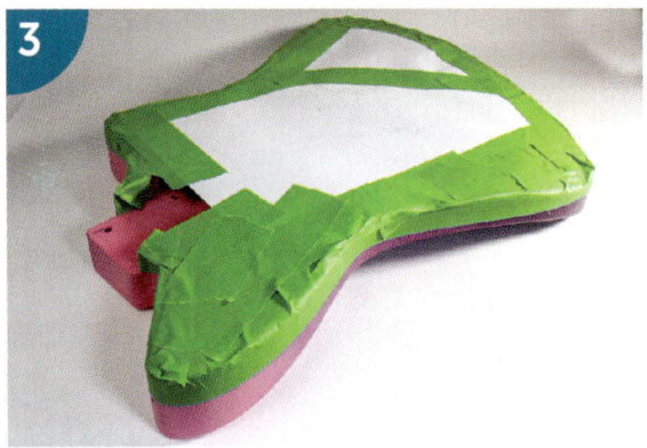

Some people will now cover the top in tape. I prefer to use as little tape as possible (so that less is actually stuck to the guitar) and instead use paper to block in the main areas, sealed around the edge in tape.

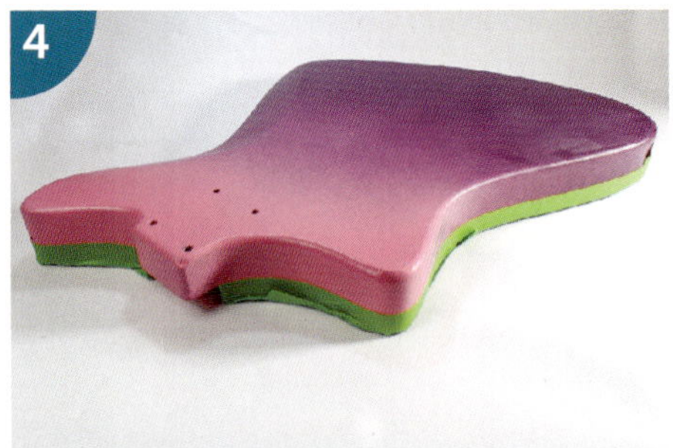

With the guitar body flipped, the neat edge of the tape is evident. Go around it with your thumb, pressing down hard to ensure no gaps. I do this again just before I spray.

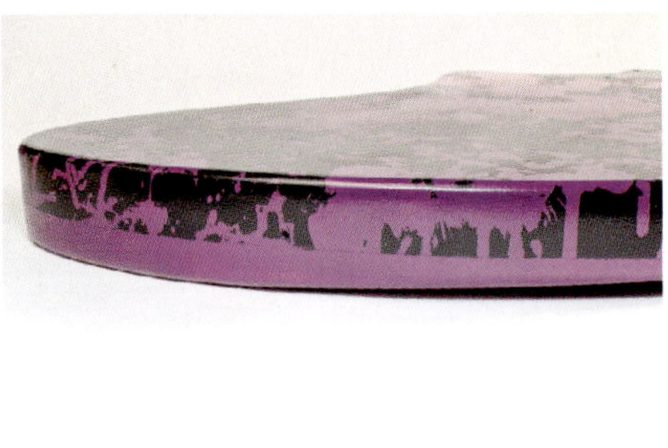

With the tape removed after the paint has been added, you can see the neat line. I really love how it works with the paint spatter effect.

Faux binding

Binding can be an attractive feature, but it's also fiddly to install and requires the use of a router (covered earlier). A simple way around this is to paint a fake binding strip. To prep the guitar, give it a light sand with 600 grit as you would before top coating. The example guitar has had a series of clear coats already applied to protect and smooth out the crackle finish.

In the example below I use a guide tape, but this isn't essential. You could draw on a line to follow; just make sure that the paint conceals the line. You could even tape the whole side and then use a scalpel to cut the faux binding gap – it doesn't have to be a straight line. Typing this I feel inspired to try a wiggly faux binding.

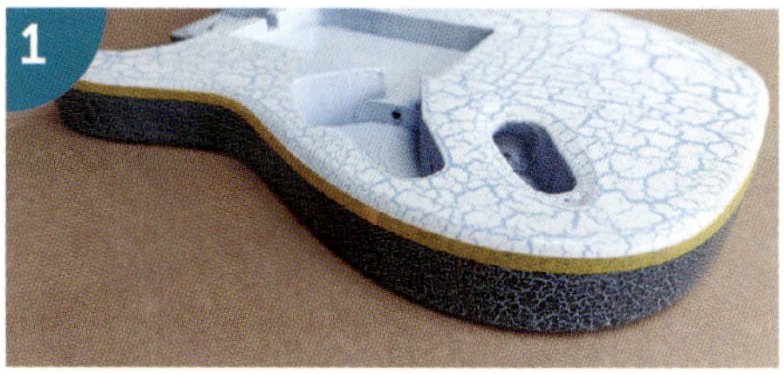

Start by running a thin tape around the edge where the faux binding will go; this is your guide.

Tape below the line. Notice there's a small gap to make it easy to remove the guide tape.

Cover the top. Small overlapping pieces may be needed to get a smooth edge.

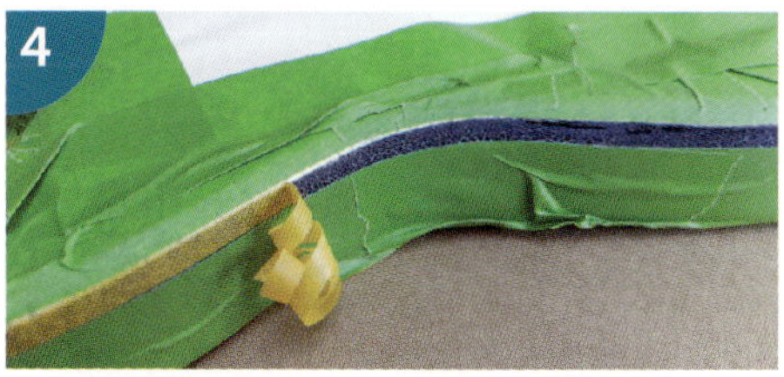

Peel off the guide tape to reveal the area to be painted.

I made two passes with Montana Gold Baby Blue, which was enough for a solid line. Here some tape has been removed.

Once all the tape is removed, the guitar is ready for the topcoats. A very light sand is needed over the faux binding with an 800-grit foam pad.

This giraffe finish was one of the most fun guitars I've worked on. The yellow was sprayed first, masking tape applied and cut, then the brown added on top. Extra topcoats were needed to help achieve a smooth finish as the brown paint was now raised from the surface of the yellow. Montana Gold paints were used.

Using masking tape as a stencil

One of the great things about masking tape is that you can draw on it. I often cover an area with tape and hand-draw designs in place, rubbing out lines or replacing tape until I am happy with the design. Then I cut through the tape and remove the stencil design. For this a sharp scalpel is essential and scoring lightly into the paint underneath as you cut the tape helps to ensure a tight join that paint won't leak through. Any indentation caused by the blade into the paint will be concealed once you have applied the topcoats.

I find designing like this on the actual body gives me a greater idea of what will work than drawing it out on paper. You may prefer designing on a computer or paper then transferring the image to the tape, or simply taping the paper in place and cutting through that and the masking tape underneath in one go.

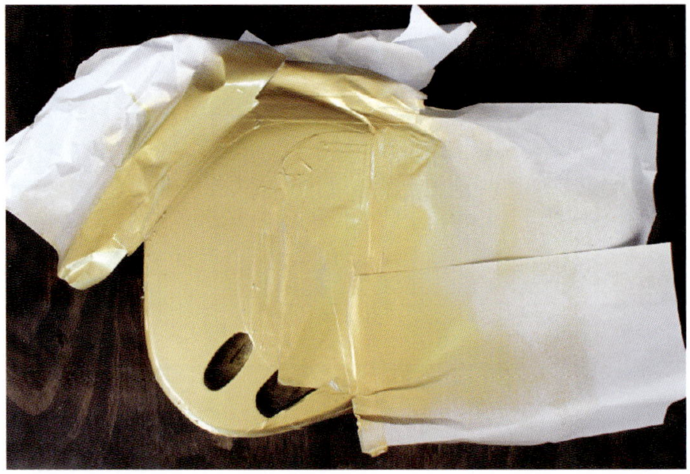

An area can be masked off by combining masking tape and paper. The gold has been sprayed on.

Masking off an area

You can use the same technique to mask off an area as we have used in the last two examples, combining masking tape and paper. On the example guitar, the gold has been sprayed on.

With the mask removed, all three colours are evident. These are Nitorlack metallic nitrocellulose colours. I had to do this in three sessions a month apart to allow the nitrocellulose to settle before putting tape on it.

Using adhesive stencil vinyl

An alternative to covering a large area with lots of strips of overlapping tape is to use stencil vinyl. You can buy rolls of it for use in vinyl cutters and some companies like Frisket sell it in sheets too.

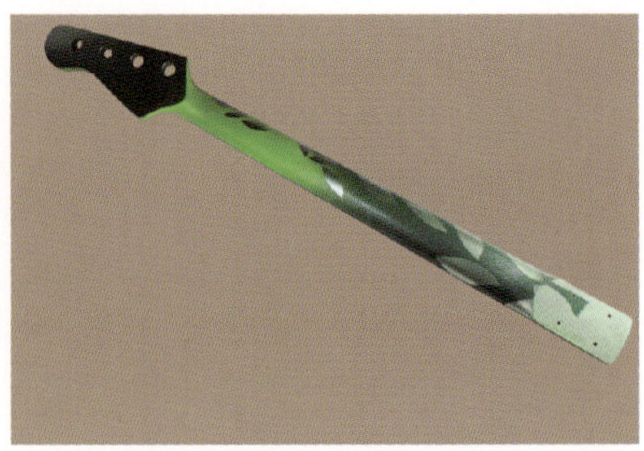

Here I have drawn a leaf pattern on the back of a bass guitar neck. You can see the pencil marks where the designed developed.

The Frisket sheet covers most of the body, with paper and masking tape used to cover the rest. For spraying small details like this I feel confident paint won't get on the sides of the guitar, otherwise I would mask a wider area coming out from the body.

The leaves have been cut out in the same way as when using masking tape as a stencil.

After the paint has been sprayed and the film removed.

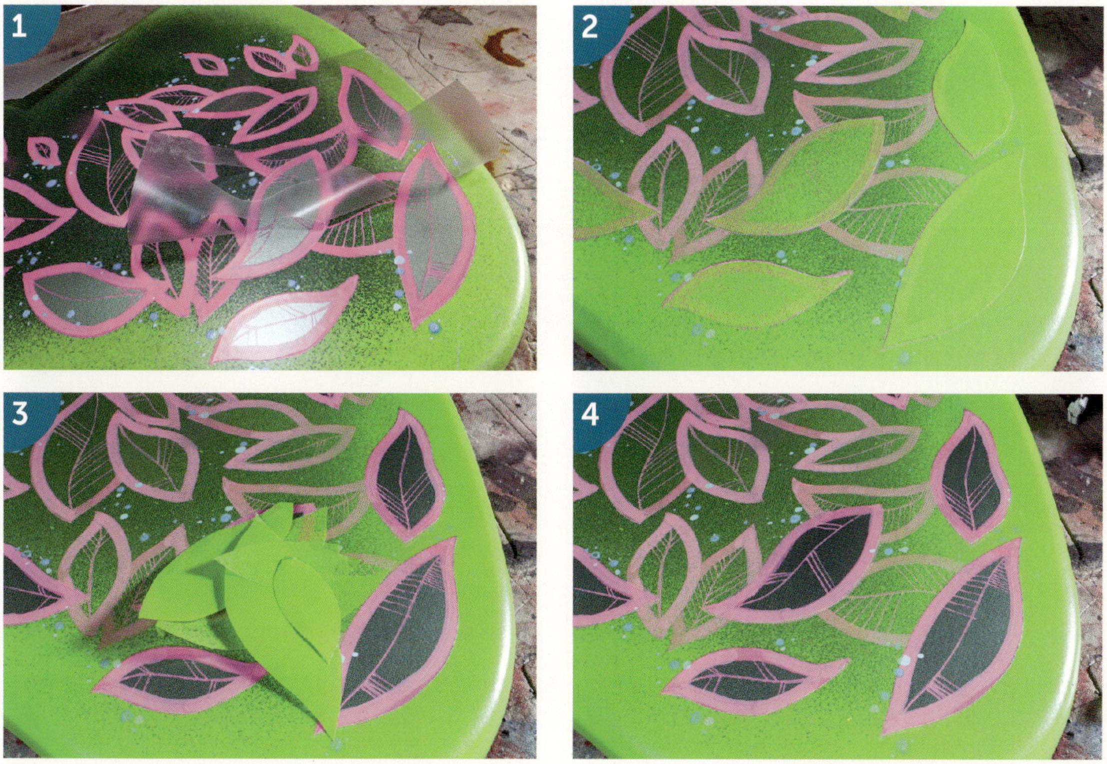

This is a reverse use of the stencil, masking over areas as I spray a burst border to conceal some of the image painted on, but to keep the masked elements vivid.

Vinyl cutters

I bought my Cricut Explore Air 2 second-hand and haven't looked back. It's a vinyl cutter that can take the digital drawings I make and cut stencils from them into various types of vinyl. You'll see things it has cut appear throughout this book. The example on the next page shows an advanced way of using a vinyl stencil. You could choose to keep it simple and just spray one colour.

The parts of the vinyl where you want the paint to come through are removed in a process called weeding. I have kept all the parts I weeded off to use again later.

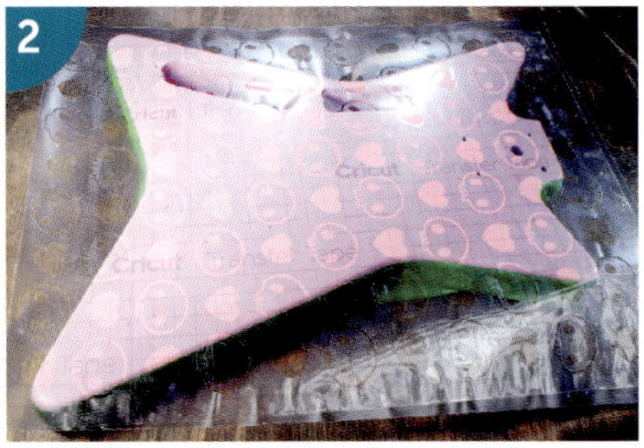

The entire sheet is then transferred on to the guitar. I have used a big sheet of transfer tape to do this. Essentially, the transfer tape is stuck on to the stencil vinyl sheet, which is then peeled from its backing. The whole thing is placed on the guitar, pressed down so that the stencil vinyl sticks to the guitar, then the transfer tape is removed, leaving the stencil material behind.

To help the stencil to fold around the edge you will need to make some cuts. Notice how the side of the guitar is already masked off with tape.

Use masking tape over the cuts to make sure that no paint can get through where it is unwanted.

Once I had sprayed the whole guitar in a Montana Gold paint and let it dry, I masked off a small area and sprayed just those with a different colour.

Here I have placed one of the skulls that I weeded off earlier back on to the guitar to mask off and protect the new purple layer.

There's a section coming up on paint pens; here I've used a black Posca pen over the stencil.

I find a scalpel is the best way to remove small vinyl stencil areas. Catch the edge and lift it up, taking care not to cut through paint underneath.

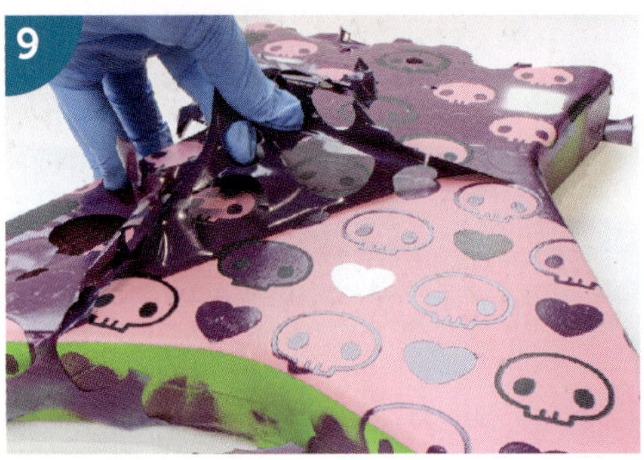

The main stencil often comes away in one piece.

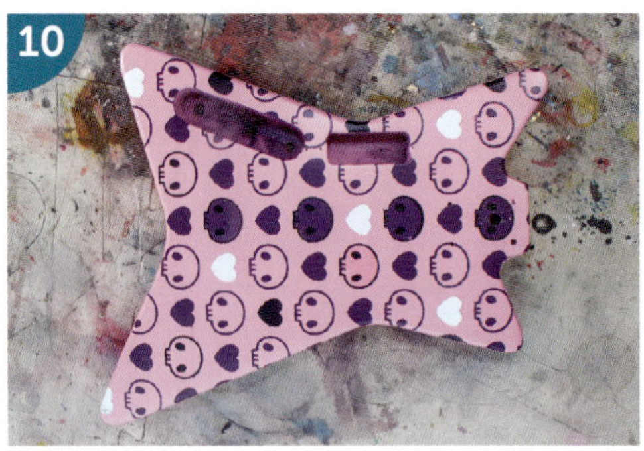

The finished design ready for topcoats. You will probably need extra topcoats to help get a smooth finish, as there will be raised paint from the stencilled additions.

CLASSIC GUITAR FINISH: POLKA-DOT RANDY RHOADS AND BUDDY GUY

Depending on your age or taste in music you may have strong associations with a polka-dot finish and a particular guitarist. For me, it's the Dot V guitar played by Randy Rhoads and built by Karl Sandoval in 1979 (based on a drawing that Randy made). The polka dot became synonymous with Randy Rhoads and his band, Quiet Riot. For some people it will be the Fender-produced Buddy Guy Stratocaster that the company has been making since 1996. Buddy had promised his mother he would buy her a polka-dot Cadillac when he became famous, so the pattern on the guitar is an homage to her.

Using a vinyl cutter is an easy way to add any pattern to a guitar. For the polka-dots, you could simply cut them out in the colour you want and place them on an already painted guitar. You could even cut them in the correct layout and spacing and use transfer tape to position them. Or you could use the stencil method for something more permanent.

This example shows two approaches on one guitar. On the left side you can see the vinyl with the circles cut out; on the right the circles only. Either works well, but I actually like them together. Another option is to make one stencil to fit the guitar and use it twice; the removed circles on one guitar and the leftover sheet of holes on another (or front and back of the same guitar). Some great results have come from the experiments I have made for this book that I will be using again.

1

2

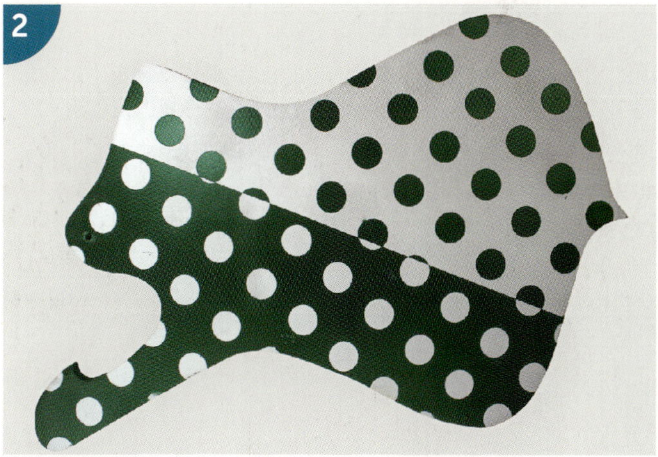

Potential issues when masking

The main problem you may encounter is the paint seeping under the mask. You can see it clearly in the photo on the top left of the next page, where strips of masking tape have been used. One solution is to change your tape. These were done with normal masking tape and not the specialist Frogtape I normally use. The best way to avoid this, though, is to spray the colour you are covering before the new colour. For example, if you are taping over white and spraying red, place the masking tape on the white and then spray white. This way, the white will seep under any gaps and fill them so the red won't get under. Then you can spray the red.

The pink circles near the skull on the headstock (in the photo on the top right of the next page) were supposed to be skulls, but I removed the vinyl stencil before the paint had fully dried. The whole area lifted and stretched, then ripped as I removed the stencil. If you start peeling away the mask and the surface of the paint seems to stretch, stop and come back later when the paint is fully dry. You can also try scoring or cutting the edge of the stencil in places with a scalpel if the problem persists.

Here the dye has seeped under the masking tape.

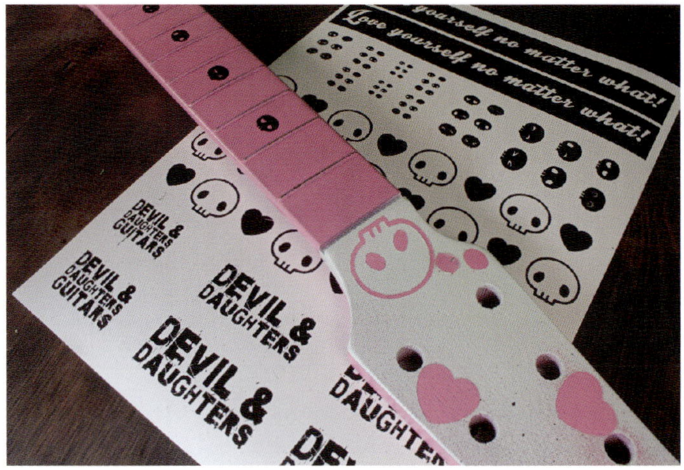

The pink circles were meant to be skulls.

Masking with stains and dyes

Masking with stains and dyes is a bit harder than with paint, simply because as they sink into the wood they can spread under the masked area. Better quality masking tape can help. You can also fill the grain, although that makes only a slight improvement. Using a primer will seal the surface to create better adhesion for the masking tape, but will prevent the stain from sinking into the wood.

I made three simple test pieces to show the difference, using Nitorlack's Nitoraqua stains. As covered in the dyes and stains chapter, these can be mixed with a water-based clear coat and sprayed, meaning that you will still have access to the colours, but can use the previous masking methods.

Stain applied with no prior wood treatment over a masking-tape strip.

Stain applied with no prior wood treatment over a Frogtape multi-surface tape strip.

Filler then primer applied. You can see the marks left from the cloth when the stain was applied. It doesn't sink into the wood, hence the much lighter colour than the previous example.

Masking fluid

My preferred technique for working with stains is to use the masking-fluid method. Masking fluid is commonly used by watercolour artists to mask off areas on paper, I'm going to use it later for one of the paint-spatter methods, but for this example I'm using liquid latex, simply because I can buy it in bulk. They are the same thing, a liquid which dries into a rubbery solid that can then be peeled away. In this case, it won't let the stain soak through and will fill the grain.

When applying, use a brush you are happy to dispose of. You can wash the fluid off in soapy water, but I have never had much success – the fluid is normally dried on to the bristles by the time I remember to wash it! You also don't have to mask off the whole area, just the edges. When applying the stain, be careful not to slip over the masked area into the area you want left untouched.

I recommend testing this technique, especially the process of painting the fluid and removing the tape; for example, if the fluid is too wet it can flow under the tape as you remove it. Practice will assist you in recognising when it's ready.

Start by masking off the area where you want the stain to go, a reverse mask. I'm using a straight line, but you can cut the tape just as you would when making a masking-tape stencil.

Brush up to the tape and don't worry if it overlaps slightly. The edge of the tape should act as a barrier for the fluid to push against.

Remove the tape before the fluid is dry (otherwise the whole dried rubbery mask will come up).

Stain can be applied with the normal method and don't worry if you overlap the masked area.

Once the stain has dried, the masking fluid will rub away. I use my thumb, but a stationery rubber will work well too.

The fluid will be harder to remove from a more open-grain wood such as this, where it breaks up. In other cases, you may find it rolls off in one.

Comparing this test piece back to the others you can see the sharpness of the stained edge.

CLASSIC GUITAR FINISH: EDDIE VAN HALEN'S FRANKENSTRAT

Eddie Van Halen and his unique playing style not only inspired people around the world to play guitar, he also inspired them to customise their own instruments. In 1977, he began customising his 1961 Fender Stratocaster. For the first two years it was a white finish with black stripes, but in 1979, as a response to seeing so many copies of the guitar, he added the red layer. The customisation continued to evolve, with scratchplates and hardware changing over time. I'm going to focus on the paint job, starting with a simple version inspired by what has become known as Eddie Van Halen's Frankenstrat.

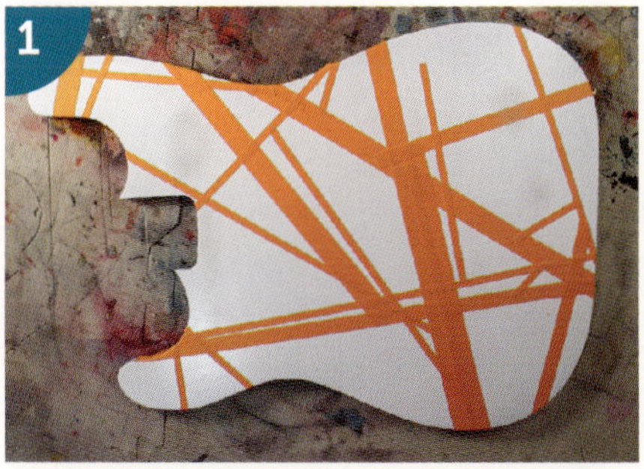

1 Starting with a white finish, I have applied some tape. I'm using three different widths for variety. The first base colour will look like the top colour on the finished guitar.

2 I've chosen a green Montana Gold spray can for the next layer. I could have sprayed the white again to ensure that the sides of the tape are sealed, but I just pushed the edges down hard before spraying and crossed my fingers.

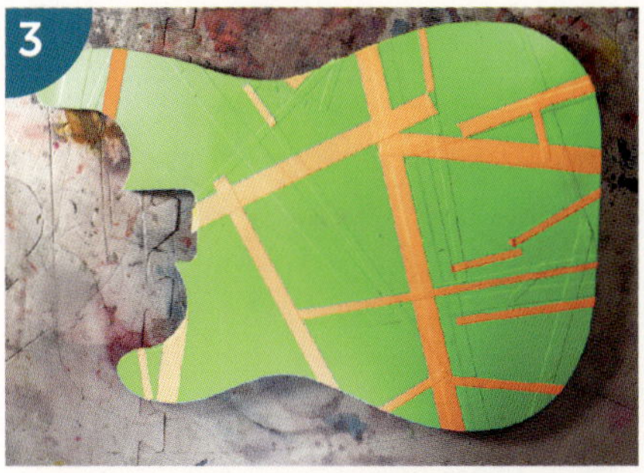

3 More tape is added. The lines under the tape will look green on the final guitar, except where they overlap tape that is already there. The green lines will appear to be behind the white.

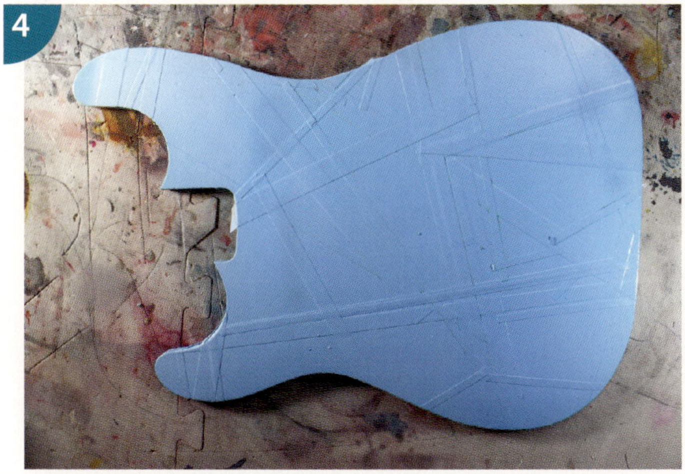

4 For the final coat I opted for a Montana Gold blue, which will appear to be the base colour of the body.

5 In the finished design, you can clearly see the Frankenstrat-inspired finish, despite the fact that I didn't try to copy the pattern exactly and used a different colour scheme.

Even knowing that Eddie painted his guitar with the black and white stripes first I couldn't work out how the masking tape had been applied. I think it's likely that the guitar was black and the tape applied before a coat of white was put on. Then over the few years before the red was added some wear happened to the paint, causing some of the blurriness and rough edges. If you look at photos of the original and not the licensed copies that came later, some of the black stripes can be seen through the red. If you want that authenticity, make sure not to spray too many coats of the red. In the example here, I'm trying to get closer to the original without going for an exact copy. Removing all the tape between paint layers helped me in visualising the finished result.

Note that the surface of your guitar is going to show the tape lines and have a texture. This will disappear when you put the topcoats on, although you may need a few extra coats to get a smooth finish.

I've started with a black body and added the orange tape on the areas I can see black on the original. Then, I will spray it white.

Once the white has dried, I've peeled back to reveal the black lines. If you want a true copy, start by using photos of Eddie's guitar in 1977 when it was just black and white as a guide.

Here I'm trying to hide some of the black, partly mirroring the wear on the guitar and partly to help create the black lines that aren't an equal width for their whole length.

I then sprayed it white and removed the tape. At this point my head hurt, but it looks really cool. You can also see the tape marks where the paint edge is raised from both tape stages. I used these as a guide for the next stage.

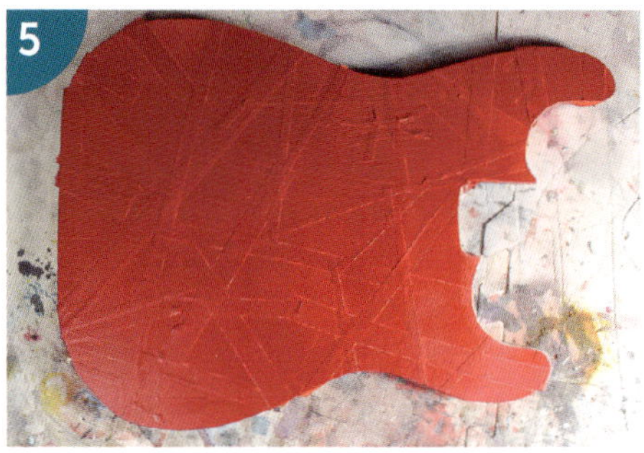

More tape and the red.

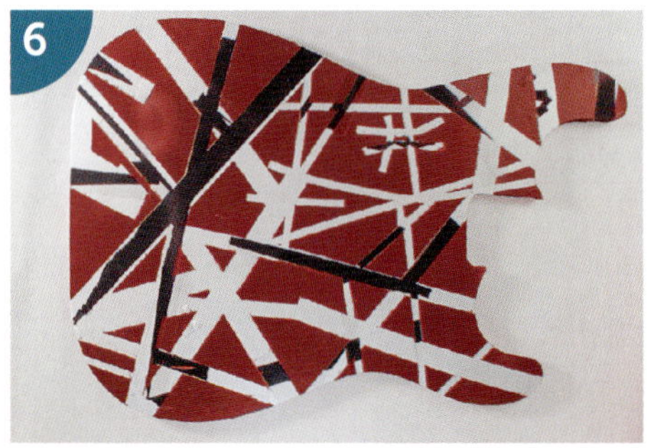

Once I removed the tape, I compared back to Eddie's guitar. Although I'm not copying it exactly, I do feel this needs a bit more black.

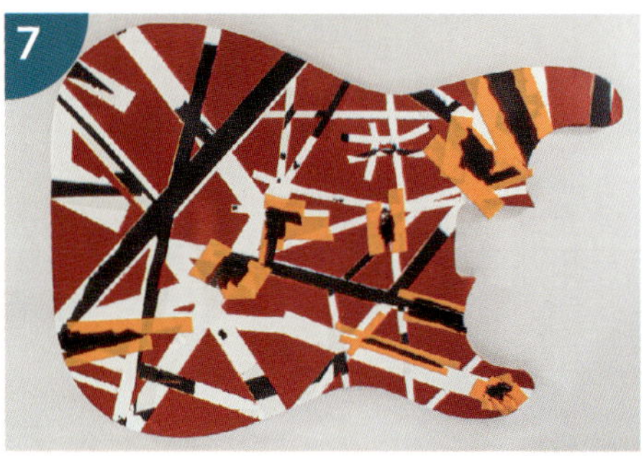

I went back in with some tape and black.

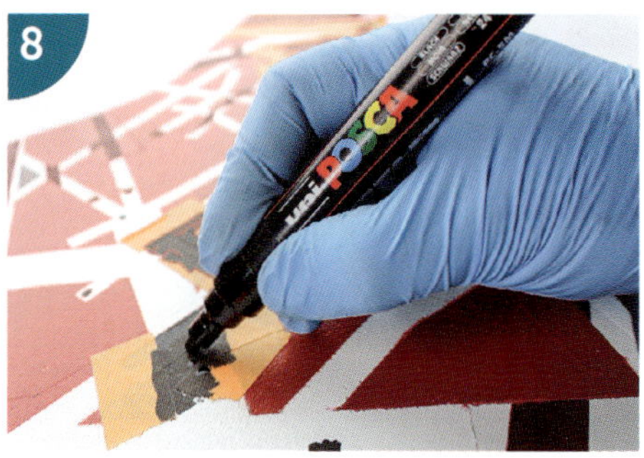

The black was added with a Posca paint pen.

The final result.

Masking with other things

If this were one of the art sessions I run, I would suggest experimenting with masking in as many ways as possible. I'd prepare several guitar-shaped templates, some spray cans and a pile of materials for you to place on the guitar body and spray over. As it isn't a workshop and you're not here with me, I've done it myself (it really was fun).

I sprinkled the surface with screws and bolts from my bits box, sprayed and removed. I like this effect. Flat things leave a more solid shape.

Wrapping the guitar in garden twine reminded me of the Eddie Valen Halen Frankenstrat finish. The string further from the body looks hazy and 3D.

I sprayed the body with paint but not too thickly, then immediately pushed the bubble wrap on to the surface. It's tricky and requires practice.

INSPIRATION: K ULTIMATE GUITARWORKS MASKING WITH CRYSTALS

Recently I was looking back at the posts I'd saved from Facebook guitar finishing groups for inspirational examples to drop into this book and noticed that several very different techniques I'd been really impressed with were done by the same person, 于溯 'Kayl' from K Ultimate Guitarworks.

This incredible crystal effect was created by Kayl using a homemade urea and water mix. He applied the mix (normally a 1:1 ratio with a small amount of dish soap or ammonia added as a wetting agent) to a guitar body and let the crystal effect form. It can be applied with a sponge. Once the effect happened, Kayl was able to spray colour over the top, the crystal acting like a mask on the surface. Once dry, the urea crystals are removed with a light wet sand.

You can buy formulated crystal-effects paints that do the same thing from companies such as Stardust Colours, which make special effects paints.

Another finish of Kayl's that I love is this one, made with alcohol inks applied to the surface and blown around using heat guns.

INSPIRATION: HILDITCH HANDMADE GUITARS SNAKESKIN PATTERN

Mark Hilditch of Handmade Guitars' cool burst finishes were mentioned earlier in the book. When I saw Mark's work on this snakeskin finish, I knew I had to include it here. This truly unique finish has been created by the ingenious use of a pair of tights!

It's not the pattern of the tights alone that creates the snakeskin effect. Mark has used his spray gun to add the light, twisting pattern that appears on the skin. It looks as if the air from the gun has slightly shifted the tights in places, creating a 3D effect where the white sometimes overlays the black. He put out a call on Instagram asking if he should keep the texture created when the tights were removed. You can see it clearly where the light catches the surface above the neck pickup. The response was to keep the texture. This is a great example of where social media can help in decision-making, or gathering opinions to help inform your own.

Masking an area for sanding

Masking has other uses. Sometimes you may need to sand off a big paint drip, splash, filled area, or a stain you don't like ... just like I did here with the Les Paul from The Guitar Fabrik that has appeared throughout the book so far.

Master Shield is a non-sandable tape from Glu Boost. You could use a few layers of masking tape instead, replacing as it wears through.

Run the tape over the area you want to protect; here it can be cut to follow the lines I need.

I'm using a sanding pad because the surface of the guitar is curved.

I didn't need to sand the stain away completely, just enough to lighten the body.

The tape has doubled up as a mask to protect against the new stain. It's not actually as good as masking tape for this, but it does the job.

A final coat of Nitortint Teal to unify the whole body.

INSPIRATION: MAYBURY GUITARS

Throughout this book I've referred to the guitar body as a canvas for creativity, a place to showcase artwork and consider how your customisation can complement the design of the guitar and hardware choices. Artists may want to see their work on instruments. While they can create the art, they might not have the skills or confidence to build the instrument. This is one strand of Maybury Guitars that I really like, the collaboration between luthier Jason Snelling and various artists. Jason will supply a guitar body for the artists to work on, which he'll then finish into to a complete guitar. It's the attention to detail, both from the artists matching the artwork to the shape and layout of the guitar and from Jason in deciding the wood and hardware finishes, that makes these so successful.

The front of the guitar is painted by artist Eddie Rifkind. Jason stained the back in a complementary colour using a signature technique that appears on many of his Upscaler line of guitars.

This collaboration with artist Christopher Williams involved artwork on the front and the cavity cover on the back. I really like hidden details that only the guitarist will see.

One of Maybury's Cholla guitars with a custom paint job by artist Christopher Williams. Here the lines of the flag line up with the pickups to help ground the work as part of the guitar.

PAINT-BASED TECHNIQUES

Painting by hand

Treating the guitar body as a canvas means that you can paint anything on to it. You can paint directly on to the bare wood, or on a sealed or primed surface. If you're using a mix of paints, it may be a good idea to put a sealer coat on top before topcoating. Always test the paint and sealer or topcoat's compatibility on a scrap piece first. Remember that a hand-painted surface is likely to be uneven, so take care in sanding back clear coats that are over the top.

Paint pens

Paint pens come in different sizes, colours and types of pen. Posca are one of the most well-known brands; they're water-based acrylic paints and I've used them throughout this book.

Before applying the paint pens on to a painted body, prepare the surface with a light sand (as if preparing for the next coat of paint). Do not sand once the paint pens have been used before applying the topcoats, as this will ruin your work. I often find that multiple applications are needed. Sometimes going over your design can lift some of the previous paint pen colour, in which case I will apply a clear coat between them (three coats in one session, left to dry, then sanded with 600 grit).

My daughter drew on this guitar, sometimes free-hand and sometimes using vinyl cut stencils.

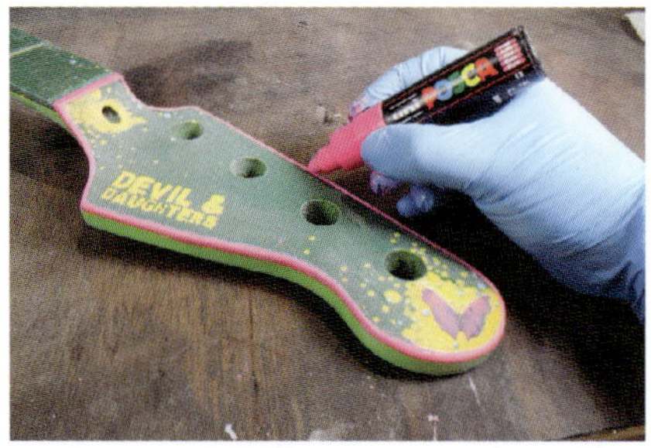

A pink Posca was used on this bass to add details to the areas I had stencilled. Using two thicknesses of the same colour really adds to the dimensionality of the leaf pattern.

The pink line around this headstock resembles binding. To achieve this, I simply ran the thicker-nibbed pink along the edge without masking.

For guitars like my Craftcaster series I mixed hand-painting and paint pens. The green detail was first painted by brush, then highlighted with multiple green and yellow paint pens.

INSPIRATION: RICHARD FAY SWIRLS

Richard is an artist and guitar maker whose work I first discovered in a guitar-finishing group on Facebook. Social-media platforms like this are great places to find inspiration. Richard has been creating swirl-art guitars since the early 2000s and his expertise is evident when you visit his website. It's filled with examples of his work and serves as a real mood board of swirl inspiration. Richard summed up his experience for us:

Swirling is an unpredictable process. Some days it goes well, other days less so, but practice is the key to getting some consistency in the finished article. It's dependent on lots of factors; the paint you use and its thickness, how much paint you put on the water and how quickly, water temperature and hardness, air temperature and humidity, the surface area of your water tank, etc., etc. So the main thing is to practise and find a process that works for you. You have some control over the patterns, by choosing how you put the paints on the water, and how much you swirl them around before putting the guitar in. The guitar can be put in straight downwards, where it'll take the patterns directly, or zigzagged from side to side as it descends (steady hands needed, whichever way you do it). All those things will have a big effect on the final pattern. But ultimately, it's still unpredictable and the result often feels like it's in the lap of the (swirling) gods.

Richard's advice is to move the paint around in the water with a dowel and not to move the guitar too much when dipping, maybe just a single zigzag from one side to the other if you want the overall pattern to have that 'swoosh' across the guitar. Most of his patterns are caused by the way he moves the paint around with the dowel before dipping.

It's not just the mesmerising patterns in Richard's swirls that captivate me, but also his use of colours. They evoke vivid imagery of molten lava, psychedelic dreams, nostalgic childhood toys, whimsical animations and futuristic science fiction. Each swirl is a portal to a different world, inviting us to see something unique and personal in its hypnotic dance.

Swirl finish

Marbling might be a familiar craft technique. Various colours of paint are dropped on to the top of a tray of water, often using pipettes. The colours swirl on the surface and interact, but don't blend; instead, they push against each other. It's quite hypnotic to watch. Then a sheet of paper is placed on the surface. It absorbs the paint and the image is transferred from the water to the paper. For a swirl finish, we essentially replace the tray with a large tub and the paper with a guitar body.

The method I am going to demonstrate is the one I have had the most success with, using Humbrol enamel paints. These little tins are the same make and size that I used when painting Airfix models as a child; a great memory to get me in the mood.

The tub you dip the guitar body in needs to be deep enough for the whole guitar to submerge into. I use a large storage box; I have seen some people using large waste bins. You could line the box with a thick bin liner if you don't want to get paint on it. My tub has approximately 100ltr of warm water in it. You will need to add bicarbonate of soda to prevent the paint from sinking into the water and diluting. (In the US, borax would be the additive to use.) I add a 1kg box of

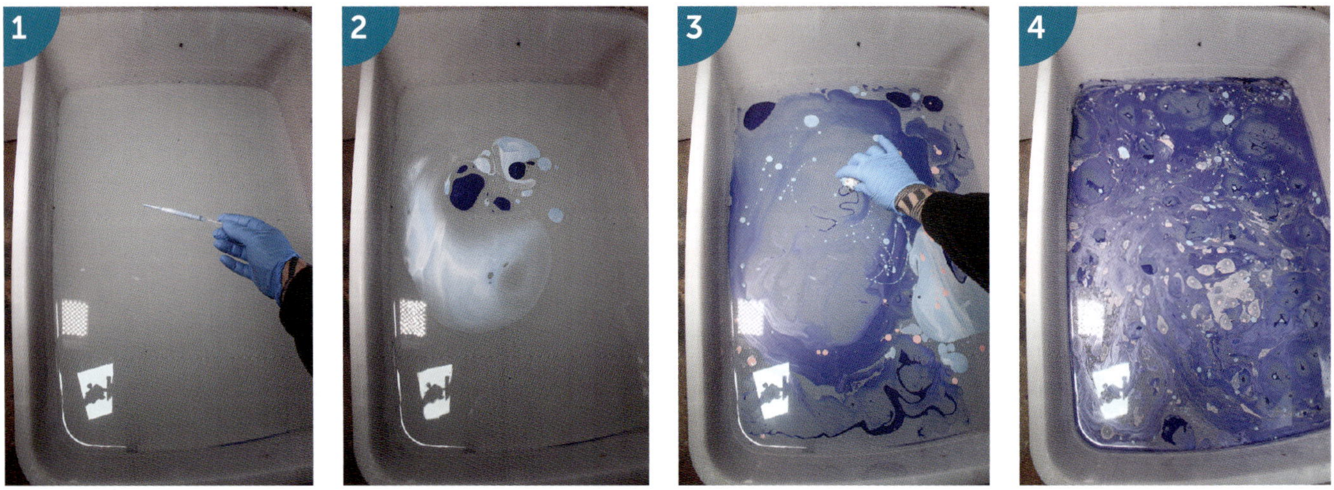

I'm using both a pipette and pouring directly from the can. Work quickly. The paint will move around, begin to clump together and paint shapes will contract the longer you leave them.

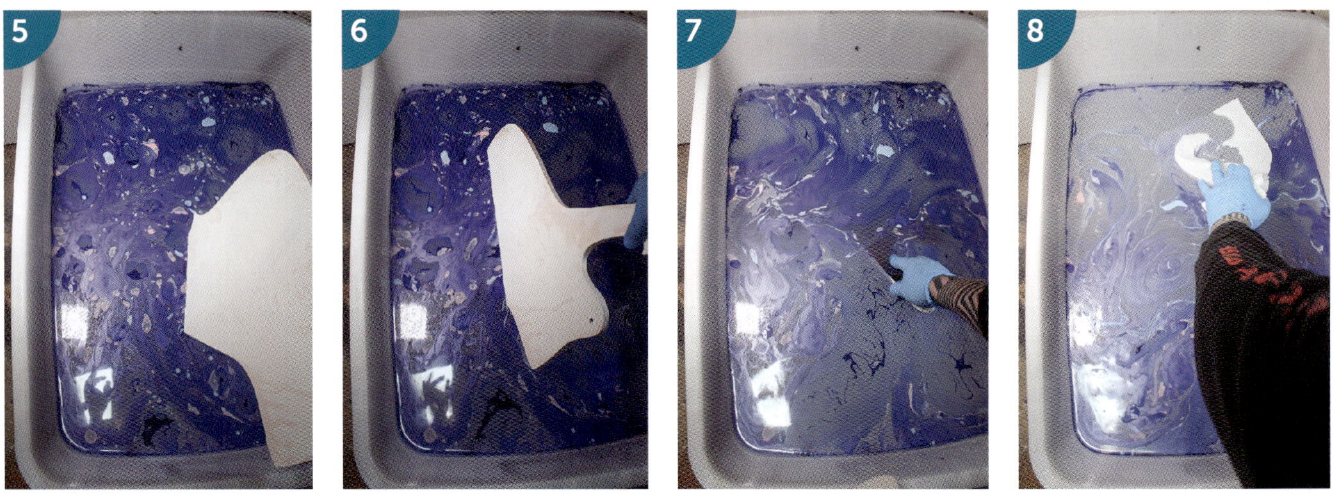

When dipping, move the body around so that it gets covered all over. The paint moves, so look for interesting shapes to push the body into. Wipe the paint off the surface before removing the guitar.

bicarbonate of soda premixed in hot (not boiling) water. There are companies that make acrylic-based marbling paints which you may want to use instead. The process remains the same.

Avoid water pooling on the guitar body by hanging it vertically whilst it dries. Don't be tempted to wipe away any surface water.

EXPERIMENT FIRST

I highly recommend that you run some experiments first. Marbling is a random process, but you can control it to some extent by the number of colours you add, how you place them in the water, and how you move the guitar when submerging it. Screw a short length of wood to the neck pocket of the guitar as a handle.

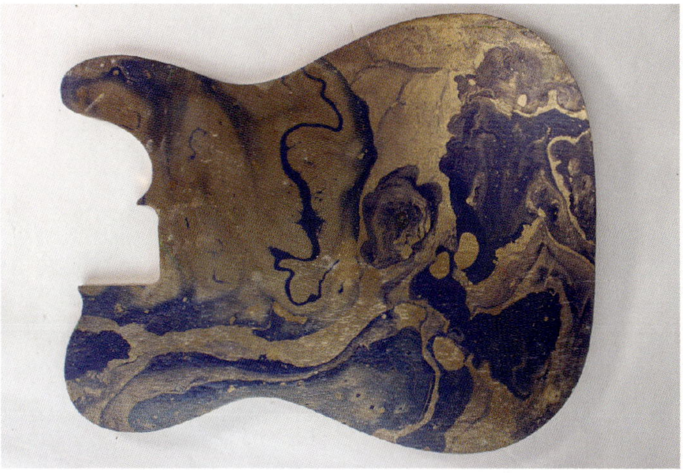

The finished body pattern is partly dictated by the small drops and pools of paint I added and by the movements made when dipping it in.

Here I have used Humbrol blue enamel only on a sample body sprayed with Montana Gold gold. Using a single colour can be just as effective as multiple ones.

Acrylic pouring

I first encountered the acrylic-pouring technique on YouTube in 2020 during the Covid-19 lockdowns. I spent many hours watching people demonstrate this mesmerising and meditative process; it was a bit of an escape from the world. Like many art techniques, as soon as I saw it, I wanted to try it on a guitar.

The process involves layering paint into a cup or jar. I've found one standard jam jar of 180ml is enough for one side of the body. You can buy acrylic-pouring paint, which is already at the right viscosity, or pouring medium to which you add standard acrylic colours to help it flow. The key is to pour the paint down the side of the jar so that each colour lays on top of the previous one (although as with any artistic techniques, rules are there to be experimented with and broken).

You now need to position the jar upside-down on the body. I do this by placing the body over the opening of the jar and flipping them together. The magic happens when you lift the jar from the surface and start to move the guitar, allowing the acrylic to flow over the body.

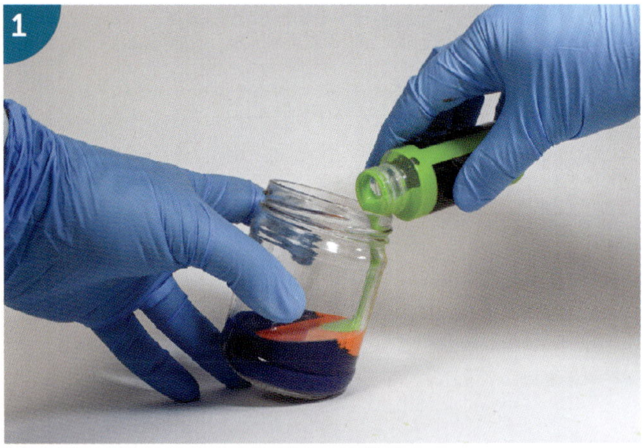

Pour the acrylic down the side of the container so it settles on top of the previous colour.

The layers of paint ready for pouring on to the guitar.

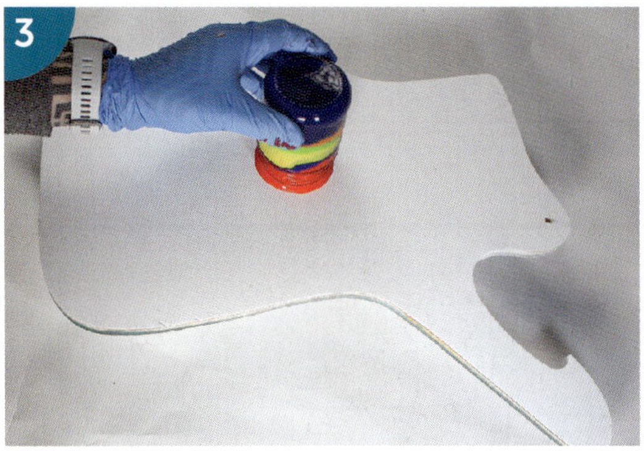

The jar of paint is upside on the surface, ready to be lifted away.

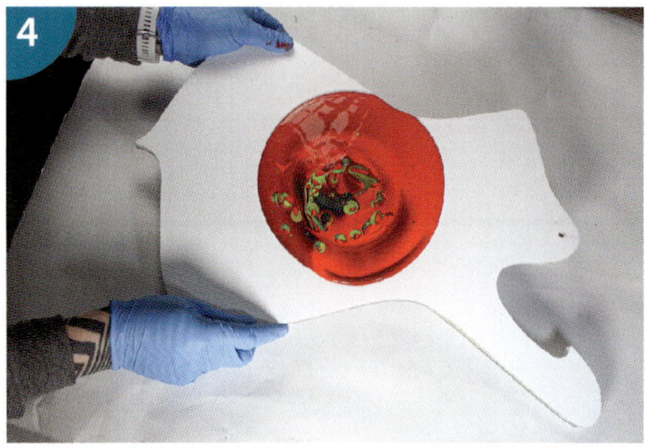

Once the paint is released, hold the body firmly and tilt it in all directions.

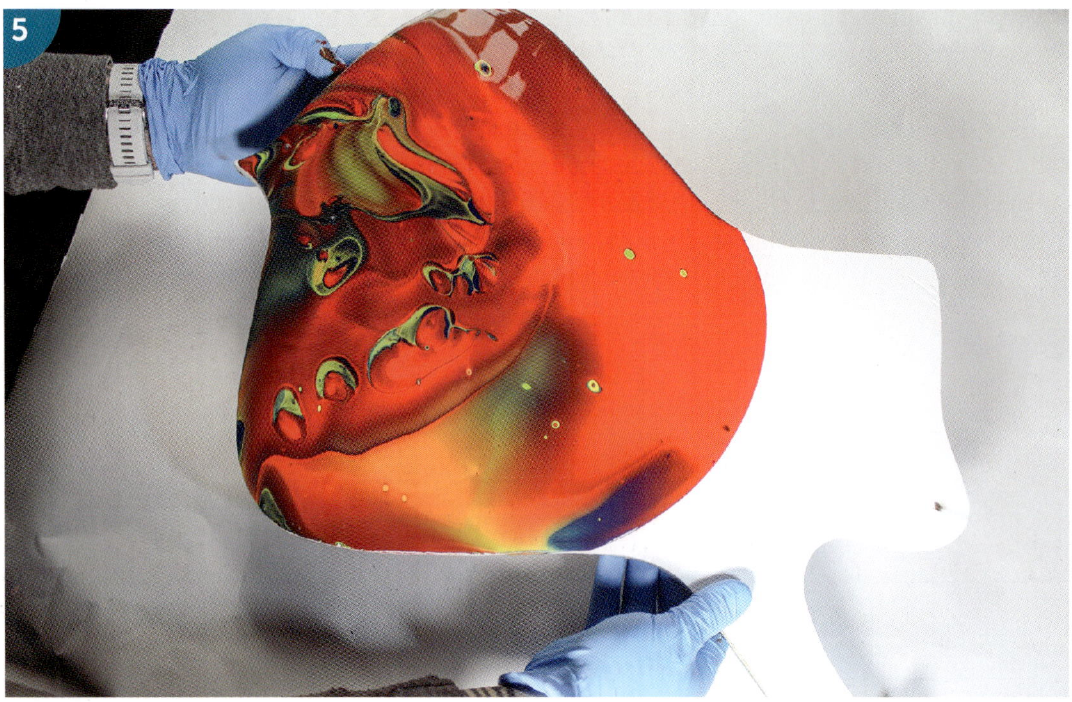

With experience you can control the pour patters to some extent.

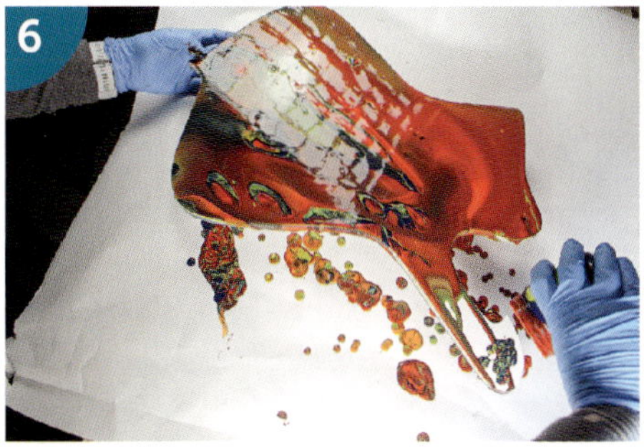

If the paint doesn't flow all over the body, which is very likely on a body with control and pickup cavities, add more paint from the jar. There's normally some left in there.

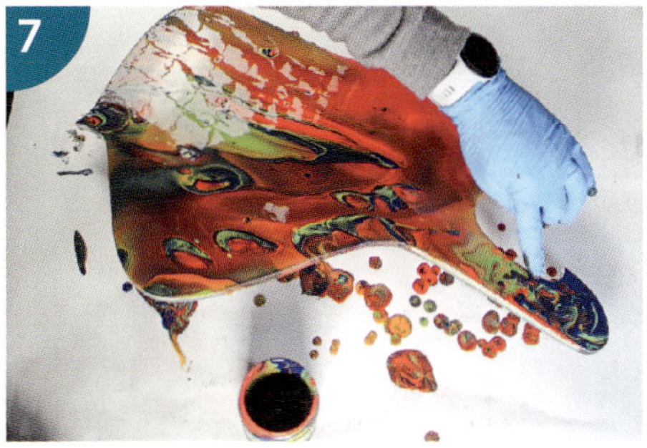

The paint will slowly level out and blend naturally into an area with paint, but sometimes won't flow into an empty space at the edge. Tease the paint into spaces with your finger.

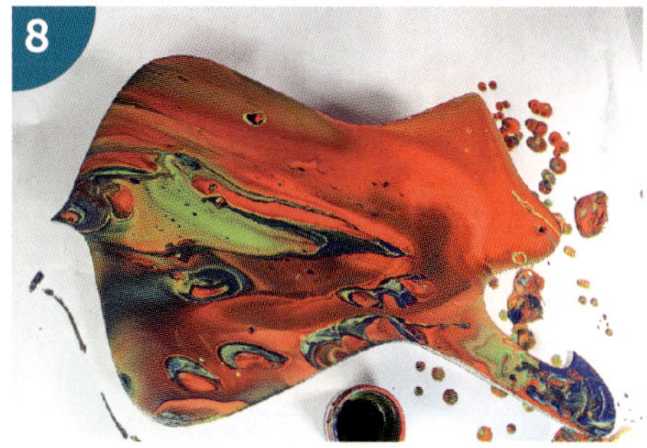

When you are happy with the result, you can stop moving the body and paint around. Expect it still to shift a bit when it is drying.

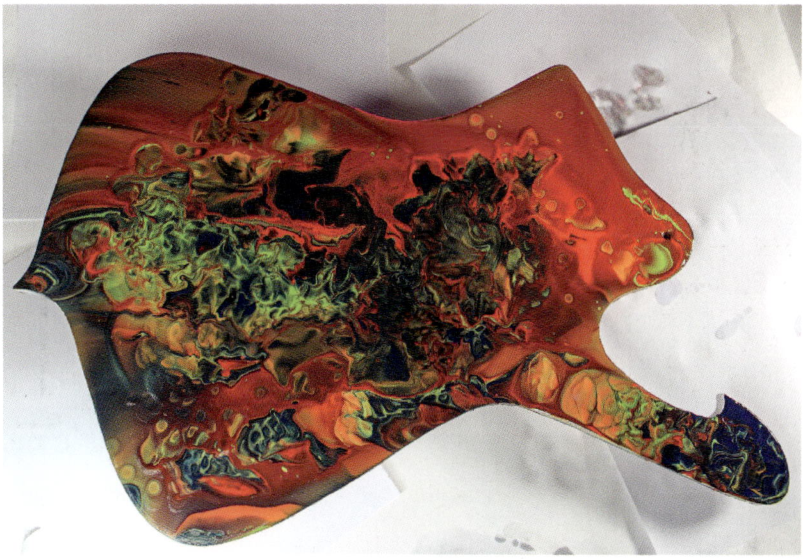

Another way of moving the paint around the surface is with a hairdryer or hot-air gun. It causes the paint surface to ripple and wave, resulting in a very different effect, such as shown here.

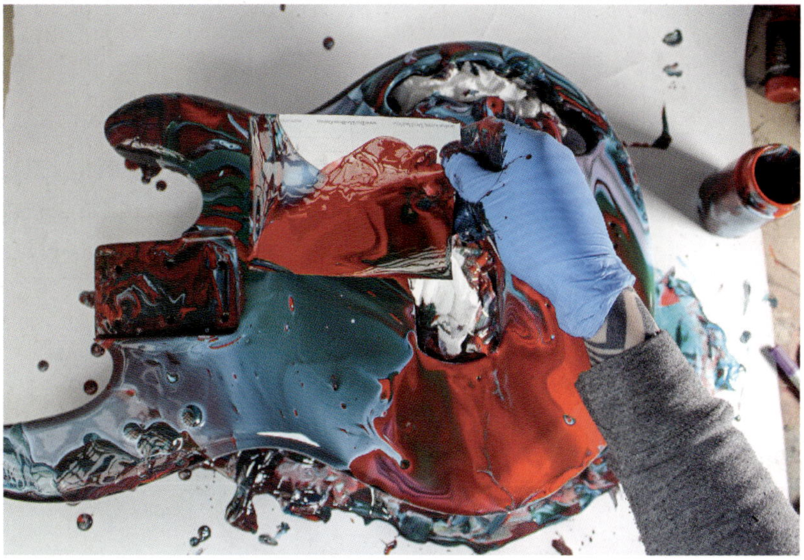

On this bass body I used a postcard to scoop up some of the paint that had overflowed and poured it back on to the areas that weren't covered.

Using silicone to create bubbles

Using a pipette to add drops of acrylic-pouring silicone causes bubbles to form in the paint, separating out the layers. Some people add drops to the original mix in the jar, but I prefer to add it the paint surface, as it allows more control.

The silicone is going to leave an oily residue on the surface, which will cause issues when you come to topcoating. It's easily removed by wiping, then buffing with isopropyl alcohol over the surface once the paint has dried. Use a lint-free cloth. I don't trust that one pass is enough, so I normally go over it three times, letting each pass evaporate before applying the next. You can feel when the residue has gone.

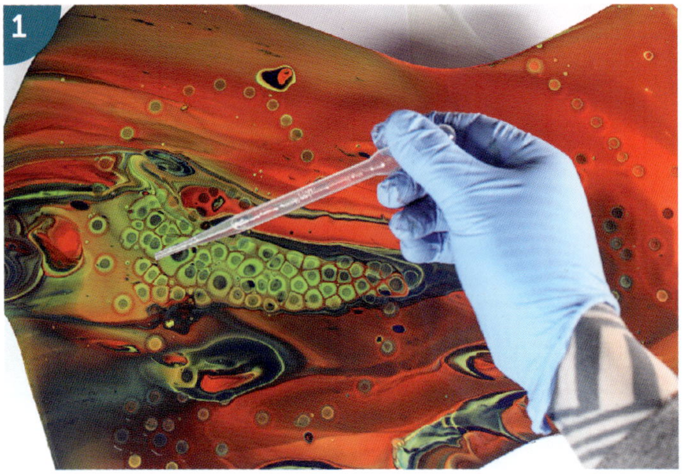

Silicone can be dripped on using a pipette.

The silicone allows bottom layers of paint to be revealed on the surface.

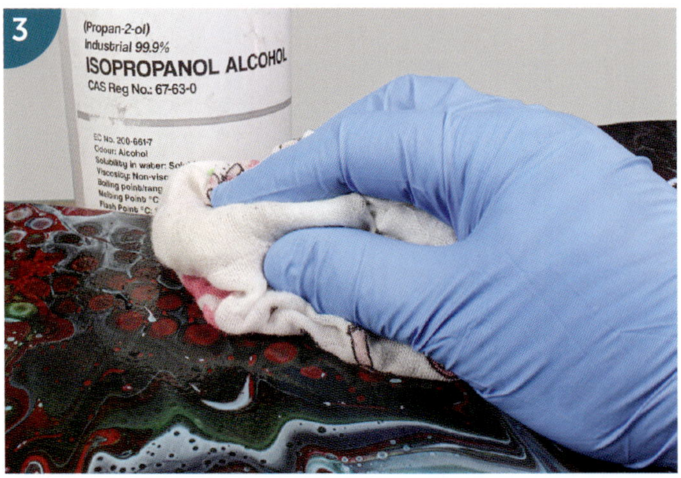

Once dry, clean the surface with isopropyl alcohol.

Applying topcoats

The bass body in the photos on the next page has had the silicone added. The surface is now rippled, even more than just pouring would be on its own. I like this texture and would consider leaving it with one spray session of topcoats added, but to get it smooth multiple sessions will be needed. Don't sand the surface too hard before the first coat; use a sponge-backed 600-grit sanding pad to allow a light texture to be added that the topcoat can bond to. Then lightly sand between the first and second, and second and third topcoats with the same pad. For this bass, I was able to use a hard-backed 400-grit paper after the third topcoat to smooth it back completely flat. I then applied the final topcoat and went through the polishing and buffing process.

The surface is really textured once the paint has dried. This finished bass is on the cover.

The finished bass shows how the layers of clear have resulted in a smooth surface.

INSPIRATION: THE FLUID ALCHEMIST

Cyrille L is an artist known as The Fluid Alchemist. He is also the visionary behind Vertige Guitars, uniquely shaped guitars that feature his artwork on the surfaces. Whilst Cyrille's artworks use the acrylic-pouring method, they aren't made directly on to the guitars. Instead, he uses a mix of processes to transfer digital copies on to the bodies. His work often also includes a mix of bursts and glitter.

On some instruments, he used nitrocellulose finishes, meaning that the process takes a considerable amount of time, as he can't mask off any areas until the nitrocellulose finish has cured. The Fluid Alchemist guitars are the perfect illustration of using a guitar as a canvas.

The intertwining swirls of black and glitter over the poured colour weave a mesmerising tapestry on this guitar's surface, evoking the potential melodies it will bring to life.

One advantage of transferring the fluid pour digitally to the guitar is the control that Cyrille has in the positioning of the shapes to fit so well with the hardware and guitar shape.

Spatter effects

To spatter something is to fling and splash paint over it. It's a word you may hear in conjunction with blood; 'the detectives examined the blood spatter at the crime scene', for example. Splatter means the same thing, although I always associate it with larger areas and droplets. It's thought that the word splatter comes from a mix of 'splash' and 'spatter'. Most guitar companies tend to opt for the word splatter, so I'm going to use spatter to stand out! Blood and heavy metal are synonymous and many companies have partnered up with well-known guitarists to make signature blood splatter models: Schecter has its Gary Holt series; Kiesel makes the Dan Sugarman models; B.C. Rich partnered with Joey Jordison ... the list goes on. In my examples, I'm going to avoid the blood finish and go black.

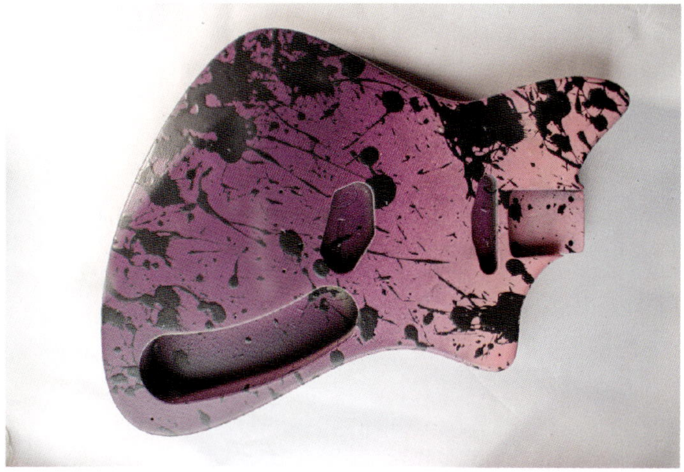

Spatter finish on the 3D printed guitar from earlier in the book.

Spatter, splash and fling

This guitar has had a spatter finish applied using a brush. I'm using undiluted Nitorlack Nitoraqua in black. It's quite thick, which means extra work to get it level for a smooth topcoat at the end, although the texture may be something you want to embrace and keep. I recommend experimenting with different dilutions and the following techniques on anything scrap until you are happy with the results. The body is painted in Montana Gold paints using a fade-burst technique and has been lightly sanded ready for the next coat using 600-grit paper. It's important to sand before the spatter is added; you don't want to sand the spatter before the topcoats as it may remove some of the subtle splashes.

Use a brush dipped in paint and simply fling it at the body. Different-sized brushes, amounts of paint and their viscosity will alter the effect.

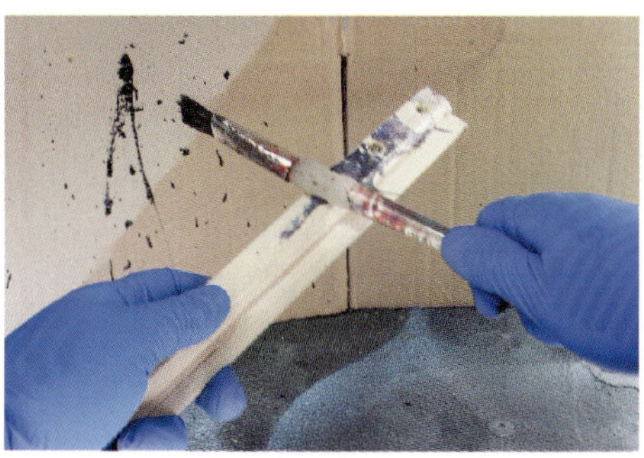

Bang the brush against something like a ruler or piece of wood away from the surface. The impact will cause the paint to fling off. Vary how hard you hit to change the spatter.

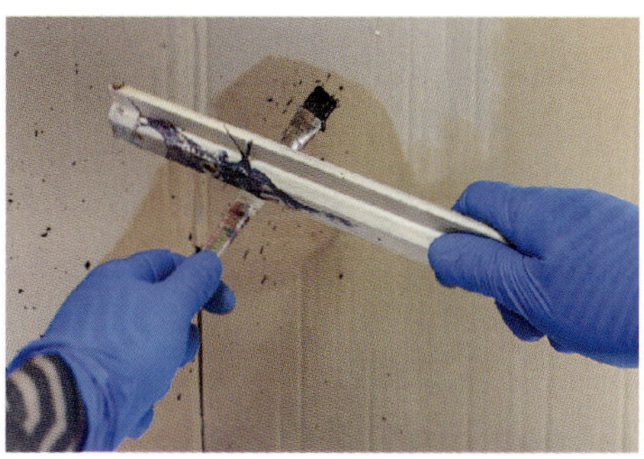

Use the same brush and stick, this time banging the brush with the stick. I find this normally gives smaller splats.

Use a spray bottle with diluted paint. Some bottles have an adjustment on the spray that can help to create thicker droplets.

Reverse spatter: the masking-fluid method

This method results in a reverse pattern because the mask is used to create the spatter. You can use the same liquid rubber or latex that I covered in the section on masking. Here I used an artist's masking fluid and applied it using a brush banged against another brush. I'm working on the back of the guitar from the first technique example. Once it was dry, I sprayed it with the same Nitoraqua black from a spray gun. Avoid spaying a thick paint because it can conceal the masking fluid too much, making it hard to remove. I only applied two coats in one sitting. When the paint is dry remove the masking and prepare for the topcoats with a light 800-grit sand.

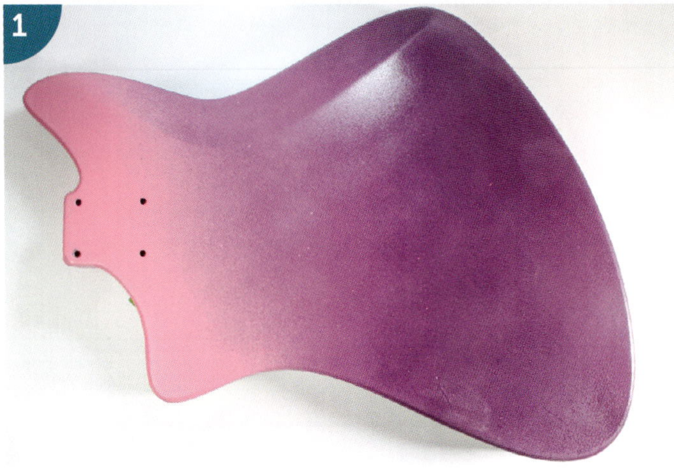

Once the base colour is put on, lightly sand with 400 grit.

Add the masking fluid using your choice of spatter technique.

Spray the next colour once the masking fluid is completely dry.

Once the next colour is completely dry you can remove the masking fluid.

ALTERNATE USES OF MASKING FLUID

You can use the masking fluid in many ways not just by spattering it. Perhaps drips, a painted design, or in combination with a vinyl mask or masking tape?

TOPCOATS OVER SPATTER

Using the spatter method results in thick paint where it has been splatted onto the guitar surface. Using the reverse splatter method you end up with a much more even and flat surface. The spatter is only as thick as the layers of paint you have sprayed on.

If you want to end up with a flat finish for the first method, the best option is to apply the first session of topcoats as normal. When dry, apply more sessions with a 600-grit sand between each. As the layers build, the clear on the flatter areas will start to be higher than the raised paint spatters and at some point the clear all over the surface will be thick enough to sand flat. Look carefully at the dust created by sanding – if any colour comes off it shows that the clear isn't thick enough. When no colour comes off in the sanding, change to a flat block and 600 grit to level it out.

You will most likely sand through the topcoats and into the paint spatter, in this case the black. However, because it's a thick, solid colour it doesn't matter that you are sanding the top off; it's not like a hand-painted design where you would lose the detail. Once the surface is flat, treat the guitar as if it hasn't had any topcoats yet and apply two sessions in the normal way, ready for the polishing and buffing process.

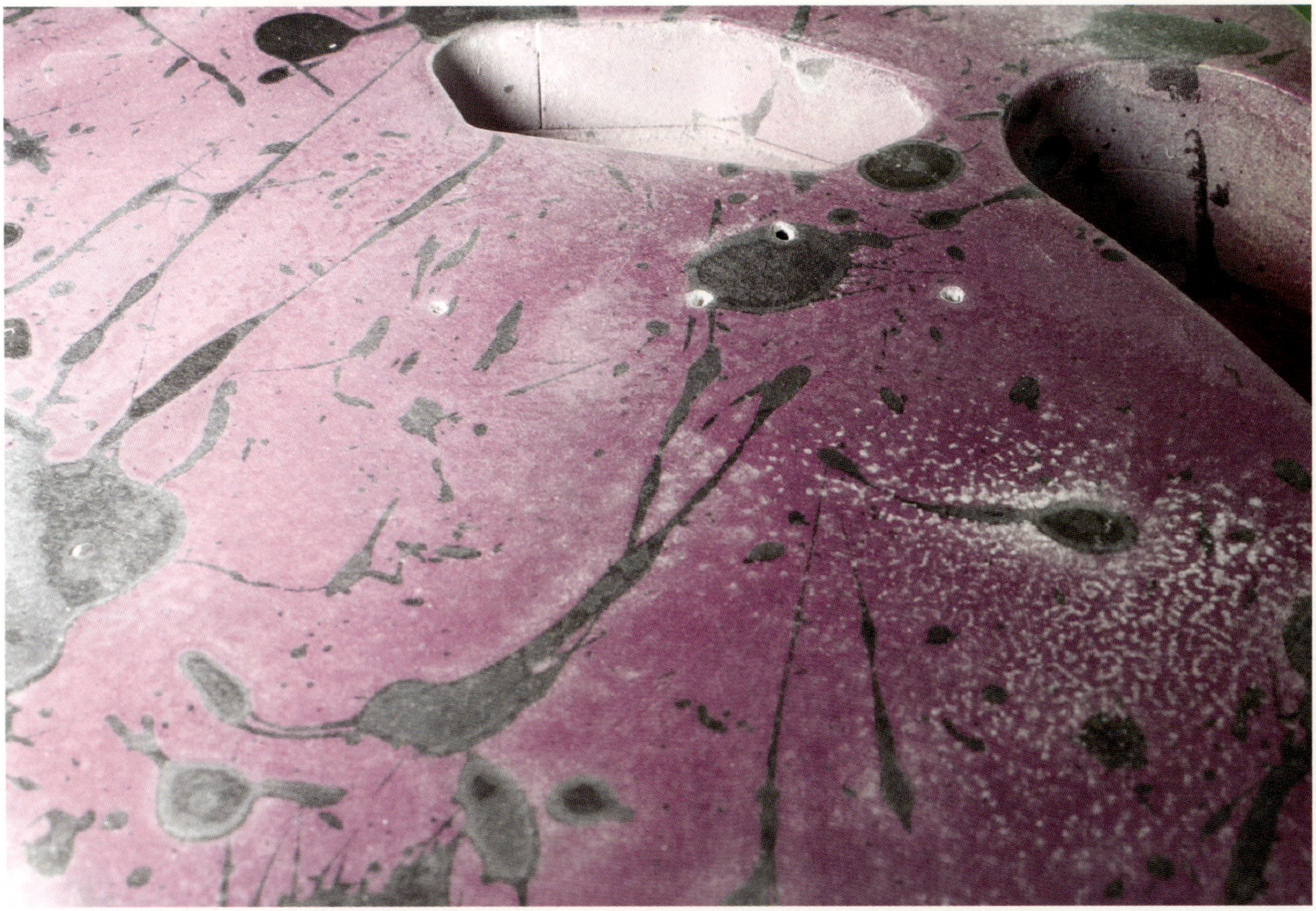

The left half is flat now, but the right is still raised. The way that the powdery sanding residue gathers around the black spatter gives it away.

EMBOLDENING THE EFFECT

Remember that some paints, particularly lighter colours, are translucent and some of the base colour will come though. This may look great, giving the spatter a 3D look, but it might not be what you want. One way to fix this is to hand-paint over the spatter with multiple layers of the colour. The original technique will create the realistic effect, whilst the additional coats will make the colour bolder.

CASE STUDY: THE SPATTERED METEORA

The Fender Meteora is the first guitar I have seen in a very long time that I wanted. It's probably the first new shape from a major manufacturer that I like. I think it works best as a bass, but in their Paranormal series Fender combined the guitar version with Telecaster hardware and it rocked. Ray from Tasmaniak Guitars designs 3D-printed guitars and he made the files for me to use in this book. I needed to demonstrate multiple techniques of spatter, so it made sense to use a different one on the front and the back. This contrast has worked so well that I will be doing it on guitars to sell. The pickguard is made from 2mm clear acrylic and has the paint spatter added to the back. Those skull and cross bone decals are stickers, which will be covered later in the book.

The soap-spatter method

This is less of a spatter and more of a drip and flick. The end result is very distinctive and it's a technique I hope more clients will ask me for because I enjoy it. Essentially, I splashed washing-up liquid directly from the bottle all over the body, sprayed it, then washed the soap off once the paint was dry. I recommend spraying straight after the liquid is applied, as it can begin to spread. Washing it off can take a while because there is so much soap there, but it's worth it for the end result.

I took this technique further by combining it with tape masking, as used for the EVH Frankenstrat, in order to add a second layer of colour on top, opting for harsh straight lines against the curvy fluid pattern that the soap makes.

Liquid soap is dripped over the guitar.

The sprayed paint doesn't settle on the soap.

Once the paint is dry and the soap has been washed away.

With the extra EVH technique applied on top.

Crackle finish

Crackle-finished guitars regularly appear in my Instagram feed. They were a big thing in the 1980s, but are still popular. The finish is achieved by spraying a specially formulated paint over a basecoat. Several companies make these finishes. In these examples, Montana Crackle finish cans have been used. Essentially, the paint shrinks as it dries, pulling itself apart. The process takes some practice, so I recommend having some test pieces with the same basecoat paint. I can get three guitars out of one can, so you potentially have some to spare.

My process comes from the advice of Kalle from Mord Custom Guitars – his experience helped me when I first experimented with this process. The basecoats are Montana Gold sprays. Although Kalle and I have used a single colour, I think it looks particularly good over a multicoloured finish. I encourage you to experiment with the basecoat when you are experimenting with the crackle. Here is Kalle's check list:

* The guitar needs to have the base colour applied. Three coats in one session, left to dry, then lightly sanded with 600 grit ready for the crackle.
* Make sure that the area in which you are spraying is warm. The warmer it is, the quicker the reaction takes place.
* Add an extra layer of the basecoat colour to the guitar no more than 45 minutes before spraying the crackle finish. This is a medium on which to help the crackle work.
* To achieve larger cracks, the paint must be applied more thickly. Spray from the normal hands-width away distance, but apply two or three coats in one area before moving on.
* Use a hair dryer or hot-air gun to encourage the cracks to move around.
* Plan the paint application route around the guitar. Sides first, then back, then front.

Topcoats over crackle

The crackle surface can be very fragile, with paint peeling away if handled too much. You must apply the topcoats without first sanding the surface at all. The cracks themselves will give the clear enough surface to bond with. Apply three coats in a single session as normal, lightly sand with a 600-grit sponge-backed pad, then continue. You will most likely need two or three more sessions of topcoats to get a flat finish like this one from Mord Custom Guitars. Follow the same process as applying topcoats over the spatter finish.

DON'T GO BACK

Don't go back over an area once it starts to crack. This can result in new paint cracking between the cracks that are already forming, leaving you with tiny close-together cracks that appear to be a blurred haze from a distance. Letting an area dry and spraying over the top creates a similar result. It's much better to sand off and start again if you aren't happy.

These are two guitars customised by Kalle of Mord Custom Guitars.

The gloss finish on this Mord Custom Guitar really makes the finish pop. The smooth surface hides the texture of the paint and makes the process seem more mysterious.

CASE STUDY: DEVIL & DAUGHTERS CRACKLE STRAT

This guitar is a Partscaster. The left-handed body was donated to me by Lewis from LT Custom Guitars. It was green originally and appeared in the sections on stripping paint, filling cavities, sealing the body with filler, routing cavities and priming. What a workhorse! The neck came from the pile in my workshop that has accumulated over the years, from guitars stripped for parts. The scratchplate is custom-built. I have a lot of cheap pickups that come from guitars that have been upgraded. Some sound awesome, some don't. The awesome ones get kept for builds like this. Most of the hardware was bought in for the build. Some of it is new but unused from other custom jobs where I had changed my mind about the components whilst assembling. Inside there's a Mars-Tronic variable treble bleed, a great piece of kit for controlling the way a guitar's volume affects an amp.

I've used Kalle's approach for the crackle finish. I started by applying a basecoat of Montana Gold Baby Blue to the body. Then I masked off the front and applied a Montana Black Crackle finish to the back. After a session of topcoats, I switched the mask to cover the back and sprayed the front with Montana White Crackle. Initially there was a hard line between the two sides, but I decided it was too harsh. You can see how I added the faux binding in the relevant section of this book.

One detail I particularly like about this guitar is the back of neck. I sprayed it in two halves, just like the body, then used Posca paint pens over the first topcoats to colour in some of the crackle pattern, making it look like the crackle was intruding from one side to another.

I must mention my mistakes here; we all make them. It's a left-handed reverse headstock neck, but, as I have done more than once before, I put the logo on as if it were right-handed. A little bit of black paint and I put the logo on again using the vinyl stencil method. It actually looks better with the black border that I had to make to cover the original upside logo, so this was a happy mistake.

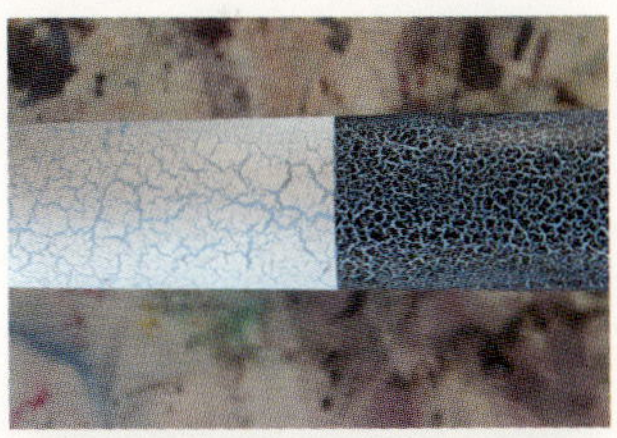

Hammerite finish

I like to experiment with non-traditional paints. Hammerite is a paint designed for use on exterior metal. One version of it dries with a textured finish, often called a hammered finished. I've used it several times, taking advantage of the texture to create a weathered metal appearance.

Once the Hammerite is dry, I spray over it, then sand the surface back. The new top colour stays in the divots of the texture; the raised parts are sanded through to reveal the Hammerite colour. You can vary the effect by the amount you sand back. Hammerite comes in a variety of colours for even more options.

A close-up showing the textured finish of the Hammerite paint.

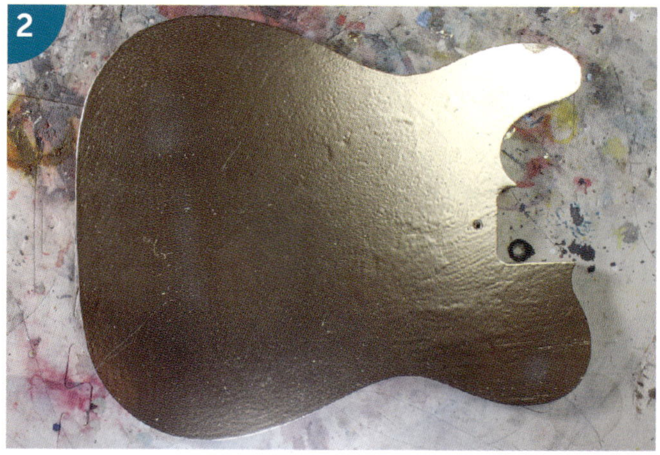

I've sprayed Montana Gold gold over the surface.

Sanding back with a 400-grit block has revealed the Hammerite on the high parts, leaving the gold in the dips.

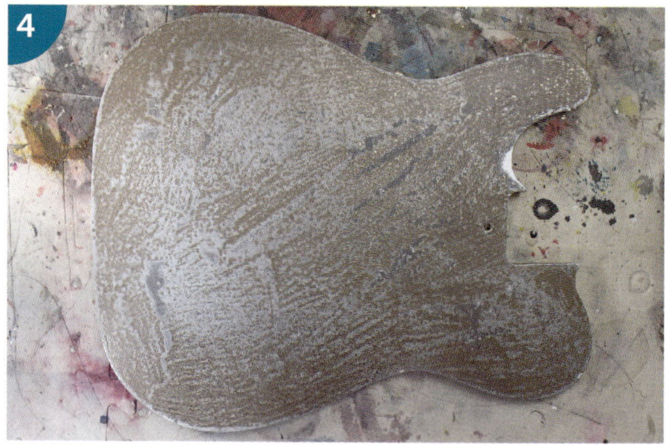

I really like using this technique for a weathered finish, but it would also look great with a bright colour instead of the gold.

This body has had a design painted on it using the tape-masking technique. The texture of the Hammerite is visible under the Montana Gold colours that have been applied.

After a light sand, the weathered look is revealed. This paint job was for a client who had given me a mood board based on a rally car. This technique really achieved the finish he wanted.

CLASSIC GUITAR: ZAKK WYLDE'S BULLSEYE

Zakk Wylde is another guitarist who doesn't just have a signature sound and style of playing, but an aesthetic too. Schecter produces several variations of his Bullseye and Buzz-saw paint finishes. Here I have recreated the Bullseye design using two techniques from the book – the vinyl cut stencil and the Hammerite finish.

I've applied the Bullseye pattern, cut on my Cricut cutter out of stencil vinyl. The missing parts could be used to create the reverse pattern on the back.

The black has been sprayed and the stencil removed. I like the contrast between the solid black lines and the textured gold/silver finish.

I couldn't resist lightly sanding the black. I used a 600-grade paper on a hard block.

SPECIALIST PAINTS THAT REQUIRE A SPECIAL APPROACH

The next three paint finishes – glitter, metallic and flip – all share a similar property, which is that the surface is essential to the finish and must not be sanded back. This can be an issue as you will want to topcoat over the paint, but at the same time need to sand to ensure that the topcoat bonds. There is an easy solution, though – simply apply a single topcoat layer in the same session that you lay down the specialist paint. These paints don't need many layers, normally only two to make sure there is full coverage, so there's no risk of putting too much paint on in that session. That single coat will be enough for a light sanding with 600 grit before starting the normal topcoat process. If you want to be cautious, apply four coats in one session, two of the specialist paint and two of the topcoat.

Glitter paint

There are actually several ways to apply glitter to a guitar surface. You can buy off the shelf glitter paint, either in a spray can or ready for use in a spray gun; this is by far the easiest option. There's a wide range of colour glitter too, which is normally suspended in a clear paint. You can mix glitter in with a clear coat when you spray it from a gun, or a translucent colour. Finally, you have the option of sprinkling it on to a wet coat of paint. Whichever method you use, remember that a topcoat needs to be sprayed as the final coat in any spraying session to protect the glitter when sanding.

Glitter mixing for a spray gun

Whilst you can use your own choice of clear, it's vital to use high-quality fine glitter, so as to avoid clogging up the gun. Some paint manufacturers make glitter especially for adding to paint. You don't need much in the mix and stir it thoroughly right before use. It's best to give the mix in the gun cup a stir between coats. Always start with less glitter than you think you need and test it; you can always add more. Often, very little is needed for a great finish.

Sprinkling glitter on to the wet surface

I advise doing this with a clear coat over your choice of colour basecoat that has had a 600-grit sand. Apply the first

GLITTER FROM A CAN

This guitar has a glitter scratchplate, backplate and fretboard. There are specific sections on painting the elements of a guitar later in the book, but here I'll cover how the glitter was used. Remember not to cut corners when shaking the spray can; a full two minutes is essential to ensure that the glitter is well dispersed.

The fretboard was given a basecoat of white, then red, then glitter from a spray can, then topcoat. It's that straightforward. The same process would be used for the entire body. The scratchplate and backplate are clear acrylic, so they were sprayed on the back in reverse – glitter, colour, basecoat.

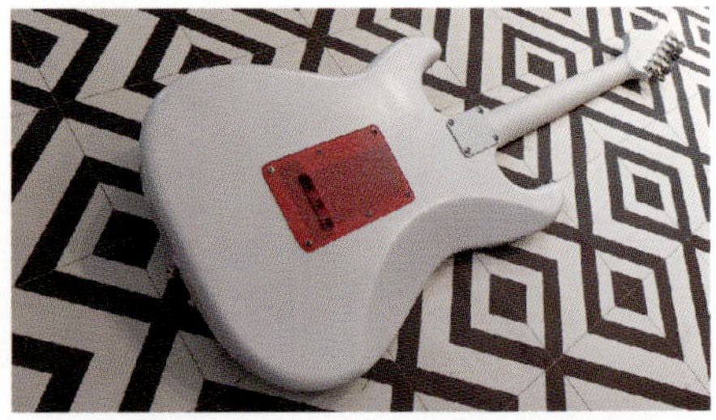

coat, sprinkle on glitter sparingly, apply the second coat and add more glitter if you think it's needed. End with a clear coat and no glitter, ready for sanding before the final topcoat process is applied. You could replace the first clear coat here with a coat of colour, but I would only advise that if you know the colour will cover evenly in one coat, or the body already has the same colour.

One coat of clear with glitter mixed in was applied over this body, followed by more coats of just clear. This allows the design underneath to still show clearly through the glitter.

ADDING DEPTH

Layering the glitter can add depth to the finish. By sandwiching the glitter-spray sessions between clear-coat sessions, a deeper field for the glitter will be created. Remember to stick to established drying times between each session and sand with 600 grit between each.

Metallic paints

Not all metallic paints are equal. The Montana Gold range that I use a lot makes metallic finishes; these (like many art sprays) don't have the same quality of finish as the professional paints such as those made by Nitorlack. I use Nitorlack's nitrocellulose spray cans and polyurethane mix from a spray gun in the examples here. Although both have a great finish, I prefer the results from a gun (although that may be down to the fact that a spray gun tends to give better results than a spray can). Both require a thorough shake or mix to ensure that the pigments are evenly dispersed and not clumped in the bottom of the can. Shake or mix between coats. Don't forget the clear final coat in the spray sessions to help when sanding between sessions.

In this photo, I have used Nitorlack's polyurethane Silver Sparkle on both the headstock and the body. I applied two coats on each and finished the session with Nitorlack's polyurethane gloss topcoat. To me, the finish is the same on both despite the fact that the body has a basecoat of white polyurethane and the headstock black Nitoraqua. Two coats of the metallic are enough to conceal the base colour.

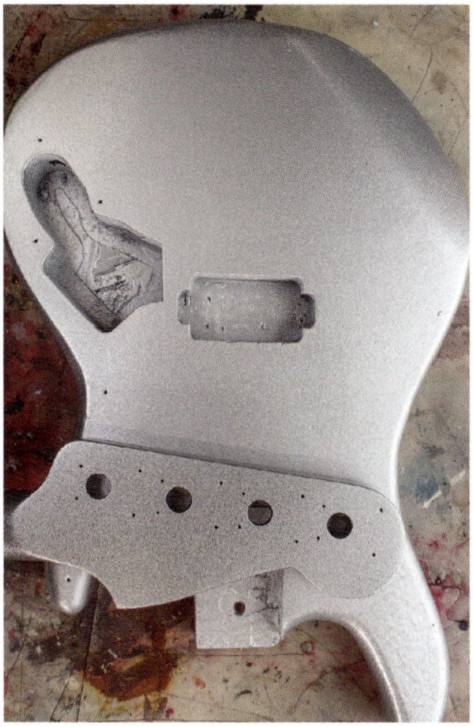

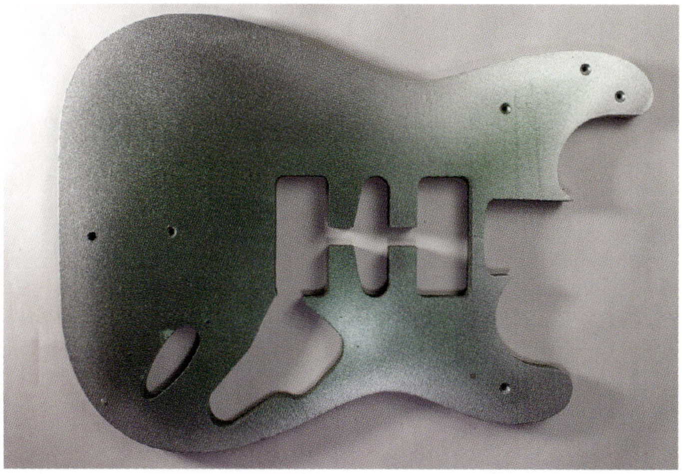

You can experiment with metallic finish by spraying it thinly, or stopping after one coat and allowing some of the base colour to come through. The body shown here has a green basecoat, with one light coat of Silver Sparkle over the whole surface and another three to make the burst.

Metallic paint and clear mix

This guitar looks like it has a glitter finish, but actually I mixed a small amount of Nitorlack's Silversparkle metallic polyurethane into their clear polyurethane. This works as a glitter finish because the metallic paint has small metallic flakes in it. For this to work, you need a good quality metallic paint and to make sure it's compatible with the clear. Using two products of the same type from the same company is almost a guarantee of this. Add a tiny drop of the metallic, test and add more if needed.

Basecoat colour

I've noticed that some companies recommend different-coloured basecoats for different metallic finishes.

CANDY FINISH

Candy finish is used to describe a transparent bright colour sprayed over a metallic finish. The reflective qualities of the metallic pigment remain, but now have a tint to them. I've used Nitorlack's transparent tint colours in a can to spray over the Silver Sparkle finish. It's the same red and yellow I used on the burst finish earlier. These are nitrocellulose, so I needed to spray the sparkle first (with a clear top as the last pass), let it dry, then add the colour. Next step is to apply the nitrocellulose topcoats.

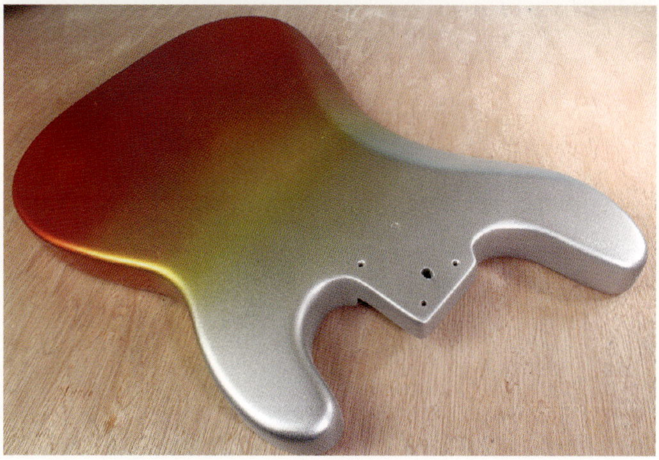

INSPIRATION: UNCLE DEATH GUITARS

I loved this finish as soon as I saw it, and that's before Nick Adams of Uncle Death Guitars told me he calls it the Evil Moss. Nick is an experienced professional automotive spray finisher and brings those techniques to his work as a luthier. He told me:

Techniques taken from custom automotive finish work have changed the way we think about building musical instruments in a custom shop setting. For the Evil Moss finish first, the substrate is prepped and sealed, and a textured two-tone metallic basecoat is created. Then, a transparent green-tinted clear coat is carefully applied, before finally building a generous topcoat of high-solids polyurethane. These types of finish work are costly to perform as well as daunting to accomplish, as there is no margin for error. Repairing a candy finish is next to impossible.

METALLIC PAINT PROBLEMS

If you don't shake/mix your paint well enough, you may end up with sections where the paint and metallic flakes separate. This can also happen when paint is sprayed too thickly, so that it drips or pools. It's far better to shake for longer and apply thin coats. If you're not happy with the coverage after two thin coats, add a third, then a clear. Occasionally, four coats in one session of spraying is acceptable.

Flip paints

Flip, chameleon, colour-shift and colour-change are all terms to describe the same paint finish – one that appears to change colour depending on the angle at which you are looking at it, or how the light hits it. The effect is achieved by having metallic flake with a special coating dispersed in the clear paint medium. The coating refracts light differently depending on the viewing angle. The flake is often aluminium and the coating magnesium fluoride; combined, they act like a prism. For these paints the base colour can noticeably affect the colours you see in the finished surface, so follow the supplier's guidelines.

I have used a few makes of this type of paint over the years. Most have recommended a black basecoat and just two layers of the flip finish. As with the metallic paint, you must not sand the final finish, so applying the two coats of flip followed by a clear in the same session is essential. With every make I have used, the paint has settled in a very thin coat and, due to the way the effect works, any blemish, dent or ding in the basecoat becomes visible in the final finish. A slight dent will effectively look a different colour, as it will be refracting the light at a slight angle to the rest of the body. It is essential that you achieve a perfect finish with the filler, primer and basecoat before using the flip.

This is my personal guitar. It was my first electric one and I have experimented with finishes on it several times. Here you can see that I have applied the flip paint over the resin-embedded shattered glass. The paint has less effect here as there is no black basecoat.

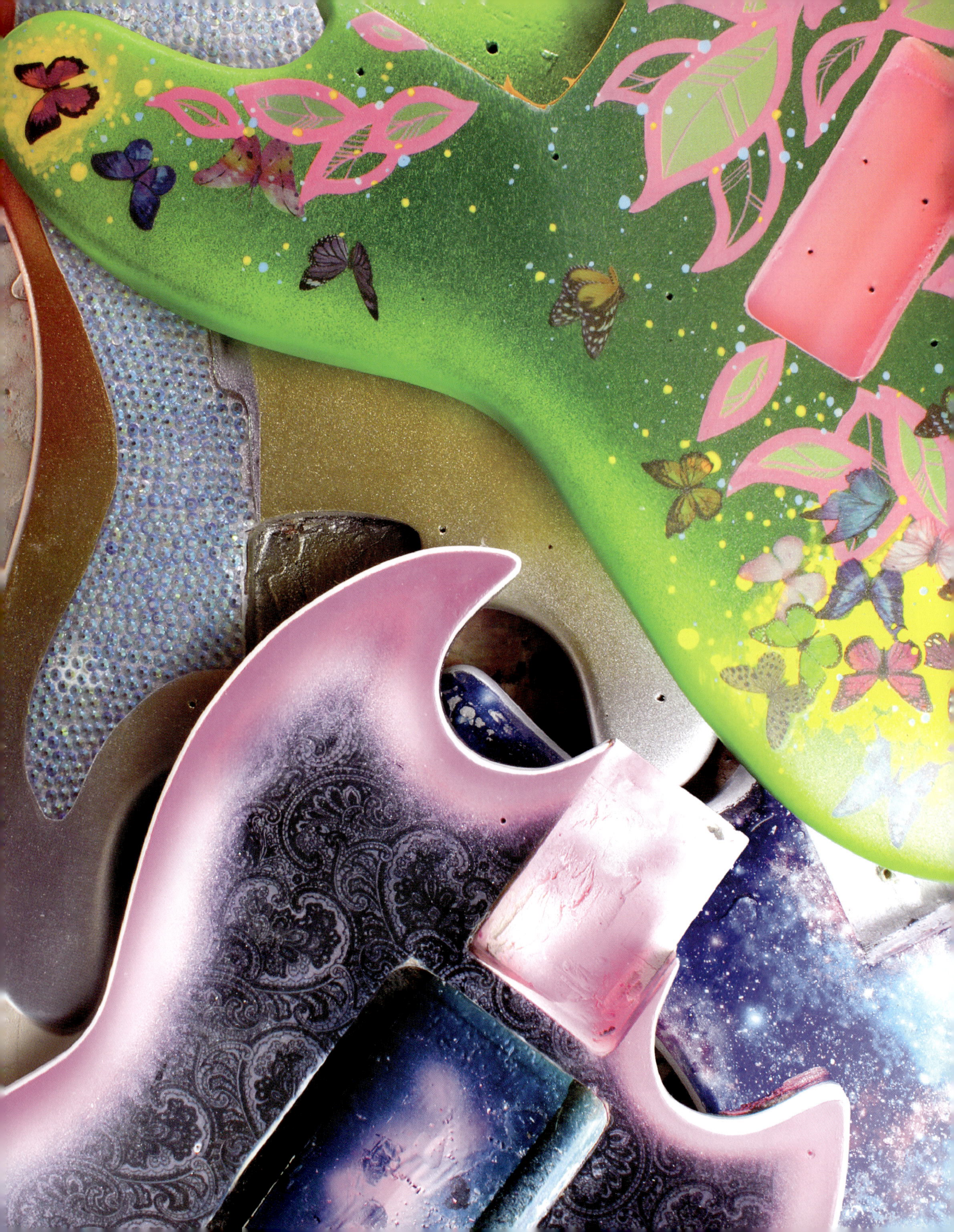

CHAPTER 5

OTHER CUSTOMISATION TECHNIQUES

The first technique we will look at here is resin. I started using resin when I was at university in the late 1990s. At that time, I could only get it from a supplier for sculptors and ceramicists in London called Tiranti. I still get it from them sometimes because it's great quality. However, the range of suppliers has dramatically increased, as the popularity of resin pouring has surged. We used to call it resin at university, but I notice many people calling it epoxy. Either way, they are the same thing.

EPOXY RESIN TECHNIQUES

Epoxy resins cure by mixing two parts together. The resin sold by Tiranti involves measuring a tiny amount of catalyst by weight and adding it to the main mix. I find this to be a bit of a nuisance, which is why I don't always use their epoxy. I prefer the two-part epoxy resin that is mixed at a 1:1 ratio. There's less chance of the mix being incorrect, which will affect the curing time and possibly result in a soft or flexible finish. For guitars, you want a hard finish.

Most resins are toxic, but some claim to contain no VOCs (Volatile Organic Compounds). I haven't noticed a difference in quality with these, but I always wear a mask and pour in a ventilated space.

Resins come with different cure times. I would normally recommend a slow cure for deeper and thicker pours, as this will resist cracking on the surface. Many companies sell specialist resins for deep pours, which I would advise for any of the examples I show that are the thickness of a guitar body. For fabric tops and embedding mirror pieces and so on this isn't necessary; some companies make resin specifically for pours of up to 10mm thick, which is ideal.

You can add colour to resin, swirl it, add glitter and even metal flakes. I used to incorporate powdered metal in my artwork using a process often referred to as cold casting. While I've experimented with mixing various types of paint and ink in resin, I recommend sticking to products specifically made for resins. Whenever possible, buy from the same manufacturer or supplier as the resin, as they will have tested compatibility. I still have some test resin elements I made two years ago for my Protoncaster guitars (they look like the *Ghostbusters* Proton Packs) that have remained flexible because the paint and resin were not compatible. These parts are no good for a guitar, but they still look cool on my shelf!

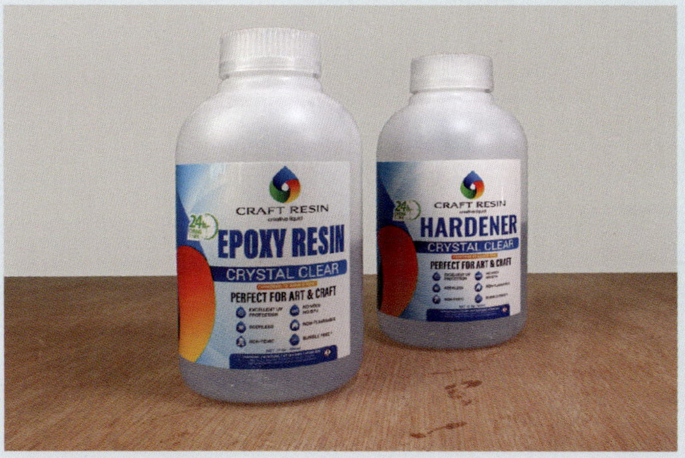

Two-part epoxy resins.

Finishing for the resin can be done in different ways. You can simply sand and buff the resin, or cover it in a topcoat and buff that as normal. I used to wet-sand, but now use the Abranet and Assilex method, working through grits up to 2000, essentially the same method as I covered in the section on finishing topcoats. Then apply your polish or wax in the same way as normal. You can get polishes designed especially for epoxy resins, but I find the guitar polishes like Axe Wax are just as good. An alternative is to go in using a hard wax oil after sanding to 600 grit, building up layers to get the desired finish, as you would with any wax finish.

A RANGE OF OPTIONS

I recommend that you read all the sections using resin, even if you are only interested in one of the techniques. Each section has a slightly different approach that will inform the choices you make for your customisation.

Fabric-top finish

Using a fabric as a finish offers a massive range of designs. The process I'm going to show you here involves a thin layer of clear epoxy resin, no more than 5mm. This clear surface really adds depth to the finish and helps it pop. The first stage is to prepare the body for having binding added, but don't put the binding on yet. There's a section on applying binding earlier in the book, so I won't repeat it here. Some of the photos in that demo use the fabric-top guitar.

If the positioning of the pattern is essential, you could first cut the material roughly to shape, which will help to line it up. You could also mark a central line on the guitar body in pencil; this will show through the glue. Start by placing your folded material with its centre line abutting the marked line and unfold from there.

APPLYING THE FABRIC TO THE BODY

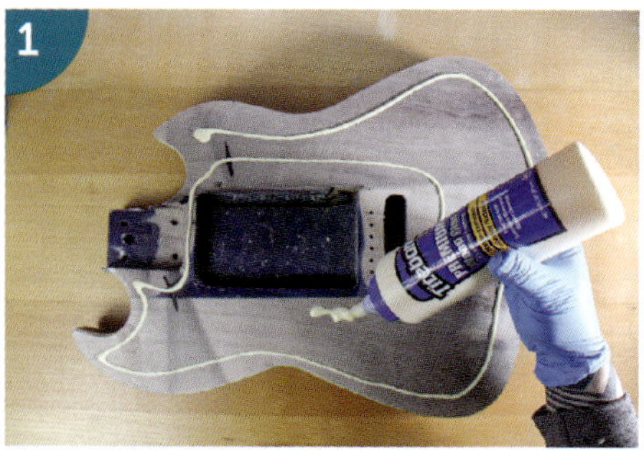

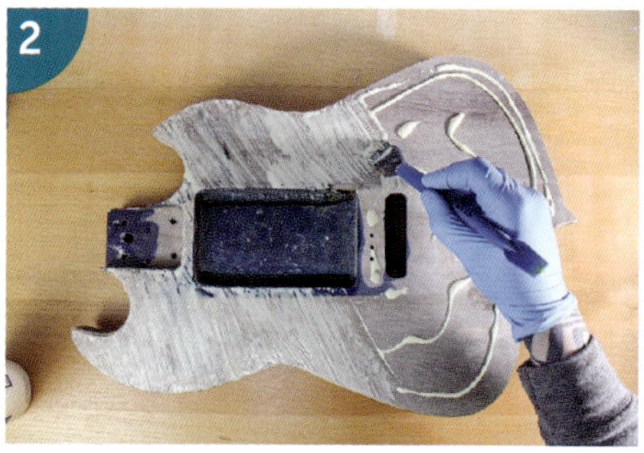

Cover the surface of the guitar in PVA or wood glue. The glue shouldn't be too runny, otherwise it will soak through the material.

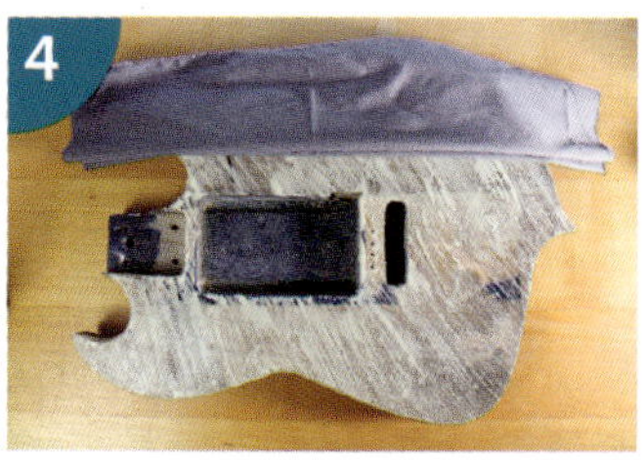

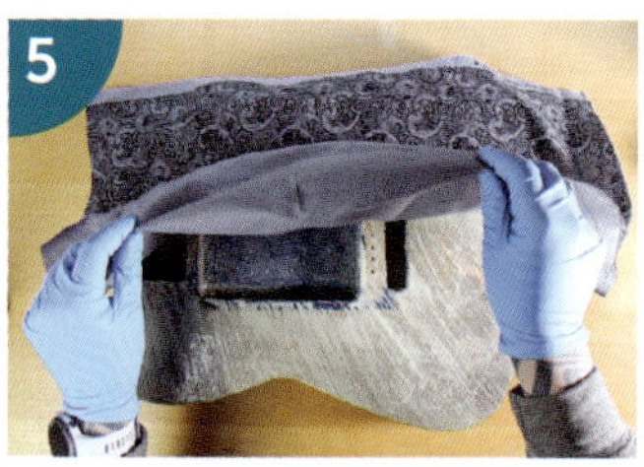

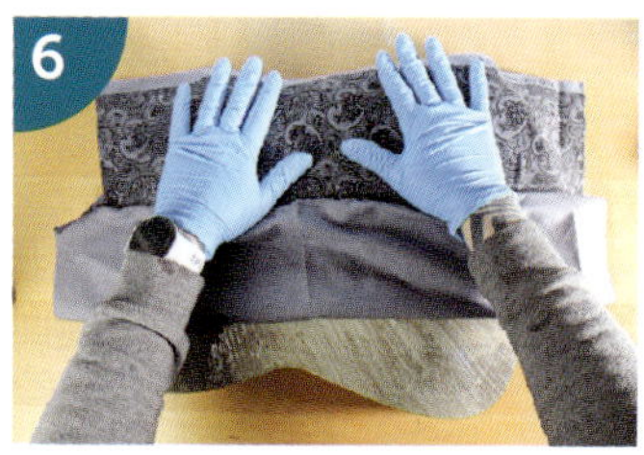

Place the folded material on the guitar. Start at one edge, unfold it and press down. I prefer this method to just draping the material over the body.

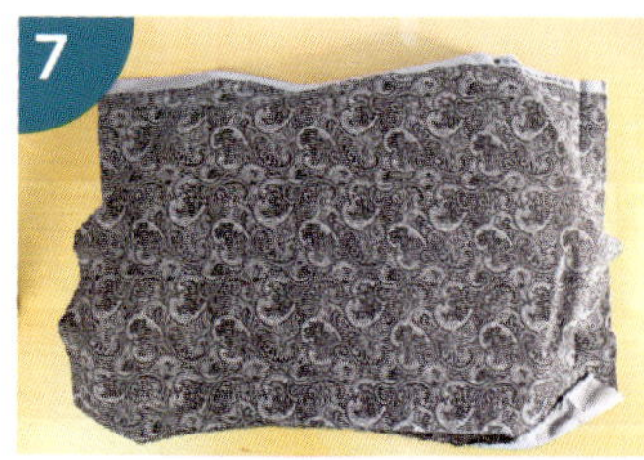

Check that there are no lumps or creases and that the pattern hasn't distorted anywhere through stretching. Leave the material in place and allow the glue to dry.

PREPARING FOR THE ACRYLIC POUR

One the fabric is dry, go along any edge with cyanoacrylate glue.

I'm using O3A thin, as this will soak through better than a thick one. Don't use kicker; let the glue dry naturally.

Once the cyanoacrylate glue is hard, you will find it easy to cut the material along the edges using a scalpel. The edge of the guitar can act as a guide, but be careful not to cut into the wood.

Make a temporary wall in the cavities and neck pocket where there is no binding. I use duct tape, folded so that there is a solid top part, then stuck in place. I then go over it with extra tape to cover any potential leakage area.

The body is now ready to have the binding added. The binding must stick up above the surface an amount equal to the thickness of epoxy you are adding (3–5mm). This creates a wall to hold the resin when you pour it. In the example, the wall is much higher than needed so that I can show you the potential problems.

POURING THE RESIN

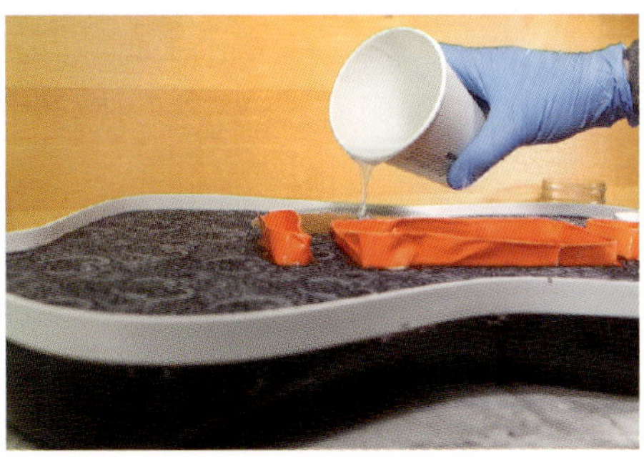

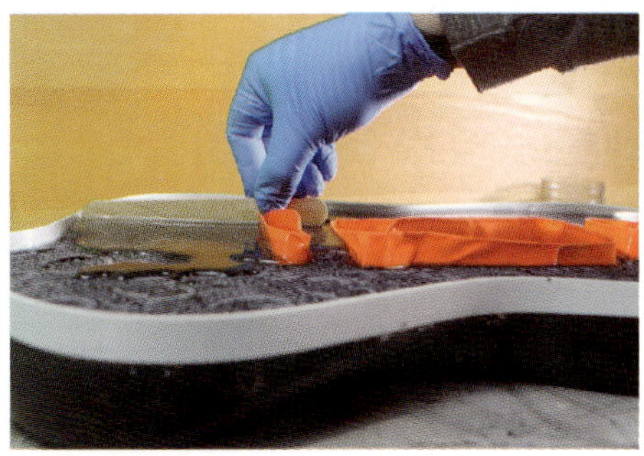

Ensure that the body is level in all directions, then pour the resin in one spot to start, letting it naturally spread. After a minute, help the resin to move around, then pour from another spot. Work in small amounts so that the resin doesn't flow over the top of the binding.

FINAL TOUCHES

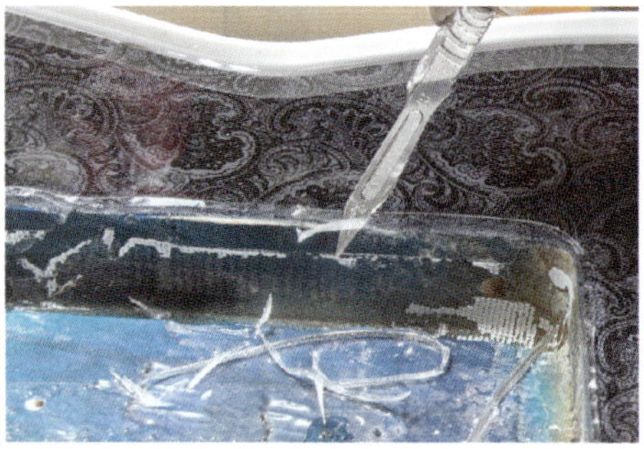

This resin takes about 48 hours to cure fully. I find that after around 24 hours, it is solid enough for me to remove the tape and cut the raised edges with a scalpel. Leaving it longer makes the resin too hard to make these cuts.

My binding was too high. It's going to take a long time to sand it down, so using a flush-cut saw is ideal. However, the motion of the saw can cause the binding to pop away from the resin if you are too aggressive, so go slowly.

At this stage of sanding, I'm using my random orbital sander and 240-grade Abranet. The Abranet is ideal for resin, but keep vacuuming the sanding pad to remove clogs. Here you can see that the edges of the resin were slightly raised due to the natural way it settles when curing. You must work all over until the sanded area is completely level before moving to the next grade.

TROUBLESHOOTING

Work slowly with the resin, pouring small amounts at a time. This will allow you to spot any leakages and patch them, as I have in the left photo in the pickup cavity. Simply adding more tape to cover the small spill and seal the edges should be enough.

Use a hot-air gun or hairdryer on a light blow setting to pass over the surface and remove any bubbles that form. Do this a few minutes after pouring.

RAISING THE NECK

Using this method has increased the guitar body's thickness. The neck will therefore have to be raised an equal amount to compensate. In this example, I have used spare binding to do that. A piece of wood cut to fit is the normal method. Pouring extra resin into the neck pocket (if you block in the holes and put a wall up first!) will work too. It also means that you can use this approach on a guitar with a bolt-on neck only. A set or through neck won't allow you to compensate its height; instead, the bridge will have to be recessed, leading to a whole series of more complicated adjustments to consider.

Polishing resin

Resin can be polished just like any finish from a can or gun, by continuing the sanding with finer grades, then using polishing compounds and wax. Another option is to stop at 800 grit and apply a wax, such as a hard-oil wax. Use it the same way you would on a wood finish.

INSPIRATION: MILEHOUSE STUDIOS

I'm often asked to feature certain guitar builders on The Guitar Builders Collective Chat podcast. In mid-2024, I received many requests to invite Paul from Milehouse Studios, who had just started his YouTube channel. It quickly became a favourite of mine for its inspiration, new techniques and truly unique entertainment value. Like many of the builders featured in this book, there's a lot you can be inspired about from Paul's builds, but I want to focus on one aspect – his method for fabric tops.

In the method I've explained above, the fabric is put directly on to the guitar. Paul, however, makes his tops separately on boards of plywood, referring to them as epoxy panels. The material is glued down to the plywood, sides are added to hold the epoxy in place, then the resin is poured in to create a thin layer. One cured, these panels are then cut to rough shape and applied to the body in much the same way as the drop tops I covered in the lamination section. This means that you would first have to reduce the thickness of the body unless you are happy with a really thick guitar. Since Paul is making his guitars from scratch, this is less of an issue for him.

There are many advantages to using Paul's method. The rectangular fabric boards he makes are much easier to pour on to than the shaped binding we have already covered. You can achieve really neat edges once the top is on the body using a trim router to match the top to the body contours. The binding is also much easier to apply, as the traditional method already covered in this book can be used.

Should you decide to check out Paul's YouTube channel, just a note that it may contain some extreme content!

A selection of some of the many guitars Paul has created with this method.

Here you can see the thickness of the top that Paul has added and at the same time how the guitar itself isn't affected because the body is already thinner.

CLASSIC GUITAR FINISH: THE PAUL STANLEY FROM KISS RHINESTONE GUITAR

The band with the most recognisable and biggest variety of custom guitars has got to be Kiss. I'm not going to cover how to build a rocket launcher or smoke system into your guitar like Ace Frehley used, but Paul Stanley's rhinestone-covered guitars are an excellent customisation technique. The original version was a star-shaped guitar built by Steve Carr in the 1970s; the top is covered in rhinestones except for the black edge that contains them, a bit like a thick binding strip. Steve Carr also customised Paul Stanley's Ibanez Iceman model in much the same way, Ibanez went on to make signature models in this style. I've got a slight twist on it for you here.

1

A plunge router and template guide are used to create the cavity for the gems.

I've made a custom template to allow me to rout a shallow cavity in part of the body of this bass. I opted not to rout the whole body. The idea is to have a cavity just deep enough to hold the rhinestones with a thin layer of resin over the top. This is how Paul Stanley's original Star Guitar seems to have been made. Routing like this means you aren't increasing the body's thickness at all and the neck won't need to be compensated. On the Ibanez Icemans, the approach is the same as with the fabric top; a binding strip is added along the edge that protrudes above the surface to make a wall to pour the resin into. This is the best approach if you want to cover the whole body.

2

The gems are added using a CA glue.

I'm adding small diamanté crystals to this body, but before placing them the cavity must be painted. I've used Nitorlack's Silver Sparkle polyurethane. The whole body has been sprayed with two coats of the Silver Sparkle and one clear in the same sitting, then lightly sanded ready. The paint on the body will end up being sanded back after the resin is poured.

Working from one corner, it's best to put a small area of crystals in at a time, then add a touch of glue to hold them in place. As you progress, work in lines for the bigger areas. I find that three lines of crystals, followed by some thin cyanoacrylate glue between them, works well. I avoided using a kicker spray in case it pushed the crystals out of place, but with larger crystals you may find this works well. Using CA glue in this quantity means fumes, so wear a mask and goggles.

Using so much glue can leave a whitish residue on the crystals as it evaporates when drying. You can avoid this by using as little glue as possible and breaking between sections to allow for it to dry fully. When the glue is fully dry and all the crystals are in place, you can clean the surface. I like the meths-vinegar cleaning mix I have previously mentioned, as it evaporates quickly. If usinge water, make sure that it has fully dried before adding the resin. The resin does hide the white if there are still a few marks.

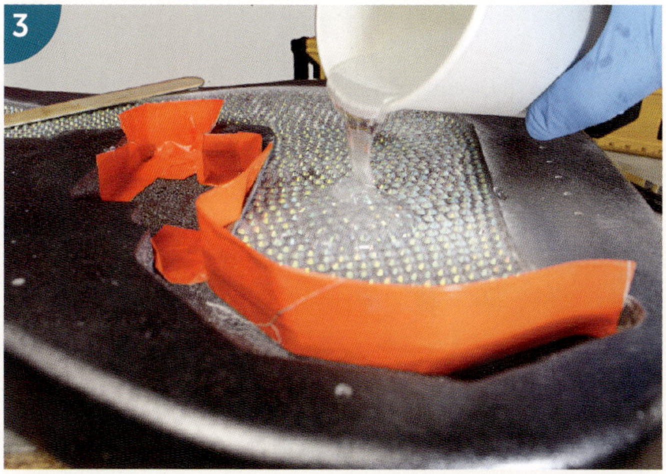

Ensure the guitar is flat, and edges walled up as with the fabric top technique before pouring.

Sand the cured resin flat to the body, working in fine grades of paper up to 600 grit.

You don't actually have to add the resin. Paul Stanley's models don't. Leaving the crystals just glued in will increase the effect of light refraction, but at the same time they are more fragile and likely to fall off. One option is to pour the resin in so that it forms a layer half the height of the crystals. Once it's poured, use a heat gun or hairdryer to lightly tease any resin stuck on top of the crystals down into the gaps.

I've filled the whole cavity because I want a smooth finish. It's best to pour the resin so that it forms a slightly raised surface above the cavity, held there by the surface tension of the resin. If some spills over on to the body it isn't an issue, as, when the resin is fully cured, you need to sand everything smooth to 600 grit. Just as with the fabric top, a random orbital sander with Abranet is great for this.

To mask off the resin before spraying, I recommend applying the tape in small sections, as this way you can find the shape you need. When cutting the tape, you want a slight edge of the resin showing for the paint to cover; this ensures no gaps between the paint and the resin. You could also mask off with a sheet of transparent stencil vinyl so that you can see what you are doing.

In this case, the best approach is to spray colour, remove the mask and topcoat over everything. This will ensure a smooth finish all over. Two sessions of topcoat are the minimum. If you sand through the topcoat into the resin when finishing it will be really obvious, so the topcoat has to be thick enough to accommodate sanding.

Mask the resin area with tape.

You can cover more are than needed.

Use a scalpel to cut the mask to the desired shape.

After spraying the body, remove the mask ready to apply the topcoat.

FILLING HOLES IN THE RESIN SURFACE

Sanding back the resin surface can sometimes reveal micro-bubbles. These can be filled with more resin or cyanoacrylate glue.

The hole caused by revealing the bubble has become dirty during the sanding process.

By using a small drill bit by hand, slightly widen the hole to reveal a clean surface.

Use a thin CA glue and dab a small drop into the hole. Don't use kicker on it.

Once dry, scrape the CA glue back with a razor blade.

Finish off by sanding to the same grit as the rest of the resin surface.

CLASSIC GUITAR FINISH: THE PAUL STANLEY FROM KISS CRACKED-MIRROR FINISH

Kiss are back! They're a bit hard to avoid really. YouTuber Henning Pauly once interviewed me discussing my End of the Road extreme relic guitars and Craftcaster sci-fi inspired guitars. He mentioned that while most people can't name many Kiss songs, they instantly recognise the band's look. Kiss's act is as much about stage presence as it is about music. Henning hadn't even seen my take on the cracked-mirror guitar, but could tell that the appearance of my guitars is the main selling point. Keeping the importance of stage performance in mind when customising a guitar emphasises focus on the instrument.

Paul Stanley's original cracked-mirror guitar was one he asked Ibanez to customise for him ahead of the band's Dynasty tour. He wanted his guitar to fit more with the disco theme. Ibanez stuck the broken mirror on to a PS-10 Iceman, making it heavy and dangerous to play. Apparently, Paul Stanley had sleepless nights due to a sore shoulder and cuts over his hand. That's why I prefer embedding it in resin.

My take on Paul's guitar are the Shattercasters. Here you can see a few of the different versions I have made over the years. I've made a lot and used a variety of techniques. All have been embedded in resin for a smooth finish, with no chance of cutting yourself whilst playing.

This Shattercaster had a shallow rout. I then laid broken mirror in it using black tiling grout.

A slightly deeper rout allowed me to layer the broken mirror – the bottom pieces in grout, the piece on top glued on.

With a much deeper rout I could lay pieces in at an angle, overlapping and seemingly more random. This is my preferred method.

This scratchplate is a mirror-finished acrylic, where I have scraped off the mirror on the back with a Dremel and filled it with black paint.

INSPIRATION: NELSON FARO DECASTRO'S SMASHED-MIRROR ICEMEN

I found Nelson Faro DeCastro's builds in a Facebook Ibanez Iceman group and was really impressed with his modern take on the Paul Stanley classic. Nelson uses coloured acrylic to make a fake smashed-mirror effect that not only brings a new element of colour to the body, but also won't add so much weight or be as dangerous.

After routing the body ready for the inlay Nelson makes a template on tracing paper that he can attach to the acrylic as a guide.

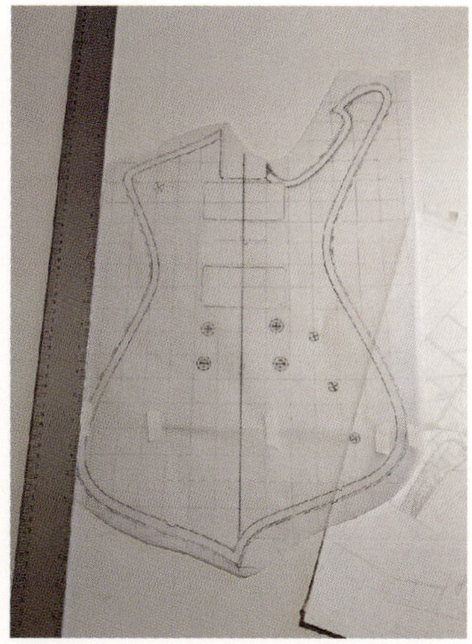

Note how Nelson has painted the routed area as you can see it between the cracks.

After cutting the main body shape in the acrylic he carefully cuts each shard and places it on the body.

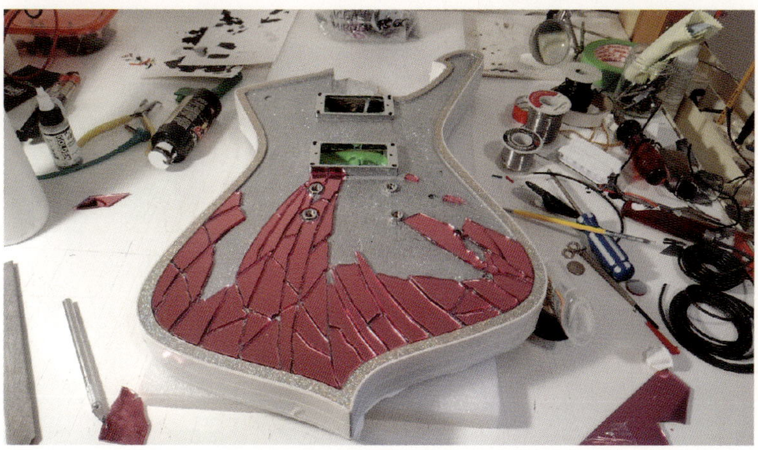

Embedding objects in resin

Embedding objects in resin is essentially the same method as with the rhinestones, crystals and mirror shards. Rout a hole the right size, paint the inside, put in the objects, then fill with resin. Sometimes, though, I have made the holes big enough to pass through the entire body of the guitar and I have some tips for you on that process.

The hole has been cut right through the body. I positioned it to miss the back cavity, but it will need to be routed on the front once I've filled it, as the Floyd Rose bridge being used is recessed.

Here, a sheet of 2mm acrylic is used to the cover the hole. It's been recessed to sit flat, then glued in place. The edges will be filled with body filler. A circle the size of the hole has been masked off.

You may recognise this body; it's the one from my example with Hammerite earlier in the book. With the paint on, the edges of the acrylic are completely hidden.

The front view shows the recess in the body for the bridge. I will have to wall off this area before pouring. Note that the inside of the hole has been painted. With the acrylic sheet as the base, I can now fill it with resin.

This is a deeper resin pour than for the fabric top, gems and mirror shards. You can buy resin made for deeper pours, or pour it in layers. If the pour is too deep in one pass, the heat produced when curing can cause cracks or warping.

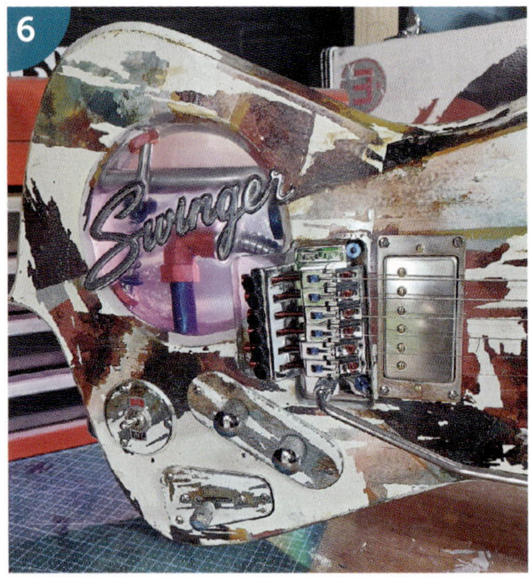

The objects in the resin where all screwed or glued in place before the resin was poured. This ensured they didn't slip around. I also avoided the area that I had to rout for the bridge.

CASE STUDY: EMBEDDING INSECTS

The photos show the two Entomology guitars I have made, entomology being the branch of zoology focused on the study of insects. I can't remember where the inspiration for the first one came from; possibly a trip to the Horniman Museum in South London, which houses a collection of taxidermy, musical instruments and torture devices, or possibly just a random search on eBay for things to embed in guitars. Inspiration can come from anywhere. The second one was made for musician Doctor Gothic, as it matched his musical style. I'm hoping my process for creating these guitars will give you some inspiration for a build, even if using different materials and objects.

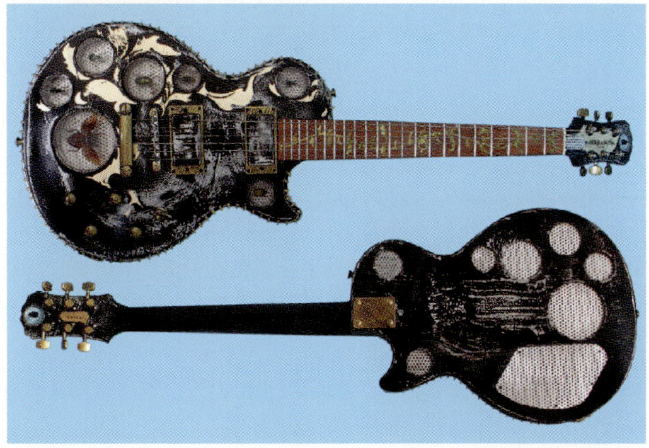

Once I'd drilled the holes through the body and painted the inside edges, I attached thin plastic to the back, sealing the edge of the circles with black cyanoacrylate glue and the outer edges with electrical tape.

I wanted this metal to be behind the plastic, otherwise I could have left this stage out. The metal is glued down with two-part epoxy glue around the edges, but no glue on the plastic circles.

A 3mm plywood back is added to sandwich everything to the main body, then filler applied to the edges. I cut this at the same time as drilling the holes through the body so that it all lines up.

It's important to mask off the resin areas when painting. It would be hard to remove any paint that went through the metal holes on to the plastic sheet.

Before placing the insects, I poured a thin layer of resin. This extra height helps the insects to look like they are floating. They are then held in place with a small hidden blob of thick CA glue.

The resin is recessed from the top of the guitar, so I painted the guitar first. If the resin were to have been level, I would need to sand it, so in that case painting the guitar afterwards is best.

INSPIRATION: INDRA GUITARS

Sometimes I come across a process new to me that's so amazing it makes me want to learn a whole new process, technique and skill set. Indra Guitars did just that. These guitars are unique in themselves, but each has custom acid-etched metal or mechanical or laser-engraved hardware on them. They are designed and made by artist Rich Legg, who is a great example of an artist using the guitar as a canvas. I've seen his work on other boutique brands who have commissioned him to produce elements for their guitars.

The intricate designs on the hardware take this bass to a whole new level.

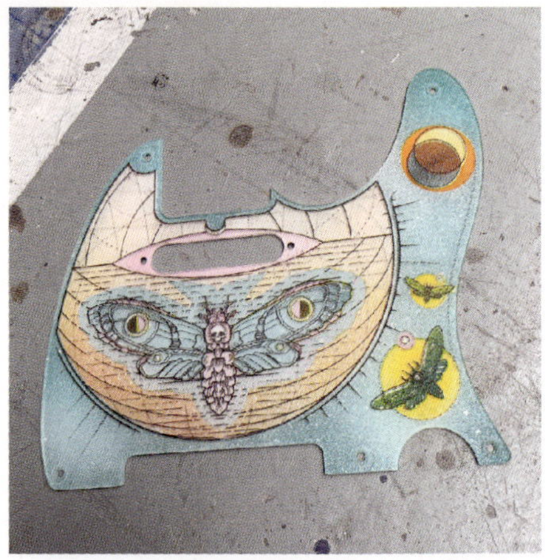

A selection of Rich's work including scratchplates, knobs and neck plates. The acrylic parts are engraved on the front and painted on the back using matching stencils.

Image transfer using waterslide decals

Waterslides are transfers applied by first wetting them so that the back layer slides off, leaving a thin layer with the image on that will stick to a surface as it dries. It's the sort of transfer that came with the Airfix models I used to make as a child, or for the Space Marine symbols I used to put on my Warhammer models as a teenager. When I use them now, I feel like I am in my youth still playing with my toys and am very thankful that I have such a cool job. I use waterslide decals regularly in several ways. I'll demonstrate the technique here with a few examples, but look out for the process in later sections covering fret markers and headstock decals. If applying decals over a painted surface, lightly sand the surface with 600 grit so that it is ready for the clear coat once the decal is dry.

A selection of waterslides I have printed and keep in a drawer just in case.

You can buy the paper and print from your computer. The paper comes in clear or white, for laser or inkjet. You can also have prints professionally made. These will be easier to work with, the image less likely to degrade, crack, or come off in the application process.

Using these materials helps to improve the process of applying the decals, but they aren't essential. The decal softener, decal fix and gloss varnish are made by Vallejo.

I have printed this pattern on to clear waterslide decal and prepared the surface of the headstock with a thin coat of decal fix, which adds to the adhesion. If the wood were bare and porous, I would first have used the gloss to seal it.

Submerge the whole sheet in water. Larger sheets are much harder to work with; as a beginner I would recommend small areas first. The sheet is ready when it starts to lift from the backing at the edges. Gently tease it whilst in the water until the whole backing moves smoothly.

Carefully place the sheet with the backing in place. Holding one end of the transfer, slide the backing out from underneath. Move slowly and adjust the whole decal if it wrinkles or moves. Avoid touching the print, as it can come off when it's wet.

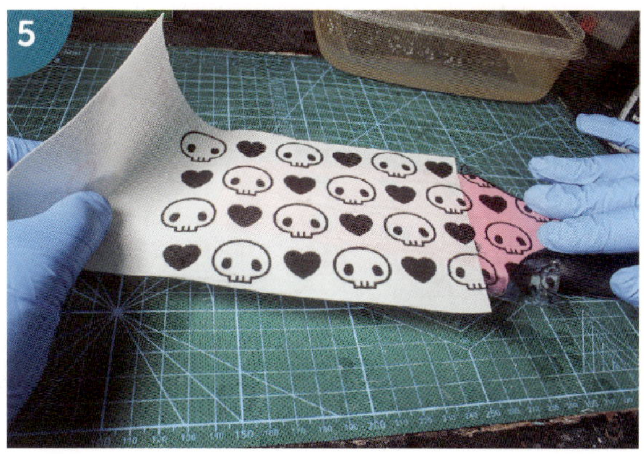

Use a dry brush to gently smooth out any wrinkles or bubbles. Don't press too hard or work for too long on the surface, as some print can be removed.

Once the water has started to dry or been brushed away, apply the decal softener with a brush in wrinkled areas. This helps to smooth the surface even further. You can go over the surface with care.

Once dry, the headstock is ready for a clear coat. Once the clear is dry, I lightly sand and use Posca pens to neaten the cracks and gaps before the final topcoats.

PROCEED WITH CARE

If the paper is left in the water too long, the print can start to disintegrate off the transfer. If it's not left long enough, it can crack when trying to slide off the backing. It really is practice getting used to doing this. I always have multiple prints at the ready. Divide large areas up into small pieces where possible. Let each area dry before applying the next. Don't touch the surface too much once it is dry, or the print will lift – you will need to spray a clear coat to protect it first.

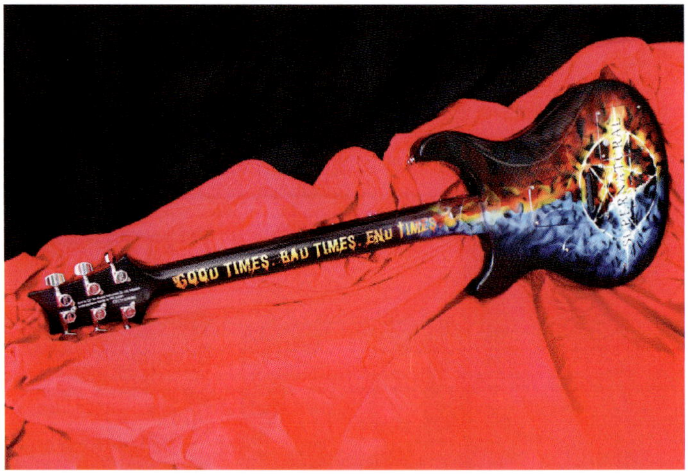

This Supenatural TV show inspired guitar uses a reverse waterslide technique for the words on the neck.

Daniel's reverse waterslide technique

I customised three guitars for my client Stefan, each inspired by a different TV show or band he likes. The one in the photo is based on the TV show *Supernatural*. The design is airbrushed using a vinyl stencil. The writing on the back of the neck is done using a method I developed and make use of a lot; you'll often see it on my headstocks and fretboards. I use a waterslide decal to print the outline and background of the words or design. The background is black and the shape is clear, allowing the colour underneath to show through vividly. For this guitar, I sprayed the neck yellow first, then added an orange fade with an airbrush. The black was added using the following process shown in the photos.

The decal is applied as normal.

I use a range of Posca pens in black.

I've roughly coloured in the neck, avoiding the decal as much as possible.

Once a clear coat has been added, I lightly sand with 600 grade.

Now the black can be neatened up.

The finished neck after topcoats have been applied.

Hydro dipping

Don't trust the internet! When you look up hydro dipping, you'll likely find swirls and marbling techniques using water baths, such as I covered earlier. Hydro dipping, or water-transfer printing, involves dipping an object (like a guitar body) into water with a print floating on it. A specialist hydrographic PVA film is used, which floats on the water's surface. It's treated with a spray that dissolves the film, leaving the ink behind, ready for the dip. You need a water bath deep enough for the guitar to go in (face down at a slight angle), and big enough for a little space on all sides of the body. You will also need an activator spray to help dissolve the film.

A customisation I did for my old bandmate Mike on his Les Paul Special. The paisley is a hydro-dip film, the colour a Montana Gold.

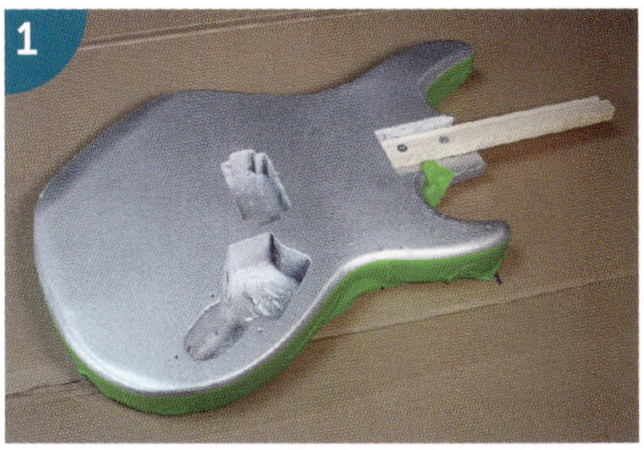

The company that made the hydrographic film I'm using, Hydro Style UK, suggested a silver base. I've used the Nitorlack Silver Sparkle; it's had a light sand. I've also taped the edge where I want the print to finish.

Cut the film to fit. It's essential to have space on each side.

I've added tape to each side to help it hold shape when dissolving.

Lick your thumb and forefinger and grip the edge of the film. One side will stick, which is the side that goes face down in the water.

Watch for these wrinkles to flatten out as the film absorbs the water.

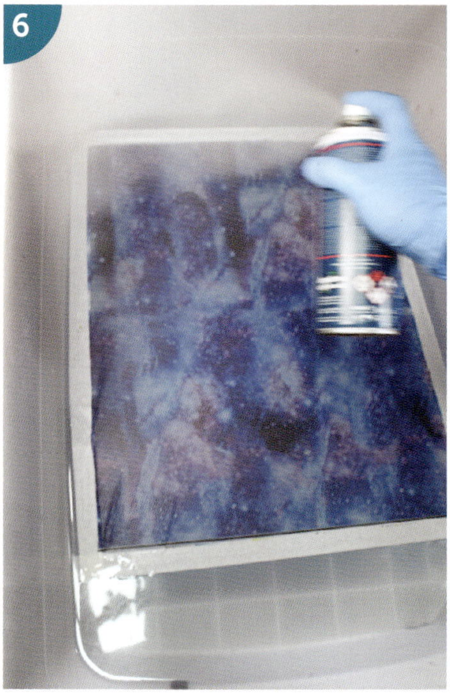

Spray the activator evenly over the surface of the film. Let it settle. If the film looks grainy or dry, it needs more activator. If it goes very glassy, you may have applied too much.

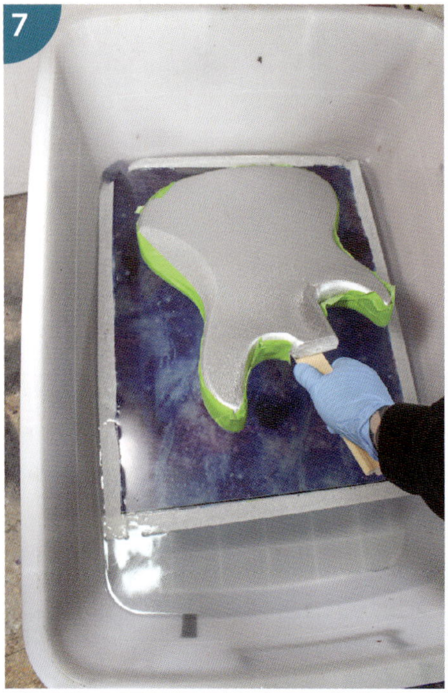

Leave the activator ten seconds for it to seep through the film. Then dip the guitar in and through the film.

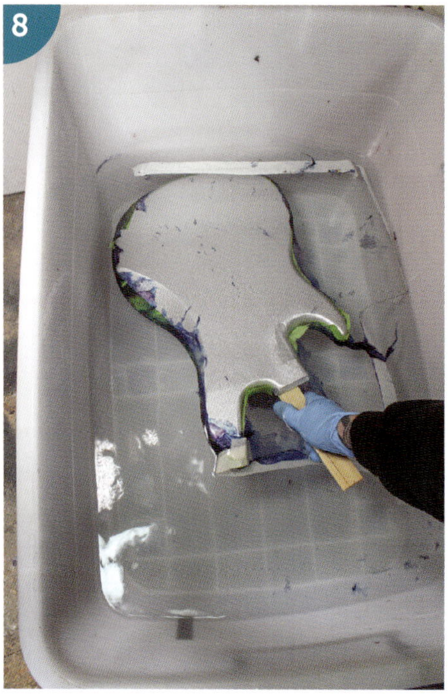

You may need to wipe excess print away from the water before pulling the guitar back out.

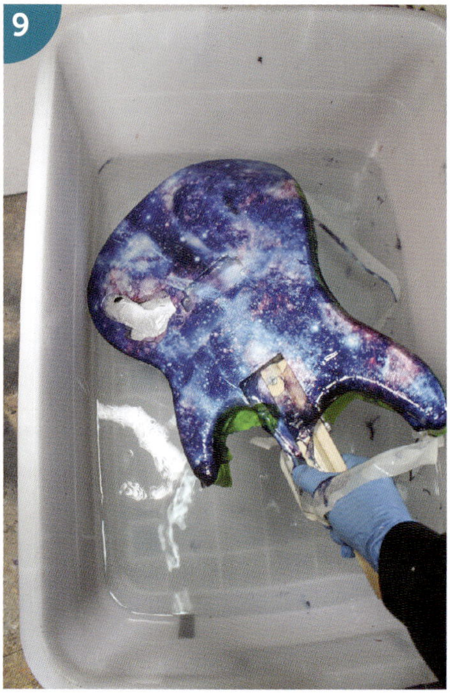

You will need to rinse off the remaining film. It's easier to do that now, although you can wash the body later.

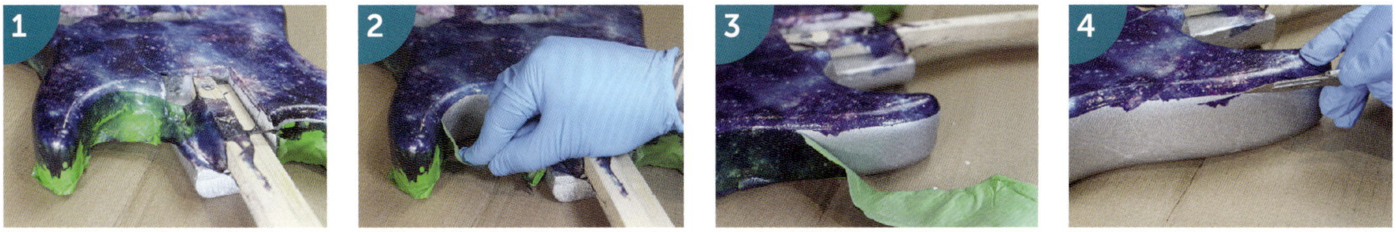

Using tape around the edge can help to ensure that the image has a neat end to it. I prefer to cut the overhanging parts with a knife once the tape is off. These parts of the image haven't stuck to the body, so normally come away easily. The guitar is now ready for topcoats – just don't sand the image.

The surface is now ready for topcoats. Don't sand it first. Start by using a water-based sealer such as Chestnut Products' acrylic sanding sealer, or test your preferred sealer on a practice piece to ensure that it doesn't affect the print.

ALWAYS TEST FIRST

This is a process that takes some practice, as the temperature of the water, the thickness of the film and various other things can affect the timing of each stage. Most suppliers of hydrographic film also sell small test models, which are vacuum-formed plastic a bit like a toy car shape. I use a scrap of plywood painted with the same base as the guitar. Always buy a longer roll of film than you think you need so that you can run some tests. One can of activator spray is more than enough for the guitar and tests. Good suppliers will provide guidelines of timing for each stage for their specific products, which will inform your first test.

CASE STUDY: THE NEGAN GUITAR

Here's another guitar I customised for my client, Stefan. It's the first one I worked on for him, with the *Supernatural* guitar being the most recent. This guitar features a mix of techniques that appear in the book.

For the front, the first stage was to use a hydrographic film of blood spatter. The image of Negan from *The Walking Dead* is a waterslide decal on white transfer paper. This means that the image isn't translucent and the colours come out more strongly. I did the head and the top of the bat as separate transfers. When using a white transfer paper, you need to cut close to the edge of the image to hide any white. I touched up the edges with black and red paint once the first layer of clear coat had been applied. The barbed wire is drawn on with paint pens, with details applied by brush.

The image on the back is also a waterslide decal, faded out with an airbrush. The only difference is that these paint spatters were added on with paint.

For the writing on the neck, I used a print-on white-backed waterslide. This allowed me to achieve the desired texture on the letters through a colour print. After applying a clear coat, I concealed the edges of the waterslide with black paint. The barbed wire was hand-painted before adding the topcoats.

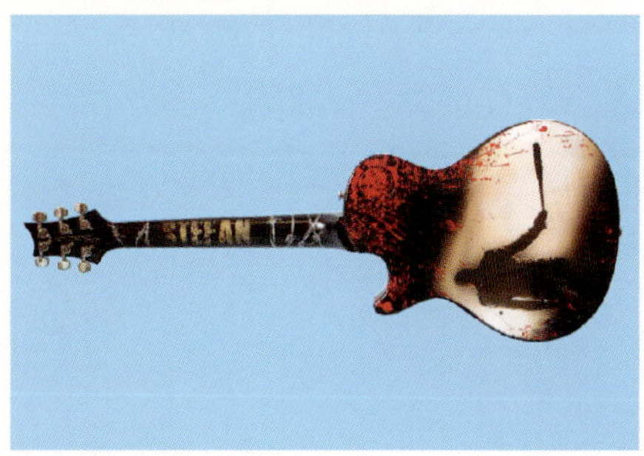

Vinyl Wrap

Vinyl wrap has been used on car dashboards for years. It was one of the first materials I experimented with when I started customising guitars. Now, companies like The Guitar Fabrik make it especially for guitars in a range of designs and they are very simple to apply with a heat gun or hairdryer. Wear protective gloves.

Run tape along the edge of the guitar. This marks where the vinyl will be cut. I used two layers of electrical tape.

Remove a section of the back of the vinyl and stick it to part of the guitar.

Pull the rest of the back away whilst pressing the vinyl down with a hard straight edge to remove bubbles.

Work around with a heat gun or hairdryer so that the vinyl wraps the edges and any imperfections can be removed.

Mark the edge where you want to cut. Ideally, cut into the tape underneath. Using more tape ensures a straight line to follow.

Cut around the edge following the guide.

Remove the tape from underneath and the guide tape, then apply more heat to smooth the surface flat.

The cavities can be cut out and the edges of the cuts pressed down whilst being heated. Then remove the clear protective film.

If you buy two of the same wrap, you can make a matching pickguard with the same technique.

INSPIRATION: MARK GUTIERREZ

Mark Gutierrez is a guitarist, producer, musician and dedicated tinkerer with a passion for creativity and innovation. He's also a regular cohost on The Guitar Builders Collective Chat podcast and a real inspiration. We first started talking when I put a call out on YouTube for help with a guitar I was designing that incorporated an iPad. Mark approaches guitar building with a fresh perspective, always seeking to push boundaries and rethink traditional methods, and contacted me suggesting that I built the pickup into the fretboard and neck. His YouTube channel is full of such unique ideas and I want to showcase two techniques he has covered on it.

Direct-to-Film (DTF) transfers

Direct-to-film transfer is a two-step process whereby an image is printed on to a specialist film and then transferred to something else using a heat press. As Mark points out in his video, 'It's used mainly with T-shirt printing, but they also use it with skateboards so I thought, why can't we DTF on to our guitar bodies?' Mark was inspired by the B.C. Rich Guitars from the late 1980s featuring artwork by Patrick Nagel. His transfers feature custom designs he generated using AI.

A close-up of a smaller image pressed on to the bare wood shows the quality of the print and how it hides the grain and colour underneath in the way that a waterslide decal may not.

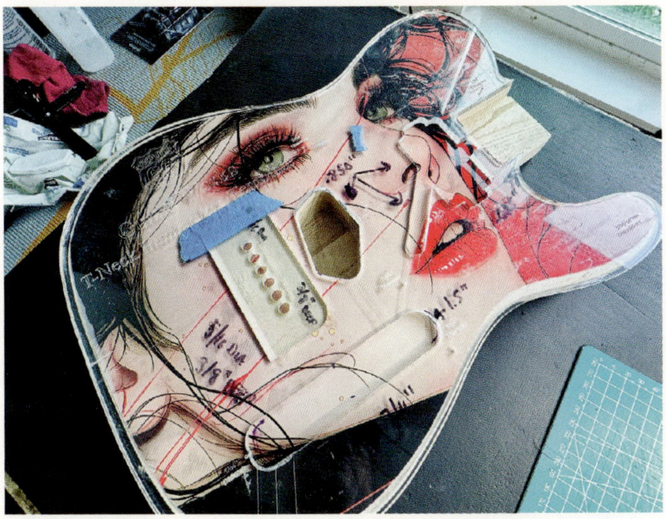

Mark used a template to cut the film to the guitar body shape. He then cut it slightly smaller to accommodate the round-over the body had, only wanting the image on the flat top.

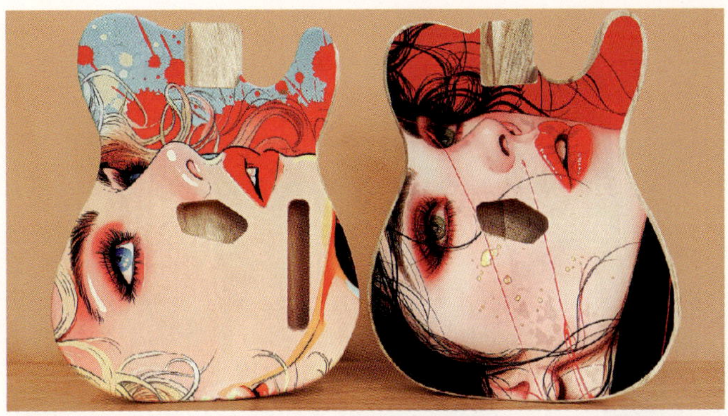

Two finished bodies. The transfer was pressed with a portable heat press, which covers about half the surface of the guitar at one time. A small craft iron will work too.

DO TEST PRINTS FIRST

You can use free samples, scraps and offcuts to do test prints first, making sure that your heat press is at the right temperature and held on the transfer for the right amount of time. Mark's video has lots of tips.

Holoflash

This is a real 1980s finish and I love it. Holoflash isn't applied in one go in the way that DTF is, but in small overlapping patches. It comes as film in various colours. Mark has used silver and gold, but you can also buy it in blue, red, pink and transparent. The base colour of the guitar will show through in areas, so plan the colour to work with your choice of film; Mark has used a black satin finish.

The process involves placing the film on the guitar, putting some parchment paper on top to protect the iron and film already applied, then applying the heat. You don't need the iron to be too hot, or to hold it on for too long. As you remove the film, some will be left on the guitar surface in a patchy finish. Simply repeat to cover the guitar. There's some cross-over to the way metal leaf is applied; this technique will be covered below.

Mark recommends not applying a topcoat, as the finish is durable. I have seen some people apply painted designs over the holoflash. If you do this, a topcoat would be a good idea to protect those designs.

Gilding

After university, I shared my first studio space with various artists. It was quite amazing looking back on it. I mainly created small paintings and drawings using inks, spray cans and masking fluid. The studio also housed a Scottish sculptor who used beeswax despite being allergic to it, a French conceptual artist working with found objects, a British sound artist, a Swiss graphic designer and a British gilder named Jo. I don't want to offend Jo with my description of gilding – she had quite a few advanced ways of doing it and used the studio to experiment and test, and what I'm about to show you is very basic. Gilding is essentially the application of a thin layer of gold, gold leaf, powder or paint to a surface to enhance it.

Use PVA glue or wood glue, applied with a brush. Keep a second brush glue-free. I'm using gold-leaf sheets. The guitar surface has had a light sand with 600 grade.

Apply the glue evenly over the whole body. I like to use a flat, wide brush. You can buy gilding glue that stays tacky for longer.

Lay a gold-leaf sheet on and press it down with the clean brush.

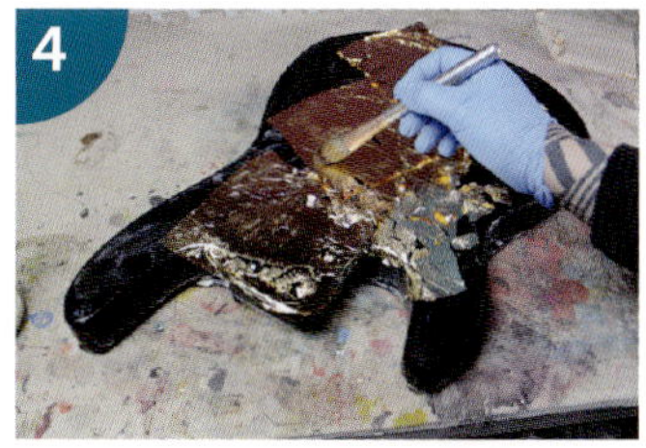

Overlap the sheets. Don't worry if they break and tear, and put ripped pieces back on. To fill gaps or leave them is an aesthetic choice.

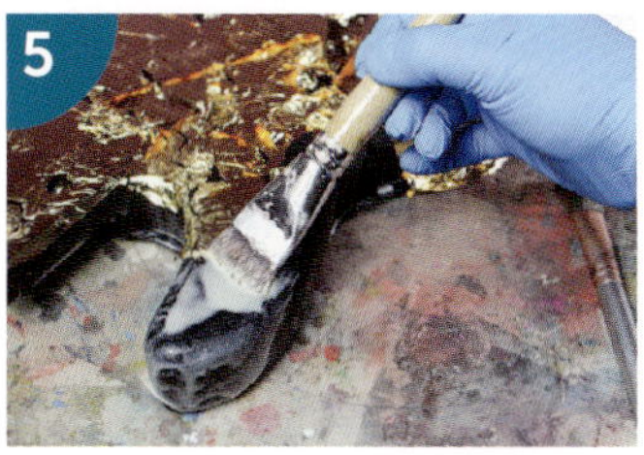

You may need to apply more glue if an area has dried up. If you get glue on the gold leaf, cover it as it will leave the area less shiny after drying.

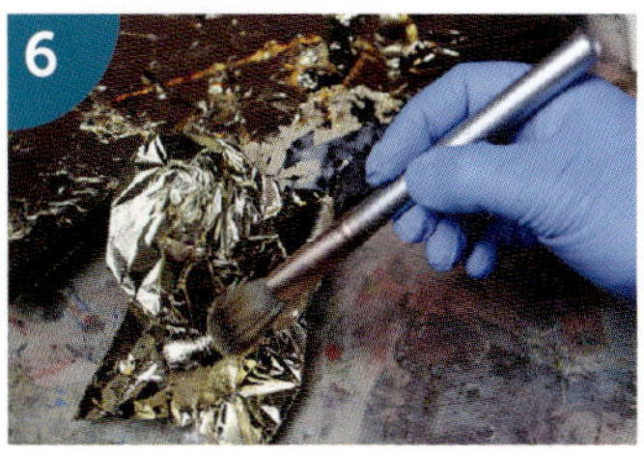

Use the brush to shape the leaf to the contours of the guitar.

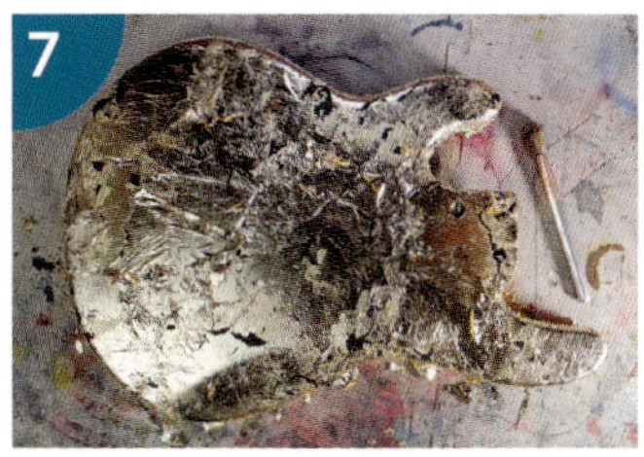

Once the guitar is fully covered, leave the glue to dry. Don't be tempted to try to remove flakes yet, as you may end up spreading the glue.

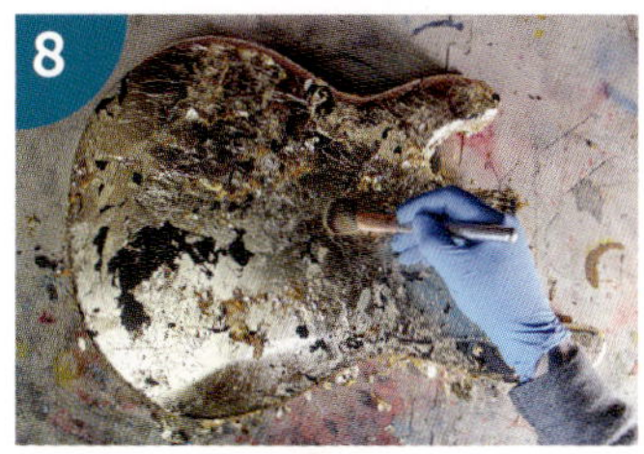

When the glue is dry, rub over it with a brush. I hold a vacuum nozzle near the brush when I do this to get all small bits away from my workspace.

The finished surface ready for topcoats. Do not sand the surface.

The back of the finished bass. I actually added another pass of gold leaf after the first clear coat layer, before the final one to hide more of the black.

REFINING THE WORK

Using paint the same as the base colour, in this case a black Posca pen, allows touch-ups and cover-ups if needed. You could use the pen to define an area.

To create a weathered patina on the surface, I lightly sprayed a coating of very watered-down water-based clear coat. As the clear coat dried, the effect started to take place. It took around 24 hours. At this stage, I would lightly sand back and apply the topcoats to seal it in place. If you want to avoid this effect, don't add water to a water-based topcoat, or seal it first. I seal my gold leaf with Chestnut Products' Acrylic Sanding Sealer.

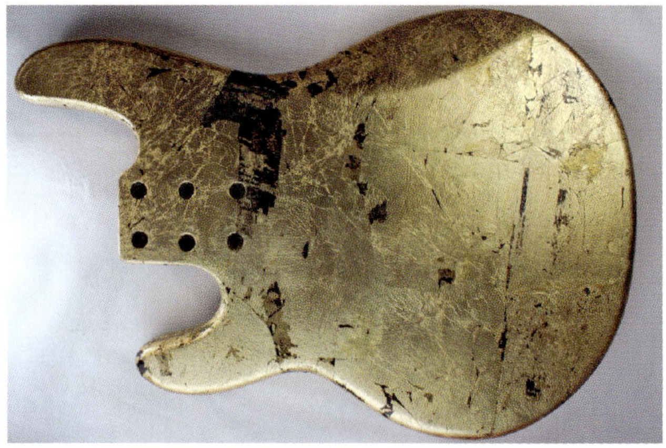

On this body, you can see some straight edges from the gold leaf. To conceal it I could put another layer on, with torn edges, or just use the leaf with torn edges. I actually like the lines, as it reveals the process. This is a problem for anything applied like this, including holoflash.

You can also buy gilt cream, like the one shown here from Chestnut Products, which is applied by cloth or a brush. It dries in 24 hours and can then either be buffed or coated in a wax finish.

CASE STUDY: CHROME UNION JACK CUSTOM FINISH

Mike, my bandmate who commissioned the Paisley effect hydro-dipped Les Paul Special, also asked me to refinish a very old and battered Gibson 335-S. He wanted a Union Jack in black and chrome. This was achieved by combining a few processes from the book.

The whole body was given the Hammerite treatment; that's the darker grey stripes on the body. Once it had been sanded back a bit and covered in clear to make it nearly smooth, I masked off the stripes and sprayed the rest of the body black. This was then sanded, so that in a few places some of the Hammerite finish shows through. It's very subtle. The lighter silver stripes and patches on the back, neck and headstock are all created using the gilding process and silver leaf. Then topcoats were applied and polished. The cool thing about this guitar is that Mike wanted a matching motorcycle helmet. I don't think he ever played and rode at the same time, though.

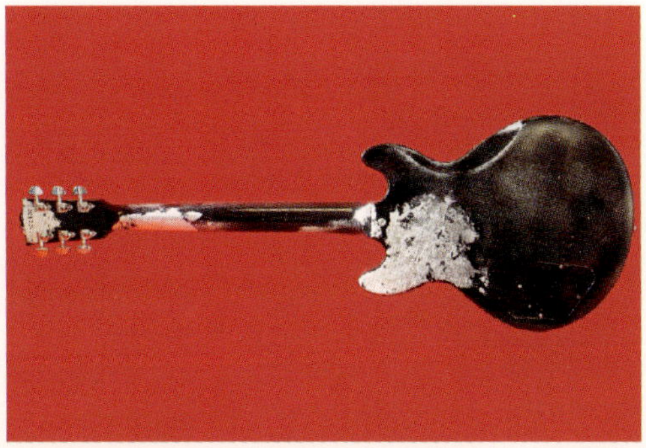

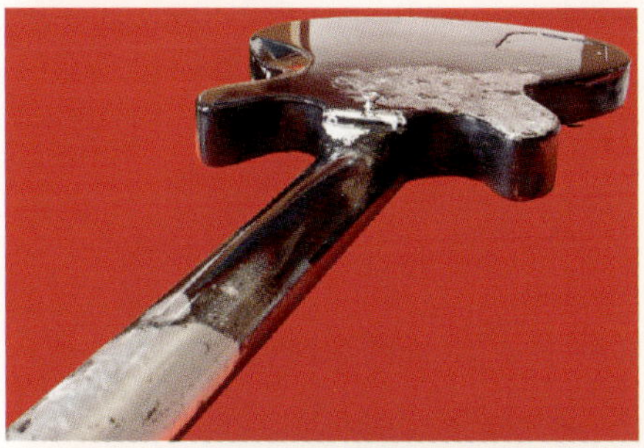

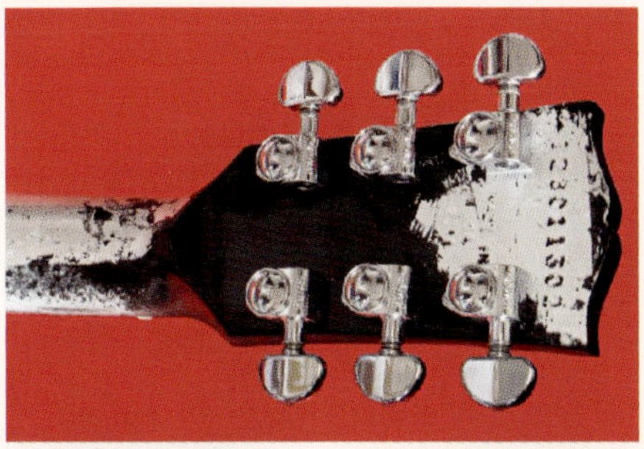

Limed two-tone finishes

This section refers to the process of creating a two-tone finish to the wood by highlighting the grain through sanding it back with a wire brush, then adding a wax and paste. You can combine this process with that covered in the dyes section, dyeing the guitar after brushing the grain then sanding back the surface. It works best on hardwoods with softer, open grains. I have stripped back guitars in the past and found that the wood underneath doesn't respond as well to the process, mahogany and maple for example.

When I was taught this process, it was called liming or lime washing because it traditionally applies to the use of lime on wood, which lightens and whitens the finish. Some makers of the pastes and waxes used in the process still refer to limed wood, but many now use the term cerused wood.

Once the body has been sanded and is ready for the painting stage, take a wire brush with stiff, coarse bristles and brush the surface. Be firm but not too aggressive and test in a hidden area if possible first. Remember always to brush in the direction of the grain for best effect. Don't brush too hard, so as to avoid gauging the wood.

Lightly sand with 600 grit afterwards to remove any raised parts. The drum sander attachment for a grinder works faster and can cover larger areas quickly, but gives less control. I use a nylon coarse brush. For one-off guitars, I prefer using a standard brush.

A wire brush and an angle grinder with drum sander attachment with abrasive wheel.

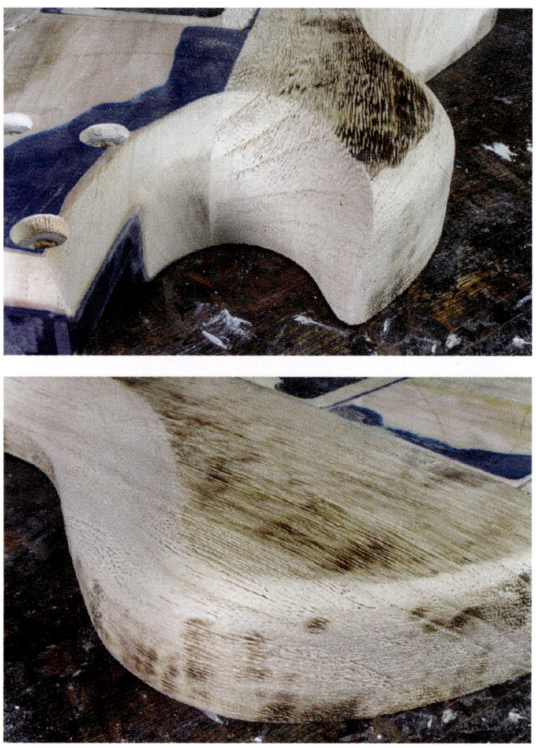

The *Paulownia* wood on the wings of this guitar is from the example in the book of changing the guitar body shape. It responded well to the sanding drum. Note some burn marks on the wood caused by too fast a setting on the grinder.

One session of colour has been sprayed. I've used Nitoraqua black. If you want the natural wood to show through, add a clear coat instead of a colour.

Apply the coloured wax with a cloth. I've chosen one of Chestnut Products' rainbow waxes.

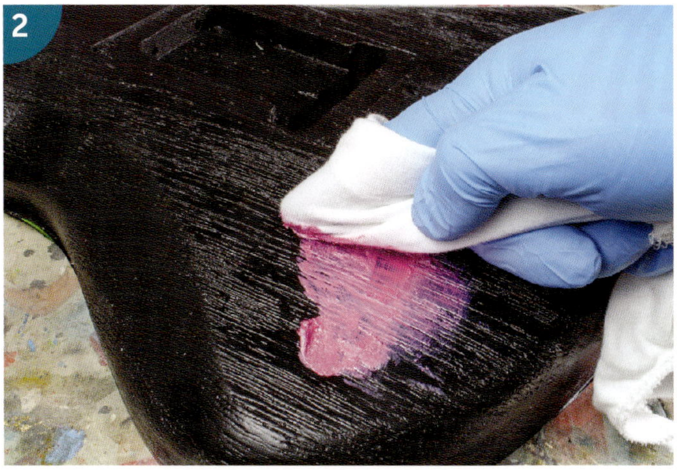

Apply moving against the grain to help fill the pores.

Leave the wax to harden, then use an 800-grit pad to sand lightly with the grain. Keep checking with each pass that enough surface wax has been removed to show the base colour. Be careful not to sand through to the wood.

Before and after. The coloured wax doesn't have to fill the pores to a level finish. If you want a level, smooth finish that can be achieved in the topcoats.

AN ACRYLIC ALTERNATIVE

You don't have to use a wax or specialised liming or cerusing paste. Acrylic paint can work just as well. Start with no added water, but add some if you find the acrylic too hard to spread. Use a damp cloth to buff the surface lightly before the acrylic dries.

Topcoats over a limed finish

In my example, the main body of the instrument is a water-based black finish, with wax filling the pores. A water-based or polyurethane topcoat is fine over the black finish, but not over the wax. If you want to spray a wax finish, you will first have to let the wax fully harden (check the individual product guidelines), then apply a sanding sealer. As so much of the basecoat is available for the sealer to bond to, the issues of adhesion on the wax areas will be reduced.

Ideally, a limed finish will have a wax topcoat applied. For this guitar, I used three coats of Chestnut Products' hard wax oil.

Limed finish on a non-wooden surface

The process of lime washing requires open grain to catch the wax when you rub it, but what if the surface had other pores or cracks? I took a template that I had experimented on with acrylic pouring and added Montana Crackle paint in white to it. I applied it thinly around the edges to allow the pour pattern to show through and more thickly in the middle so that the paint would crack there. Then I used the same Chestnut Products rainbow wax. I think it looks cool. This experiment shows the importance of keeping all your test pieces. The more you have to play with, the more chances there are of finding a new style to make the customisations your own.

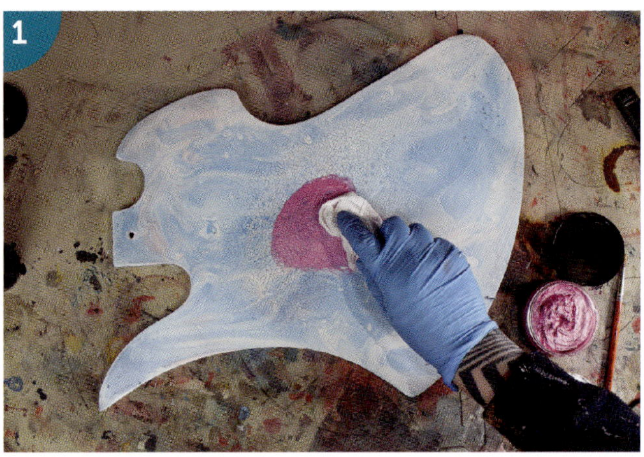

Rubbing a coloured wax into the texture of the crackle paint instead of the texture of an exposed grain.

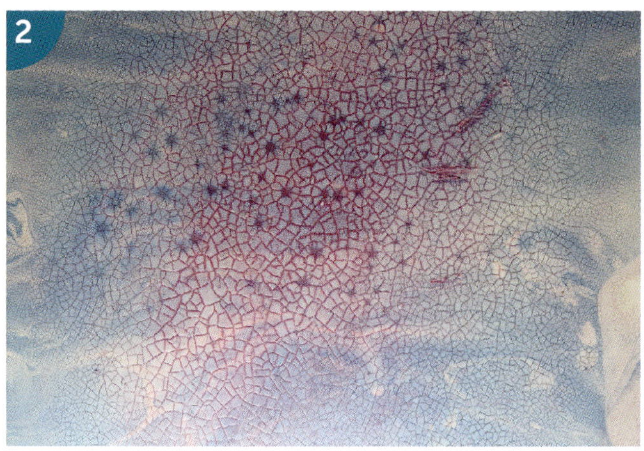

I chose just to put the wax in a small area and fade it out around the edges. Experimentation can lead to interesting and unique finishes.

INSPIRATION: ABHORRENT GUITARS

Abhorrent is a boutique brand known for its extreme guitars and basses. Here, I'm showcasing two exceptional guitars built by Alex, the mastermind behind the brand. These guitars take some of the techniques discussed in this book to an entirely new level.

Instead of applying a metal leaf to the surface as I did, Alex put a brass sheet on the surface of one of his Origin series guitars, in a similar process to adding a wooden veneer to the top. By coating the brass in sulphur, salt, distilled vinegar and paper towels, he initiated an oxidisation process that resulted in a mesmerising patina. I first saw this on his Instagram channel; it was utterly hypnotic.

The guitar below was meticulously crafted from scratch, allowing Alex to control the positioning of the grain in this ash to great effect. The surface has been sandblasted to emphasise the grain, a much more controlled method than using a wire brush, but one that uses specialised equipment. The vibrant colours were achieved through a combination of dyes and the sand-back method, and the guitar is finished with a sleek 2K matt coating. Every design and finishing choice harmonises perfectly, creating a guitar that truly lives up to its fierce name – the Bloodthirst VIII.

Sticker-bombed finish

One of the first customised guitars that I remember seeing was Billie Joe Armstrong of Green Day's Fernandes Stratocaster from the *Basket Case* video. Sixteen year-old me watched that video over and over, having recorded it from MTV on to VHS. The music blew me away, but so did the sticker-strewn Strat. Billie Joe and his guitar were the coolest combination I had ever seen in a guitarist and their instrument. Covering something in stickers probably doesn't need much explanation, but I wanted to include it in this book.

Sticker-bombing refers to the concept of covering something in stickers. Graffiti artists and punks have been using stickers since the 1970s, but it was the very end of the 1980s, after skateboarder Shepard Fairey distributed many thousands of his *Andre the Giant has a Posse* sticker artwork across the US, that sticker bombing became a worldwide phenomenon. When I see a wall full of stickers it reminds me of the green rooms and toilets at small venues my band used to play in, the signatures left behind by all the bands that previously played in the venues. It feels like a rite of passage for any young punk guitarist to add at least one sticker to their guitar.

Some of the first guitars I made used old skateboards and I covered them in stickers. I wanted to make them look rough and lightly sanded them, but then applied topcoats to protect them in that condition. The problem I encountered is that you can still peel the stickers off and potentially crack the topcoat in the process. To eliminate this possibility, you need enough topcoats to be able to sand to a smooth surface finish.

One of my guitars made from broken skateboards, with a sticker-bombed finish.

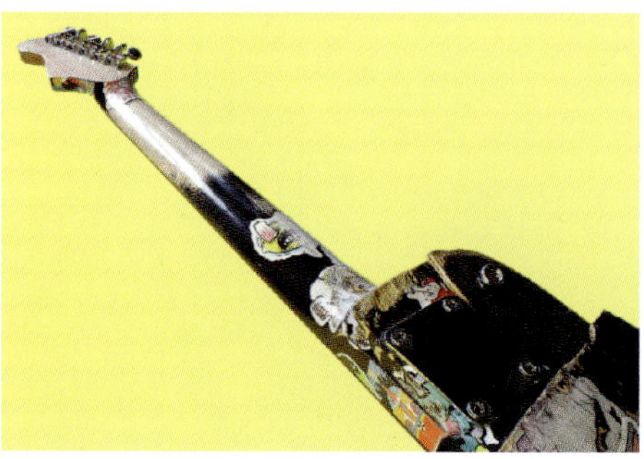

The back of the neck needed extra layers to ensure that the texture of the stickers didn't affect playing.

I wanted the stickers everywhere. I removed the pickup cover first so that I could cut the holes for the pole pieces.

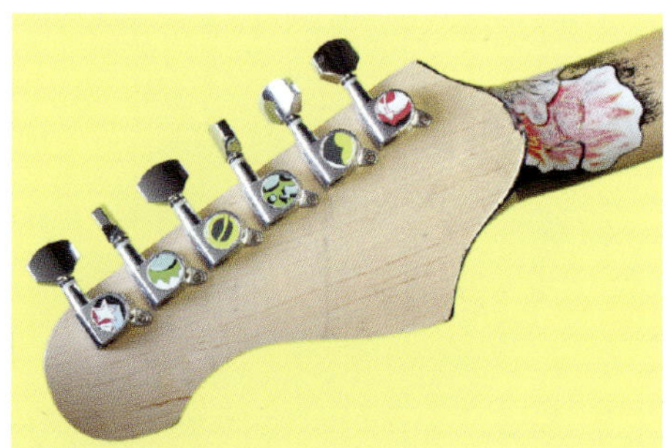

This part of the machine head can have a sticker on it, or be painted without affecting its ability to function.

PROTECTING THE STICKERS

My daughter sticker-bombed this guitar, but some of the stickers started to peel or raise, especially where they folded around the edge of the guitar. The solution is to ignore this and apply the first session of topcoat. By waiting until after the first layers of topcoat, you can protect the stickers. Once this is dry, go in with thin cyanoacrylate glue and stick back down any raised parts. I prefer using a medium-viscosity glue. I find using a CA kicker here is helpful, along with lolly sticks to hold the sticker down. Any bumps of dry CA can be removed with a blade, or when light sanding with 600 grit ready for the next layer of topcoats.

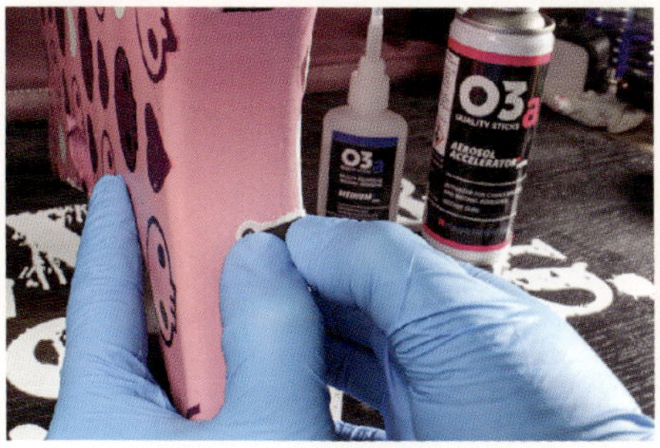

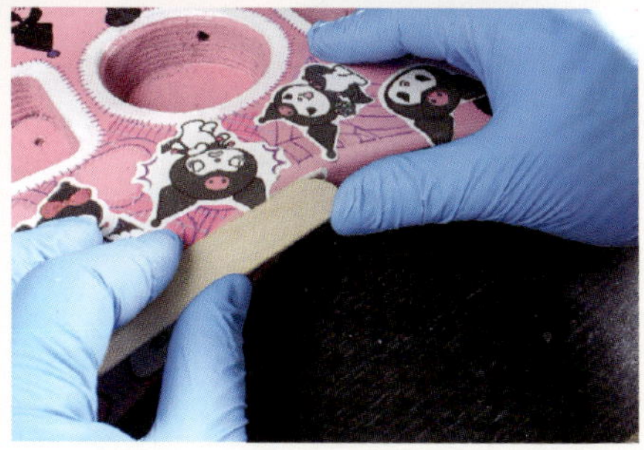

Topcoats over stickers

You will be facing the same issues with stickers as for a hand-painted surface when it comes to applying topcoats. You will need to repeat the process of applying topcoats and sanding until an even, matt finish can be achieved after sanding. Depending on the thickness of the stickers and the topcoat, this may be three or four sessions.

The light shining on the surface reveals the raised sticker under the topcoat. To achieve a flat surface, you must flat-sand without removing the stickers.

Sand with a hard-backed 400 grit, continually wiping away the dust. Where the area has been sanded will appear matt, with shiny areas where the surface is still low. Don't go too far.

Here a final top coat has been sprayed. Three coats in one session of Nitorlack's Nitoraqua Matt. I may leave it matt, or buff it to gloss.

INSPIRATION: COURT O'REILLY'S PYROGRAPHY

I'm always fascinated by artists like Court O'Reilly, who treat wood as part of the artwork itself. Court works in the medium of pyrography, or wood burning. She says about her artwork, 'I intentionally choose wood with unique grain patterns and character to enhance the pyrography artwork. Each wood slab is inspected and considerately selected to ensure the highest integrity and quality of wood.'

One of Court's nature-inspired artworks is burnt directly on to a guitar. When I first saw it, I was immediately drawn to the way her artwork and process felt like part of the guitar, not just painted on to it. All the colour and texture had been naturally created through the pyrography process.

The guitar itself was built by Evan of Trailblazer Guitar Co., who shares Court's interest in sustainability and is inspired by wood choices. He also made the leather scratchplate, inspiration for a completely different material to any covered in this book.

Court has published a book on pyrography and has tutorials on YouTube, so you can learn more about the technique directly from her. She shares her artwork across social media as Hippie North.

ADDING STUFF AND THINGS

In the words of artist and musician Martin Creed, 'I like things, a lot.' Anyone aware of my work with Devil & Sons and Devil & Daughters Guitars knows that I stick things on guitars whenever I can. There are countless items you might want to attach to a guitar (remember the giraffe guitar in the masking section that had a fluffy mane and tail?) and numerous ways to attach them. For this section, I thought the best approach would be to provide some case studies and tips on what to do and what to avoid. Then, I encourage you to go out and experiment. Following is a checklist for adding parts:

* Does the placement of the object interfere with any parts?
* Will the object be in the way when you are playing?
* How will the instrument be used? A touring guitar may be knocked about a lot.
* Could the object fall off (i.e., should you add another screw)?
* Test your materials' compatibility with the paints and finishes you are using.
* Take into consideration the overall weight.

Materials such as Milliput epoxy putty, Araldite epoxy glue and screws are essential to holding added parts on to the body.

Xenomorphs series: screwing things in place

I've made a few Xenomorph guitars using resin and vinyl model kits. This one is a great example of how I had to edit the body slightly to accommodate the chest-burster alien on the upper horn. It was then screwed in place just like the face-hugger alien. To hide the screws, I modelled over them with a two-part epoxy putty; Milliput standard is my go-to. I have faith that it will dry hard and resist any damage and wear during playing.

I was a bit more anxious about the paint finish, though, so added more topcoats than usual, sticking to three coats in one session. The final session is when I uncovered the body and sprayed everywhere with a matt topcoat. I needn't have worried about wear, however, as this guitar ended up selling to a stunt performer who had just worked on *Transformers: The Last Knight* and wanted it to display as a work of art – he couldn't actually play guitar.

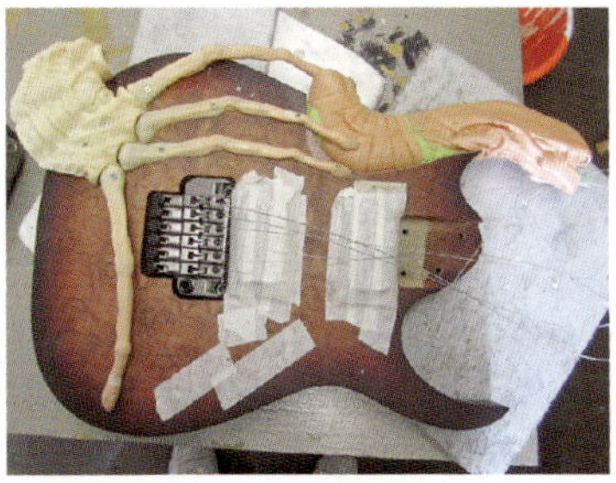

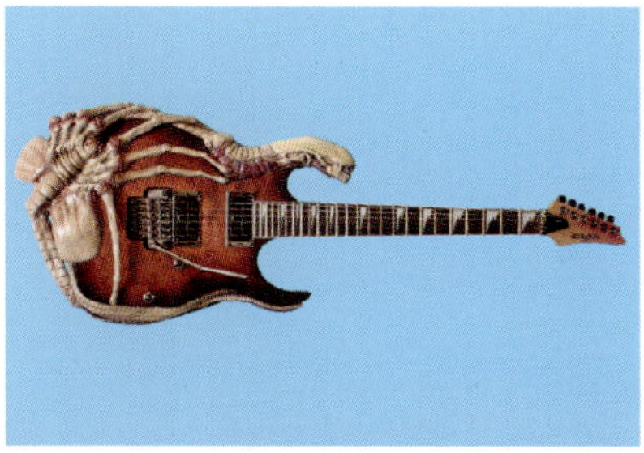

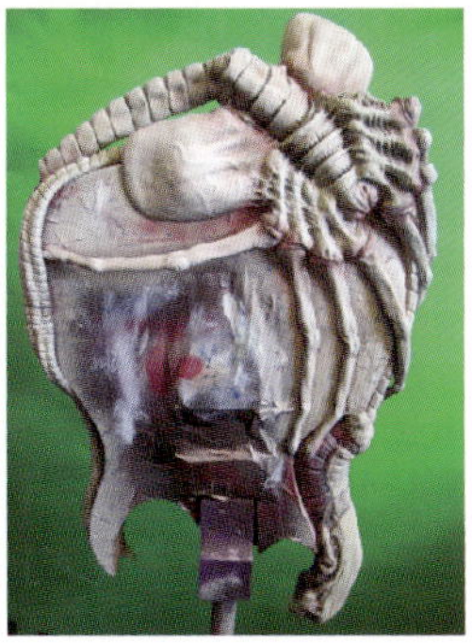

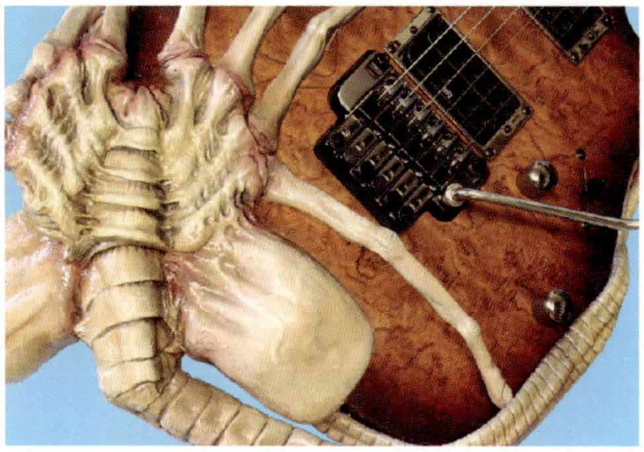

Steampunk guitars: the power of glue

I had this guitar for eight years before I sold it. I wasn't happy after the initial build that certain elements would hold in place as they were simply glued there. I also wasn't happy with the weight; it has a motorbike engine cover on it. I'd spent ages on eBay buying second-hand objects that I thought looked cool for my steampunk guitars; they were a really varied bunch of things. When I revisited this guitar after all that time, it had held together and I realised the weight wasn't so much of an issue if you let the person buying it know. In fact, it probably weighed less than a Gibson Les Paul.

Some parts are screwed directly to the body, while the rest are held in place with a two-part epoxy glue. I normally use Araldite five-minute set, but for parts of this I used their steel metal glue. The right glue in the right places does the job. The small metal exhaust parts (which are actually bicycle brake noodles) are held in place with glue and two-part metal epoxy.

Craftcasters: kit-bashing

I first came across kit-bashing via two YouTube channels around the same time. The first was Adam Savage's Tested. Adam is, amongst many things, a prop builder who worked on the *Star Wars* prequels and *The Matrix* sequels. Part of his process involves sticking bits from various kit models together to add details to his props; this is where the term kit-bashing originates. Meanwhile, Brian Thompson from The Smugglers Room and his awesome geek enthusiasm introduced me to the word 'greeblies', as a way of describing those small parts you add to a model to make the model look more complex and detailed.

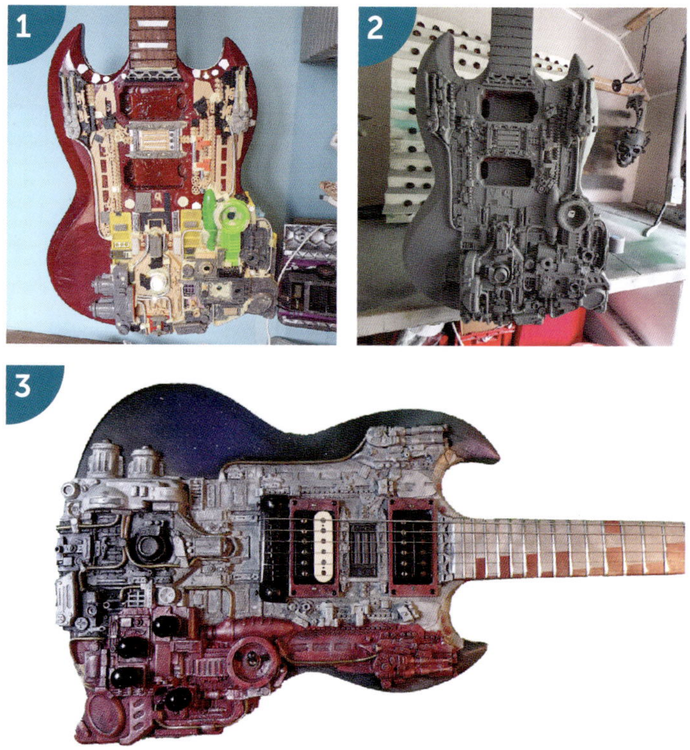

This progression shows a kit-bashed Epiphone SG. When the basecoat of primer is added, all the parts gel together, but the paint job is what brings it to life.

This is my Solar Craftcaster, named after the Solar pickup from Alchemy Pickups in its bridge position. I spent a lot of time creating a backdrop to photograph it against.

The main circular part with the holes on comes from an old vacuum cleaner. The large green and dark grey parts are from a water pistol.

The pale-yellow sections are moulded and carved in Milliput epoxy putty. The tan-brown parts are from a model tank.

The white part, hidden here, comes from a Covid test. The rest of the test is on the back of the headstock. I've also added some aluminium modelling wire as pipework.

All the white is thin plastic cut on a Cricut vinyl cutter. There are two brackets from an Ikea cupboard here and the canon from a *Millennium Flacon*.

DO YOU RECOGNISE THIS?

To kit-bash on to a guitar, make sure that each part is securely attached. A mix of glue and screws helps. Not all plastic is the same, so some may not adhere that well with glue. Others can be bonded together with special plastic cement plastic weld. Kit models are made to be glued; water pistols aren't. I always use an adhesion promoter before priming. Hycote makes both.

Always ask yourself, Is the part obviously from somewhere else? If so, it may distract from your design if people recognise the origins of it.

Hycote primer and adhesion promoter.

Mad Axe: material choices

This progression shows how I built up my first Mad Axe guitar in stages from a kit guitar body. You'll recognise it from the design section of this book. The main takeaway from this is the material choices. There are flat pieces of metal and hardboard attached to the surface. Hardboard was easy to cut and I had a lot lying around; it was light. I have avoided it since because it isn't as durable as using wooden sheets, which are widely available from hobby shops. Think ahead to the end function, for example an instrument that will get handled a lot.

RELIC FINISHES

There's an apocryphal story that Fender made Keith Richard some new guitars that he liked, but wouldn't play on stage because they looked too new and he needed to play something vintage. The Fender custom shop team then aged them, creating a relic look, so Keith wouldn't be embarrassed to play. It's not actually true, but I like the story. It's why a lot of people want a relic guitar; for the vintage look, one that tells a story and one they can't create naturally because they aren't touring musicians who mistreat their instruments.

I make a lot of relic guitars – in fact, I have a series of extreme relics called the End of the Road guitars, designed to look completely smashed but are actually still playable. They key to creating a natural-looking relic is to find source material to work from. No two guitars will relic in the same way, as it partly depends on the owner's playing style, but a fake relic is often easily spotted as no attention to detail has happened.

One of my End of the Road Guitars.

The relic masking method

You can create a relic look to the paint by masking a bare body with a relic pattern and spraying paint over it. This helps to create a thickness to the edge of the paint that looks aged and chipped.

I photographed some old wooden tables at a pub, where the paint had been peeling off.

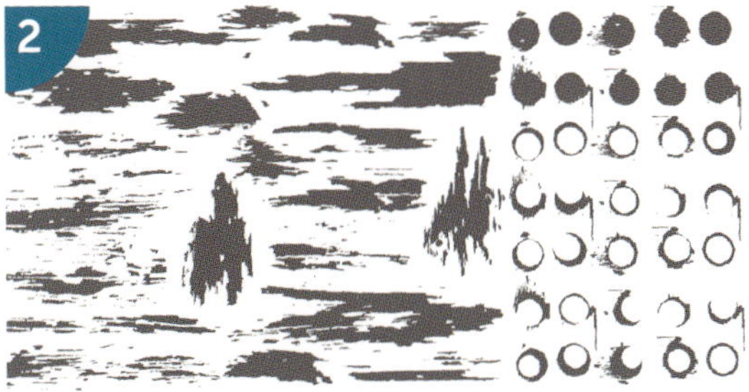

On Photoshop I created a template of the chipped paint pattern, then printed it on to vinyl stencil paper.

The body after it has been sprayed and the mask removed. It's too bright at the moment, though.

Sanding areas

Sanding paint off in areas of wear is a good way to create a relic finish that is more subtle than the harsh lines of the template (although parts of that can be sanded back too). I like staining the wood underneath before applying the colour and priming in white so that as you sand through the colour you see a white edge and then reveal the wood underneath. Some stain will need to be added back to the wood to dirty it up, especially as it's easy to sand through.

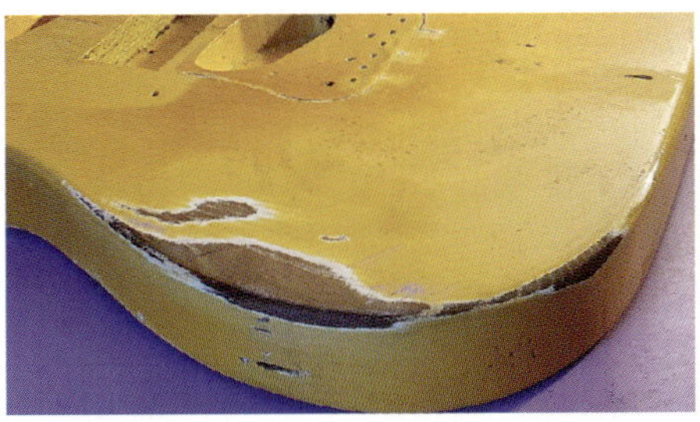

Dents and dings

The small marks that build up on a guitar over time are essential to making a believable relic. Dropping keys, bashing the surface with a bag of nuts and bolts, scraping with a saw or fine Dremel bit and repeatedly banging with a nail punch all work really well. Refer as often as possible to photos of actual relics to ensure it looks right.

Making the dents and dings.

Age tint

Using an amber or brown translucent spray can be a good way of lightly ageing the surface. Remember that nitrocellulose does yellow over time, so a light spray of the aged yellow in some areas can look great too. Here I've put an old scratchplate on the guitar and lightly sprayed around it, keeping the area that would be protected in real life from ageing.

Checking in nitrocellulose

The cracked pattern that appears in the surface of the nitrocellulose finish over time is called checking. You can recreate this if your guitar has a nitrocellulose finish. If it doesn't, you could spray a coat on it. Nitorlack makes three different nitrocellulose topcoats. Its standard modern formula is most resistant to cracking. However, its Golden Age formula is designed to check over time, so the processes I'm about to discuss work well on it. Nitorlack also makes a Relic finish, which responds really well as it's designed to crack easily; in fact, it will happen without additional help.

The finish will need to have dried out for at least a month, but then there are two options to help the cracks appear through temperature shock. You can put the guitar body in the freezer overnight, then when you take it out rapidly warm it with a hair dryer or heat gun. This process sometimes needs to be repeated a few times. Alternatively, you can heat it with the heat gun, then rapidly cool it by spraying cold air on to it. Air duster cans, designed for cleaning keyboards and electronic devices, release a cold jet of air when sprayed upside-down, so are perfect for the job. Work in small areas at a time. Remember not to hold the heat gun in one area for too long as it can cause the nitrocellulose to bubble and burn.

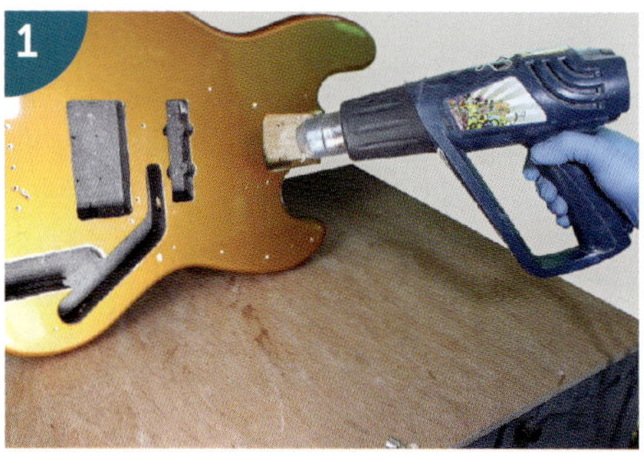

Apply the heat, possibly working in small areas but always moving the gun to prevent burns.

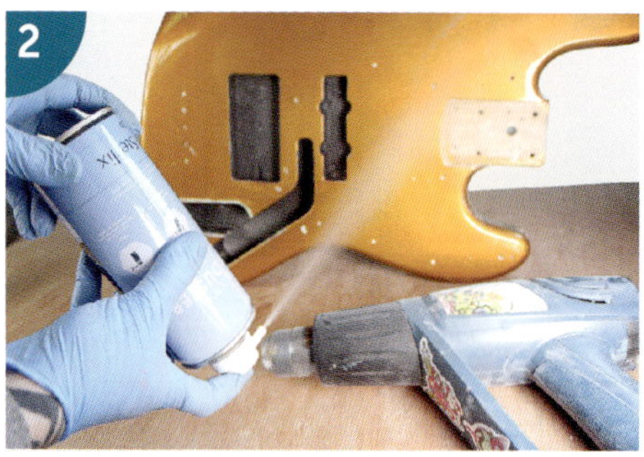

Spray cold air on the body using an air duster can upside-down.

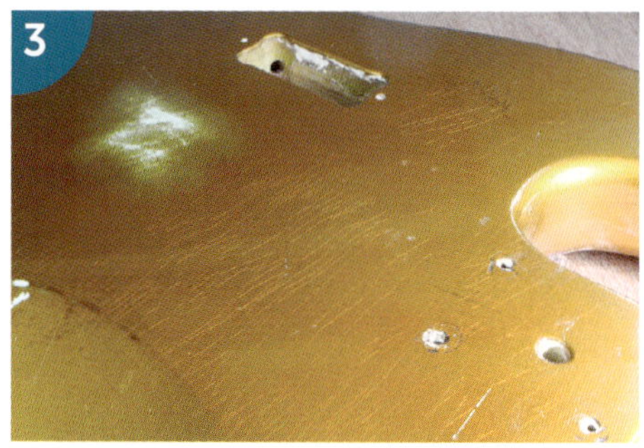

Checking appearing on the surface of the finish.

Nitorlack's Relic Patina is rubbed onto the surface with a dry cloth, then buffed out after five minutes.

Often the cracks are very hard to see, but they can be highlighted by rubbing a darker stain into them. You can use acrylic paint or dark wax. Nitorlack makes a special Relic Patina paste just for this purpose. It is rubbed in with a cloth, then buffed off the main guitar surface.

Checking in other finishes

Fake checking can easily be cut into the surface of other finishes that won't naturally crack if you don't want to give them a topcoat of nitrocellulose and check that. Remember always to use photos of an actual relic as a guide.

This body has cracks cut into it with a scalpel. A light sand and application of the Relic Patina paste, followed by buffing, will help to make the edges of the cuts more realistic and subtle.

Ageing hardware

Hardware can be lightly scuffed with wire wool or foam-backed sanding pads, but a further technique I like to use is the application of ferric chloride. Chrome-finished hardware may need more work with wire wool to prepare it, so always test. Simply add a bit of ferric chloride to the surface of the hardware using a cotton bud or brush. Leave it five to ten minutes, then thoroughly rinse off. You can experiment with the amount of scuffing and the length of time the ferric chloride is left on.

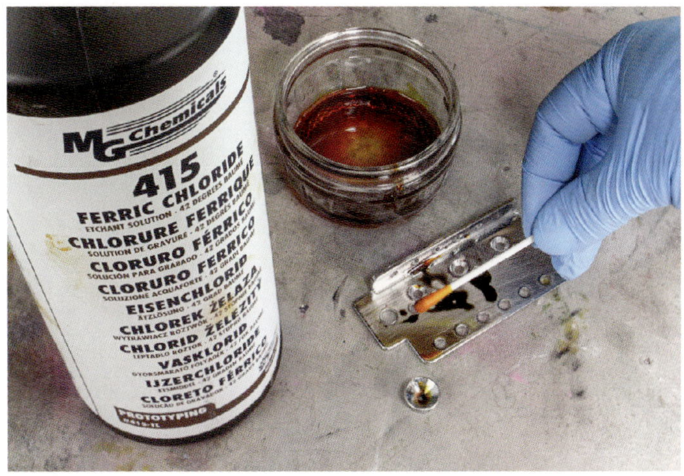

Applying ferric chloride with a cotton bud.

Hardware that has been given the ferric chloride treatment.

INSPIRATION: DOM DE PLUME'S WASTELAND GUITARS

One of the many elements I love about Wasteland Guitars is how Dom De Plume, their creator, describes it as a living art project. Dom is a practising multi-media artist who makes works for galleries. He says that the electric guitar serves as both a source of passion and a medium for his creativity, combining his passion, hobby and vocation.

The finish of all his instruments, including the hardware, is painted on using a myriad of techniques, colours and coatings that all come together to achieve his distinctive signature look. The addition of graphics and logos adds to the narrative tale the guitars tell and gives them an imagined history. As I'm sure you can tell, I think his work is amazing; I look at it, wish I'd made it and straight away want to get customising.

CASE STUDY: RELIC BASS GOLD TOP

This bass is a great case study for highlighting how you can transform an instrument. It features in the relic section of this book, but multiple other techniques have been used on it too. It started out as a body from one old bass, and the neck from another. Both were donated to me by friend Isaac as he upgraded his personal instruments. I bought it new hardware and pickups.

You can see the original Fender Sea Foam Green showing through on the body. That is a poly finish and needed a light sand back to allow me to add the nitro on top. Here I have used Nitorlack's Aged Goldtop (one spray session, about half a can), followed by their Relic Gloss (two sessions, one whole can). A month later the heat and cold shock treatment was used, followed by adding the Nitorlack Relic Patina paste. I then lightly sanded back in some areas to get the worn look, and to reveal the original colour. I then sprayed two sessions (one whole can) of nitro gloss to seal it all in and buffed it up. The texture of the cracks still showed through.

The neck had a similar process, except I first used a relic stencil on some areas, then sprayed Nitorlack's Amber Vintage, before removing the stencil and continuing with the Relic Gloss process. This time I sprayed three sessions of the nitro gloss to help achieve a smooth finish and hide the texture of the cracks. I like the texture on the body, but not on the neck.

The headstock logo was made using a vinyl stencil and a metallic silver Posca pen. The custom scratchplate is made from mirror acrylic. I scratched into the back of this to make the crack lines in the reflective surface and painted the cracks with a black Posca pen.

Love yourself no matter wh

CHAPTER 6

PAINTING A NECK

When visiting a guitar shop, you will observe factory-made guitars with a variety of neck finishes, including painted, clear varnished, waxed and oiled options. Personally, I prefer painting the necks, as it provides an additional canvas for artistic expression.

The process is essentially the same as painting a body, so make sure that you have prepped the neck by cleaning and sanding before masking. Any filling of dents or reshaping of the headstock should happen before painting begins. This chapter will cover the additional elements to think about that are specific to painting a neck.

PROCESS OF PAINTING A NECK

The fretboard

Masking off the fretboard

The sequence shown in the photos covers how to mask off an entire fretboard.

Fretboards have a thickness; you can see this on the side of the neck. The side dots are normally in the fretboard wood itself.

Run masking tape along the side of the fretboard. Try to do it in one piece, although this can be tricky as the neck may have a slight bow to it.

Fold the tape tightly over the top of the fretboard. Press down firmly and run your hand along the fold to make sure all is tight.

Repeat on the other side. The tape strips should overlap. If any fretboard is exposed, cover it with extra tape.

I make sure that a slither of the fretboard edge is still exposed, so that when the paint is applied there is no gap between the paint and the fretboard edge. The size of the exposed area is exaggerated slightly for this photo.

It's common to leave the fretboard unpainted on the headstock side of the nut.

Instead of trying to use the tape that's running along the fretboard to make a neat end, use a new piece.

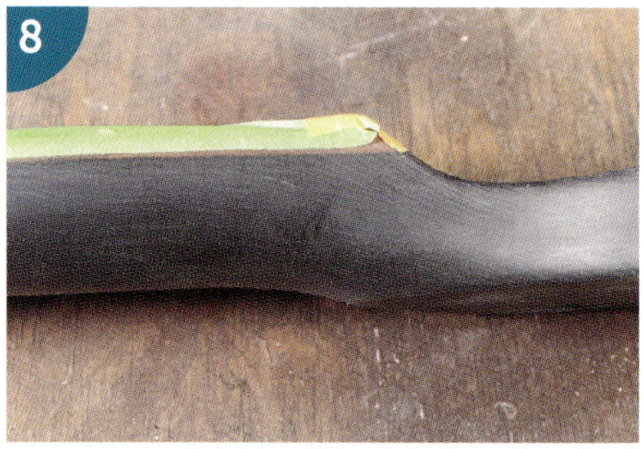

Trying to fold the edge of the new piece to line up perfectly to the side tape can be fiddly and cause the tape to lift slightly. Instead, cut it short.

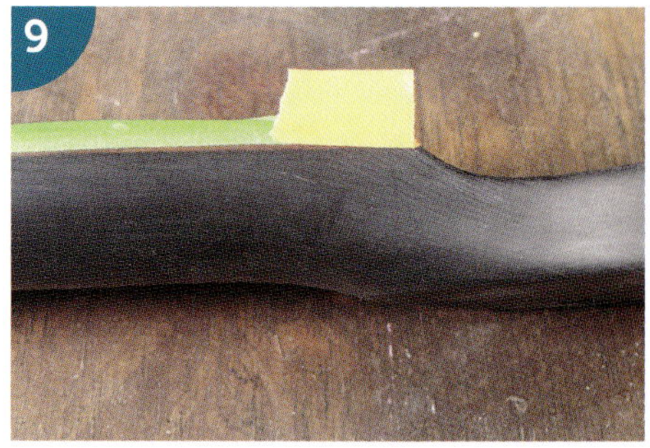

Line up a new piece of tape to make a straight, continuous edge.

Neatly fold the edges of the tape to ensure that no paint can get through when spraying.

Some necks will have a fretboard that overlaps the heel.

Although this edge can't be seen, I like to use a new piece of tape to seal it off. The devil is in the details.

It's likely that the tape will buckle and crease here when you wrap the tape around the curved edge.

Use a new piece of tape to cover any gaps. Ensuring that everything is tightly covered now will save time when cleaning up later if paint gets through.

A completely masked fretboard, including the sides.

Masking off just the top of the fretboard

There are two obvious situations in which you will mask off just the top of the fretboard. You may want to paint the neck in a solid colour, including the edge of the fretboard, or you may want to clear-coat the entire neck and need to protect the top of the fretboard in the process. There is an import third reason shown in the example here – if you have painted the neck in a solid colour and left the fretboard edge, there will be a lip once you remove the masking that will be really annoying for the guitarist when playing. In this last case, you will need to remove the entire masked-off area from the colour coats and add the new 'top of the fretboard only' mask before applying topcoats. You may need to apply extra tape along the middle of the fretboard to ensure that all is covered; the wide tape I'm using covered it all.

This neck has been sprayed black. The fretboard and its sides have been masked to protect it.

Removing the masking completely reveals the untouched top and sides of the fretboard.

It's best to start with fresh masking, so remove all the previous tape.

Mask from one end of the fretboard to the other, lining up one edge of the tape with one edge of the neck. Repeat on the other side.

Painting the fretboard

Most fretboards you'll come across aren't painted, so you'll be forgiven for thinking that they shouldn't be. Maple is a common and traditionally used wood for guitar necks. For builders, it is readily available, inexpensive and easy to work with when carving the neck. However, it isn't as durable as some other fretboard material choices and due to its light colour is likely to show up marks caused by playing. This is why it's common to see lacquer on fretboards made from it. If Fender has been lacquering fretboards since the 1950s, then why can't we?

When customising a neck, we need a technique to ensure that the fret wire does not end up covered in paint or lacquer, as this will affect playability. It's common practice for manufacturers like Fender to lacquer over the frets, scraping back just the crown of the fret wire and leaving a smooth flow of lacquer on the fretboard and sides of the fret wire.

It will be necessary to remove the paint from the fret wires after painting. The method for doing so is shown in the photos.

Once the final coat is fully dry and before you polish and buff the neck, the paint should be removed from the fret wires. The edge of each fret must be scored with a scalpel, both sides and both ends. The paint can then be peeled away.

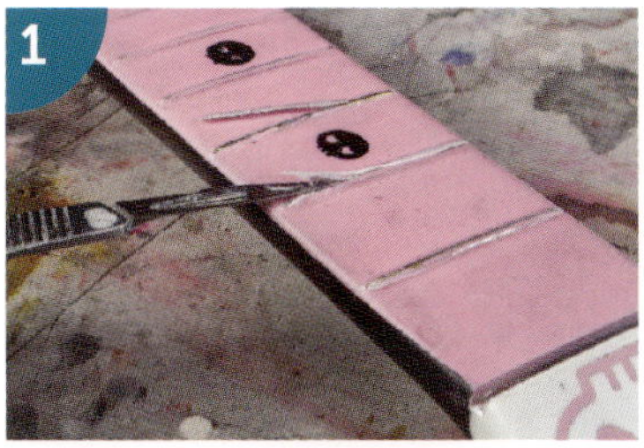

I have a set of fret rubbers that I use to work on each fret in order to remove any small pieces of paint left behind. Use metal fretboard protectors or masking tape. This can also be done with a firm stationery rubber.

Masking off the fret wire

If you want to avoid the work of removing the paint from the fret wire at the end, there is a simple alternative and it's the one I normally opt for.

The back of the scalpel is angled to help press the tape tightly against the fret wire, making a tight fold where the wire meets the fingerboard.

Run the scalpel along the edge of the fret wire as close to the fretboard as possible. Take your time to avoid slipping and cutting into the edge of the fret wire or the fingerboard.

Here you can see the ideal angle for the blade to cut at.

If you accidentally score the edge of the fret wire, it's not going to affect the way the guitar plays, as the strings make contact with the crowned top part of the fret wire, not the sides. If you mark the fingerboard with the blade, it may be an easy fix, such as a mark simply filled and concealed by the paint as you apply layers on top and sand back. If the cut is deeper, the best approach is to use cyanoacrylate glue to fill it, sand back, then paint.

It is essential to have the masking tape as close to the fret wire as possible, otherwise some of the original colour of the fingerboard will show through next to the fret wire when the tape is removed after painting. This is the main disadvantage to masking off the fret wire. A way around this is first to paint over the entire fingerboard and fret wire with one coat of the colour you will be using. You can then tape up the frets. This will mean at the end you will only have to remove one coat of paint from the wire and not the multiple coats and topcoats that will be applied.

Working from left to right, we can see the stages of masking off the fret wire and it's very straightforward. Cover the whole wire with a piece of masking tape. Apply pressure along the ridge of the fret wire only. Apply pressure on each side of the fret wire using the back of the scalpel, or your fingernails. Cut one side of the tape, then cut the other.

The fret wire has been masked off after the first coat of paint has been applied. Notice how the tape wraps over the end of the fret wire and down the sides of the already masked-off neck.

This fretboard has had more topcoats put on it than normal because the gilded surface needed the extra coats to make it smooth. As a result, it is best to cut along the edge of the masking before removing it.

Removing the mask reveals both the thickness of the topcoats and the single black coat that was applied before the masking to help ensure that none of the original fretboard showed through.

Use a 600-grit foam pad to smooth both the edge where the topcoats were just cut to remove the mask and to remove the paint layer from the fret wire. Take care not to work too hard on the wire and remove metal.

Another angle showing the foam pad wrapped around the fret wire. I'm gripping each side and not applying much pressure to the top of the wire.

Remove the masking before the final polishing and buffing stages of the paint process on the neck.

Polishing the frets

I normally leave this stage to the very end, once all the rest of the neck and fretboard has been polished as part of the painting process. The process of buffing the neck is often enough to clean the frets and leave them as shiny as possible. You may want to consider using different cloths or pads when working on the fretboard, as polishing metal will leave black marks on the surface of whatever you use.

When polishing a fret wire, you will want to protect the fretboard by using the metal fret protectors. Simply move them along each fret in turn as you work your way along the fretboard, using the one that best fits the relevant fret.

You can protect the fretboard by masking all the areas that aren't the wire, a bit like the reverse of masking off the frets to paint. Don't use this method on nitrocellulose unless fully cured, as the tape could affect the finish.

Lightly rub each fret with micromesh, fine abrasive paper or micromesh pads. Start with 1500 grade and working up in four to six jumps to 12000.

Finish with a liquid polish, like this from Axe Wax. It can be applied by cloth, with a polishing disc on a rotary tool, or using a big buffing pad if you have masked off the whole fretboard. Don't use the fret protectors held in place with rubber bands if using a rotary tool, as the bands may catch on the spinning pad.

Painting only the fretboard

The examples of painting the fretboard so far have assumed you're painting it the same colour as the rest of the neck. If you are planning to use different colours, or just painting the fretboard, you will need to mask off the neck and leave the fretboard free. Then you can decide if you want to mask the fret wire, or cut and rub the paint off the wire later.

When painting the neck and the fretboard different colours, it's usually easiest to paint the neck first, including the side of the fretboard. I normally do one session of topcoat too, so as to protect the colour when masking. When this is fully dry, you can mask the neck off, leaving the fretboard free to paint, including an edge along the side of the neck for a fake fretboard edge.

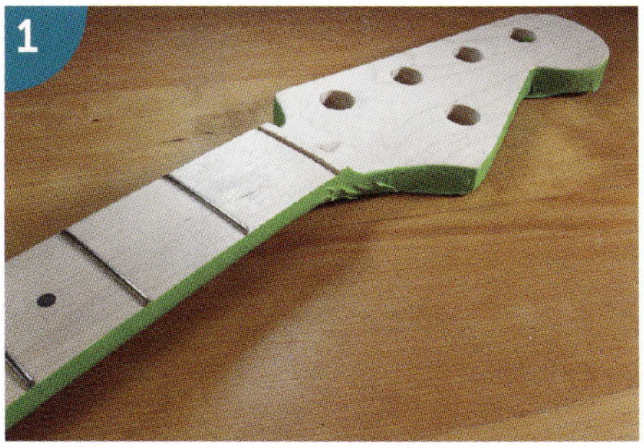

The neck has been masked, including the sides of the fretboard. When painted, just the very top of the fretboard will have the new colour on it. The face of the headstock has been left to take the same colour.

The fretboard has had a gilt finish applied, then the topcoats.

Once the masking on the neck has been removed, the edge of the paint can be sharp.

Some larger overhangs of finish can be cut or scraped back.

All edges should be lightly sanded with an 800-grit pad.

If an edge is lifting or chipped, fill with cyanoacrylate glue.

Headstocks

Sometimes you just want to paint the front of the headstock to match the guitar body. This was in fact the first change I made to my very first guitar when I was a teenager. It was a black Squier Stratocaster. I painted the headstock front and the scratchplate and stuck hand-drawn black and white stickers over the body. I still have the guitar and have repainted it several times. I've routed out areas and embedded them with smashed mirror in resin. It's a guitar I can't ever sell and will no doubt repaint again sometime soon.

The edges and back of the headstock are masked off and the neck wrapped in paper.

Once the paint is dry and the masking removed, the edges will need a light sand with 880-grade paper to smooth sharp paint edges. Then the headstock is ready for a polish.

Neck-painting technique

The process for painting a neck is essentially the same as painting a body. Prepare the wood in the same way, apply the same number of coats and topcoats and use the same polishing and buffing techniques. However, necks are long and thin, so the painting technique is slightly different. Normally you would spray a body top to bottom, then go over it left to right as a single coat. For the back of the neck, it's easier to follow the length of the neck only. Normally the back of a neck will take three overlapping passes to cover it.

Headstocks come supplied with holes in them, which makes them easy to hang and paint.

Remember to start and finish the spray off the neck so that you don't get a build-up of paint.

If you are painting the fretboard too, make sure to angle the spray towards the nozzle-facing side of the fret wire when moving from one end of the neck to the other. Adjust your positioning and spray a second pass travelling the other direction. You want to make sure that an even layer of paint is getting to the entire fretboard and that no paint shadow is caused by the raised fret wire shielding the area behind it from paint. You can hang the neck to paint it, but, be careful, this is more likely to cause drips if you over-spray the paint. It does, however, allow you to spray both the fretboard and the back of the neck easily.

Using a piece of wood a similar width and length of the neck to rest on is a good idea when just spraying the neck. You can move the whole thing without risk of touching the wet paint on the neck.

Working with the neck on a flat surface is ideal for spraying if you are just working on the back of the neck or the fretboard. In the photo, I have the neck laid out in front of me, so that I can easily spray from left to right and back. Between each coat I turn the neck around; this means that the side furthest away from me doesn't remain the same and risk either getting less paint on it or me missing areas that I can't see well. I still do only three coats in one sitting, though, with the recommended flash time between coats, and a day between sittings (remembering to sand lightly and denib if the paint requires it).

Often you will be spraying both sides of the headstock and the back of the neck, but not the fretboard. In this situation, I always spray the three coats on the front of the headstock first, then lay the neck down to work on the back. It adds time, but makes it easier.

Sanding back and denibbing

You will need to sand and denib between paint spray sessions just as you would on a body. I recommend using foam sanding pads. They can easily shape to the back of the neck; most headstocks will have a curve somewhere on them and the fretboards aren't flat. A hard sanding block would not be suitable. Remember that nitrocellulose will only need to be sanded if there is an imperfection, drip, or run to the finish.

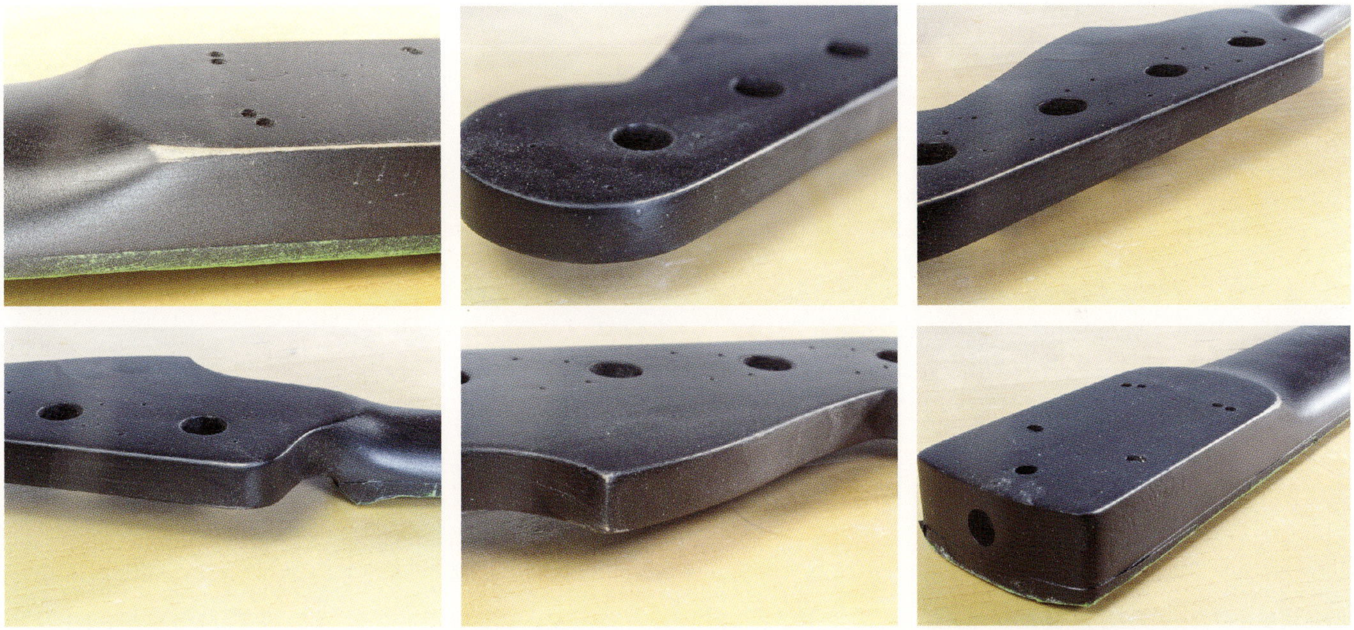

The edges of the heel and headstock are risky places for sanding. The paint is thinnest at hard edges like these and it's easy to press too hard and sand through a coat.

Topcoating a neck

Follow the same process as you would with topcoating on a body, with the same spray technique used previously on the neck. Remember that you will need to tape off just the top of the fretboard if you haven't painted it – the edges of the fretboard need to have a topcoat to ensure a smooth finish into the neck. Additional coats of clear may be needed to hide any raised edge of the paint, but remember to stick to the three coats in one session and just add extra sessions. If you're painting for someone else, check whether they like the feel of a gloss finish – many guitarists prefer the final finish on the neck to be matt for ease of playing.

FRET MARKERS

There are many ways to customise fret markers. Some of them use techniques already covered in the book, and some are unique in themselves (although I encourage you to find ways to use them on other parts of the guitar body). I have included them at this stage of the book as it makes sense with the chapter order, but some techniques will have to be applied before clear-coating the fretboard.

The use of a laser level is helpful for positioning fret markers.

Applying fret markers

Waterslide decals

Any of the techniques from the waterslide chapter can be used on a fretboard, including having a clear image for the marker with a black border, allowing you to have a colour underneath that will show through. The rest of the fretboard will be painted black to blend in with the border.

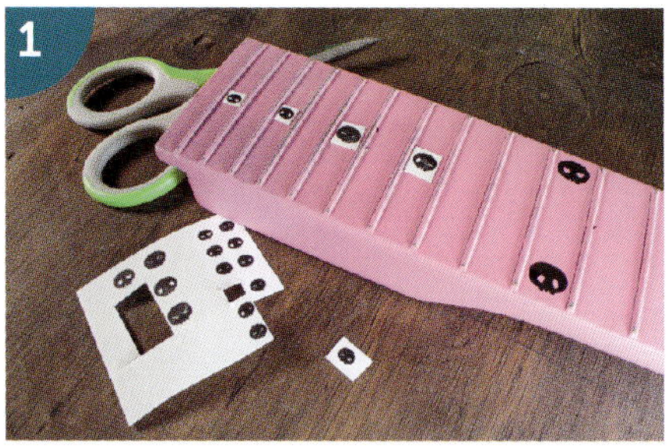

I always print duplicates of markers, as well as extra in slightly different sizes so that I can cut them out and place them dry on the fretboard before transferring them one at a time. It's often easier to gauge the right size when you can physically place them.

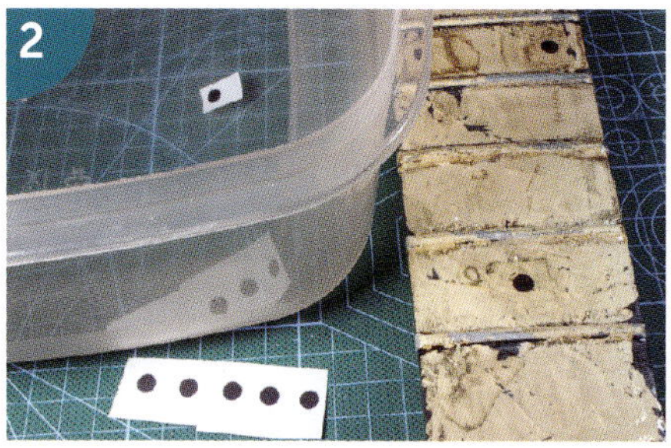

The process for applying the fret markers is the same as any decal; however, you must cut close enough to the side of the marker so that no decal overlaps the fret wire.

Cutting the decal with extra space above and below gives you more backing to grip and slide out without the risk of touching and damaging the print in the process.

Vinyl-cut stencils

The use of a paint pen makes quick work of this process. You could place the stencil, then mask off the rest of the fretboard if you prefer to spray the paint.

Hand-painted designs

This fretboard was sprayed with colour before the markers were drawn on with paint markers. I've also added some details along the fretboard. If painting with a brush, try to use thin paint, otherwise you'll need extra topcoats to obtain a smooth finish.

Inlay stickers

There are several companies that make stickers designed specifically for guitar fretboards. They are made from PET (Polyethylene terephthalate) and are usually only 0.07mm thick. This is thin enough to have no effect on playing. I have used them a lot and found them to be durable, with any marks they leave being easily cleaned off. However, I did have one guitar that showed signs of the stickers once I removed them because the fretboard wood had faded in colour slightly over time due to bright sunlight falling on it (I clearly didn't play it enough and just had it hanging on the wall!). You can apply topcoats over the stickers (just as in the sticker-bomb section), although it isn't necessary.

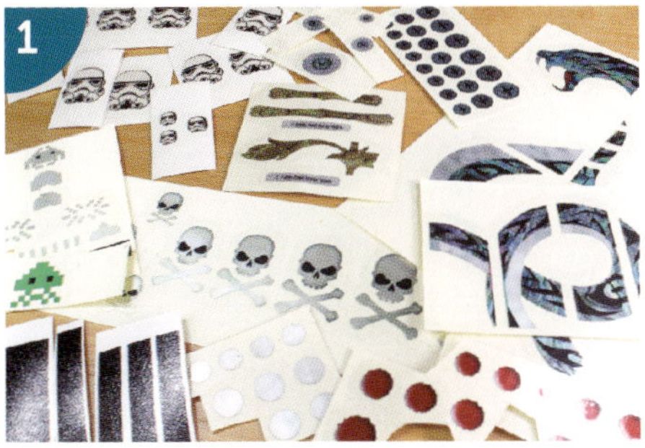

A collection of stickers from companies like Inlay Stickers Jockomo.

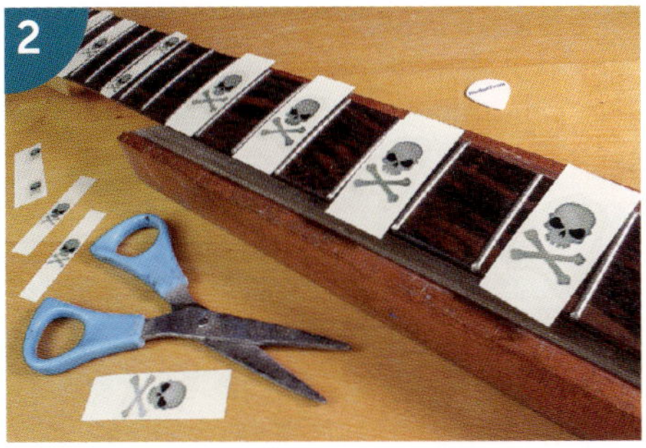

Lay the stickers across the fretboard to ensure that they are all correctly positioned before you start sticking.

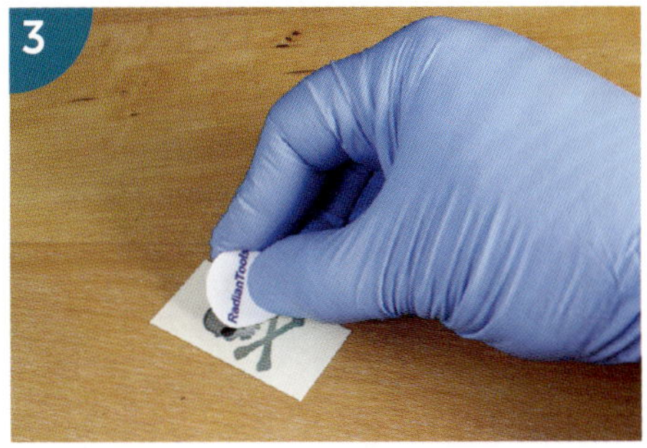

Start with a sticker from one end, press down on the top protective coating using something solid like your thumbnail or a plectrum.

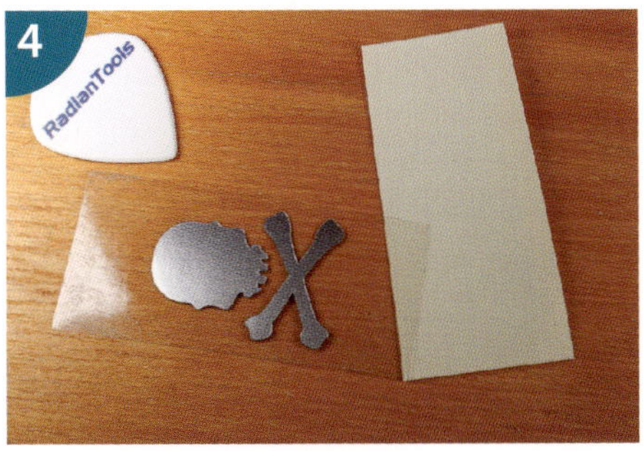

Peel away the backing, ensuring that the sticker is attached to the top coating.

Place the sticker on the fretboard and press down firmly. A plectrum is a good tool for this. Leave the protective coating on and work down the fretboard a sticker at a time.

Once all the stickers are in place, go back and remove the top coating. Peeling it back at a sharp angle helps to prevent the sticker from coming away from the fretboard.

Using the back edge of a scalpel hold the sticker in place whilst peeling off the top layer if the sticker starts to come away from the fretboard.

Press firmly on the sticker to ensure that it is all flat against the fretboard.

Removing existing fret markers

For the next techniques you will need to remove the existing fret markers. This approach is simple if they are dots, but can easily be expanded on if they are another shape, such as blocks or shark fins.

This process involves drilling into the fretboard, so you need to be careful to avoid the truss rod, the metal rod that runs along the centre of the neck. The truss rod sits just below the fretboard. By looking at the side of the fretboard, you can determine the maximum depth you can drill before risking touching the truss rod. I prefer to do this with the neck clamped in place and with a pillar drill or drill press, although it can be done by hand drill.

The hole only needs to be deep enough for whichever process you choose to follow. There is no need to remove the existing marker completely if you are worried about drilling through. Clean up the edge of the hole with a scalpel and 800-grade paper.

A brad point drill bit is good to start the hole off as it can help centre the drill bit and potentially crack the fret marker.

If the marker has cracked, fish out the remaining parts with a scalpel and tweezers.

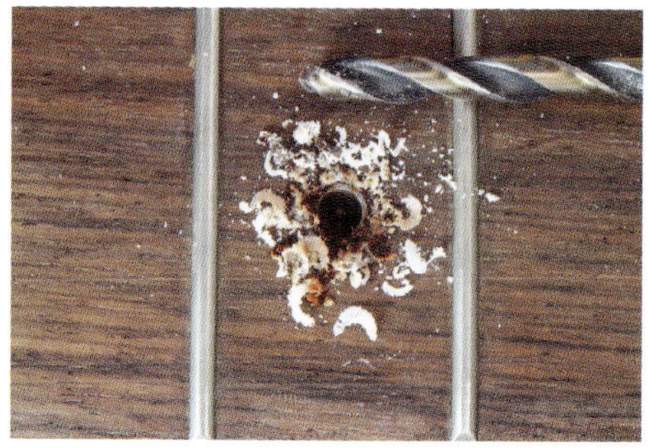

If the fret marker doesn't crack, change to a standard bit to continue; it's less likely you'll drill through the board into the truss rod with it.

Carving fretboard markers

An extension to this method is to carve a shape using the hole you have drilled as a starting point. You can use your choice of tool here. I prefer a rotary tool engraving bit, but small chisels and wood-carving knives can also do the job. Outlining with a scalpel blade first is essential, as it gives an edge to work against. I also go over the edges to make sure they are straight and perpendicular to the board top with the scalpel at the end.

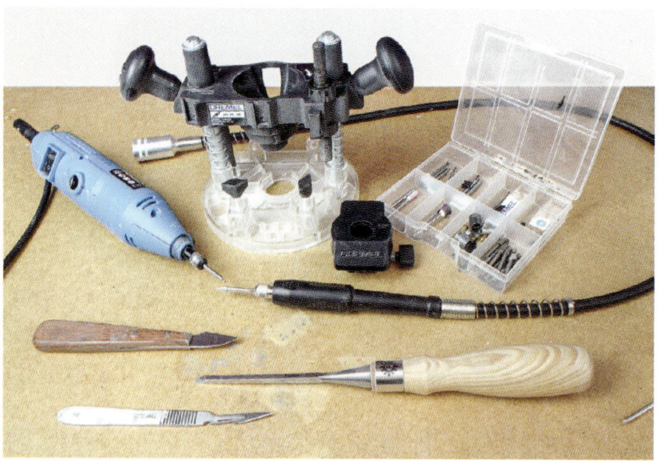

A range of tools used for carving out a shape in the fretboard.

These fretboard markers are filled with resin containing a pearlescent pigment.

Resin and cyanoacrylate glue markers

With the holes drilled out you can easily pour resin into them. The resin could be coloured by adding the pigments that a resin supplier will sell. These will include metal flakes, glitter and glow in the dark pigments. I highly recommend drilling some holes of equivalent size in a scrap of wood and running some tests first, both of the mixes you use and your finishing technique.

If you are putting resin markers into a fretboard that's to be painted, drill the hole and put the resin in first. Then mask off the resin markers once they are fully cured, apply the paint, remove the mask and finish with the topcoats over everything.

UV-cure resin is the best choice for markers, as you are working with such small amounts. If using a two-part non-UV-cure resin, secure the neck level during the curing process.

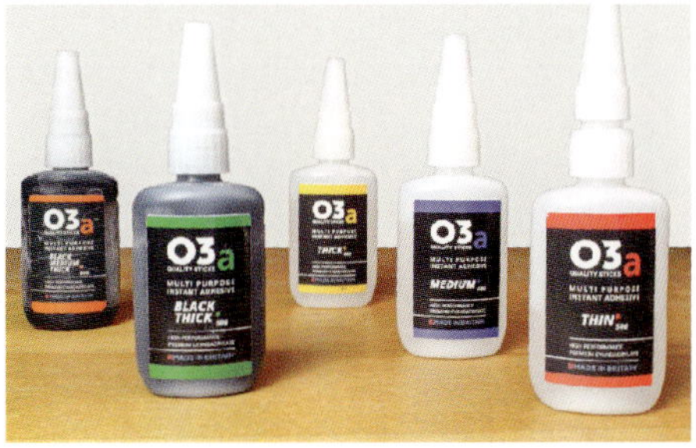

An alternative to resin is cyanoacrylate glue. Avoid using a kicker spray, as this can cause some whitening. The CA glue can still be mixed with pigment. Companies like O3a Adhesives produce a range of thicknesses.

These markers were painted in acrylic before having clear UV resin added to them. I painted the sides and base of the hole I cut.

Allow the resin or CA glue to form a slight dome; it will likely sink back whilst curing.

Lightly scrape away the excess domed resin or glue, remembering that the fretboard isn't flat, but will have a slight curve to it. Use the blade parallel to the fret wire.

Polish the marker as you would any resin finish, working through grades of paper. For the final polish, use the same lemon oil or fretboard wax that you would use on the fretboard and do the whole board.

REPAIRING FRETBOARD DAMAGE

You may not notice if you have marked the fretboard with sandpaper or scraping too hard with a blade when removing resin until applying the lemon oil or wax. This may also reveal some CA glue or resin stains too. In either case, lightly sand the fretboard with 800-grit soft-backed, then move on to 1000, then 12000. Reapply the wax or oil. You may notice the sanded area looking slightly different (potentially smoother) than other frets, so it's often best to lightly sand the entire fretboard (avoiding the fret wire).

Objects embedded as markers

This has become my favourite upgrade to a fretboard. I've embedded screw heads, washers, jewellery charms and objects I have made from Fimo (a modelling clay that is baked to harden). I highly recommend you search out a supplier of mosaic pins. They are normally used in knives, but are perfect for guitars. Mosaic pins are metal tubes with a metal shape that runs through the centre of them. I've seen skulls, flowers, bear claws, stars, circle patterns … the range seems endless.

When drilling the hole, you can match it to the size of the object you are embedding, or go slightly wider and have an outline around the object filled with a coloured resin or cyanoacrylate glue. Just remember not to go deeper than the thickness of the fretboard. Embed the object lower than the fretboard surface and have a layer of resin or glue on top.

Mosaic pins can be sliced into discs of any thickness. They will need some cleaning up afterwards with a file, a piece of 800-grade paper and a scalpel to remove burrs.

Use a small amount of cyanoacrylate glue to hold the mosaic pin (or anything else) in place before adding the resin, or the rest of the CA glue.

I use black CA glue, such as the range from O3a Adhesives, to fill the gaps in the mosaic pin. Avoid using the kicker spray as this can whiten the glue.

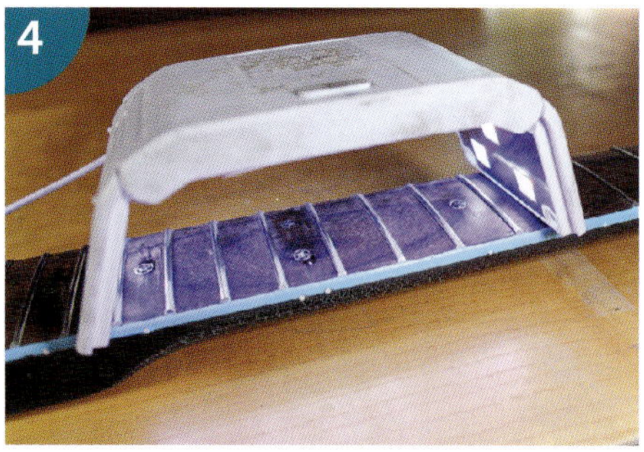

The final top layer of glue is clear to avoid obscuring the design. Alternatively, use UV-cure resin.

Here, the hole was made larger to allow for a border, filled with black CA glue.

The finished fretboard after scraping the top of the CA glue or resin and waxing the entire board.

Screw heads look cool, but make sure to use flat-headed ones and cut the shaft off as close as possible to the head, so that the overall thickness of the head isn't greater than the fretboard.

Steampunk jewellery charms are among my favourites to use on my steampunk and apocalyptic themed instruments.

SIDE DOTS

One problem with painting a neck and fretboard is that you will inevitably paint over the side dots. Whilst some players are happy not to have fret markers on the fretboard, it's essential to have them on the side. I wouldn't advise trying to mask off the side dots that are already on the fretboard before painting – they're so small that the mask can slip during painting, tear the paint around it during removal, or overlap the area you want to paint. You can scratch through your painted finish back to the original dots with the tip of a scalpel, but it is very hard to get a neat-looking circle this way. The best stage to put new dots in is before the topcoat, wax or oil is applied to the neck.

Inserting physical side dots

This technique can be used even if you aren't painting the neck. Changing the side dots to be a different colour, or embedding small objects in resin in their place, is something that can subtly transform the guitar. As a feature that the player looks at and uses all the time, this could be a practical change not just aesthetic, making the side dots stand out more, or even glow in the dark. I prefer to do all this before I apply topcoats, using them to get an extra smooth finish.

Side dot material comes as short plastic rods. Suppliers often have a few different diameters, colours and materials.

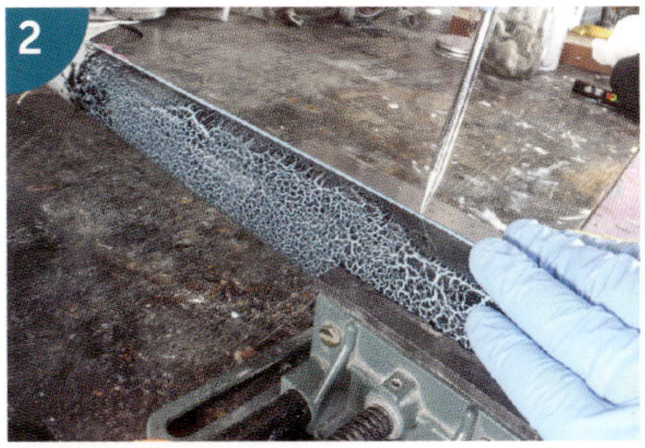

With the neck clamped tightly in place, use a bradawl to mark the dot placement. Sometimes you can use the marker that is already there.

Carefully drill a hole in each side dot. Use the same diameter as the rod you are placing.

Drop cyanoacrylate glue into the hole. Pushing the rod in will cause the glue to squeeze out of the top, so you only need a small amount. I'm using O3a thin CA glue.

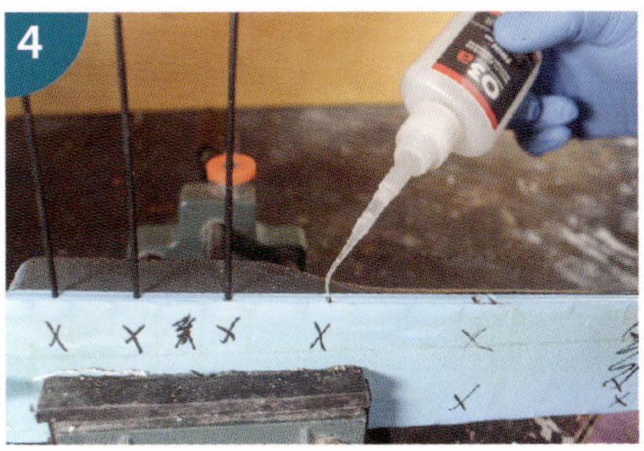

Push the rod in and wipe off any glue spill straightaway with a cloth. Then move on to the next dot. Sometimes I have enough rods to do all the frets in one go, but normally I work in batches of four or five, using a CA kicker spray on them before the next stage.

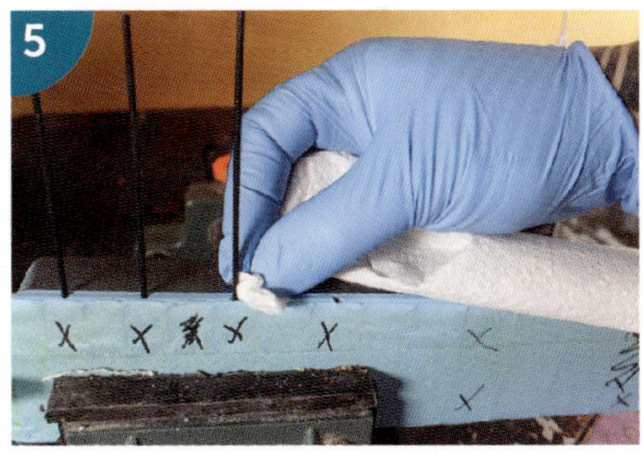

Use end cutter/nipper pliers to remove as much of the exposed rod as possible. If you don't have a pair, move straight to the next step, but they do make the process easier and quicker.

Use a scalpel to cut the dot level with the fretboard edge.

Hand-painted dots

I have often used paint pens to draw the dots on the side of a guitar. One way of ensuring a consistent size of dot across the fretboard is to make an indent that the paint from the pen can easily pool into. Usually, the topcoats applied to the neck will fill and hide the dent, but you could use a drop of CA glue after the first session of applying the topcoats, sanding it back whilst you lightly sand the neck before the second session.

EMBEDDING SMALL OBJECTS AS SIDE DOTS

As an alternative, you may choose to fill the hole you drill with a coloured resin or cyanoacrylate glue. If you want to embed a small object such as jewellery crystal as a side dot, simply follow the same process of drilling the hole, then place the object and fill the hole using the same technique as embedding fret markers.

This is the automatic centre punch I have been using for years to make side dots. It can be quite aggressive and leave deeper dents in softer woods, so a small round head centre punch and gentle hammer tap may be better for a beginner.

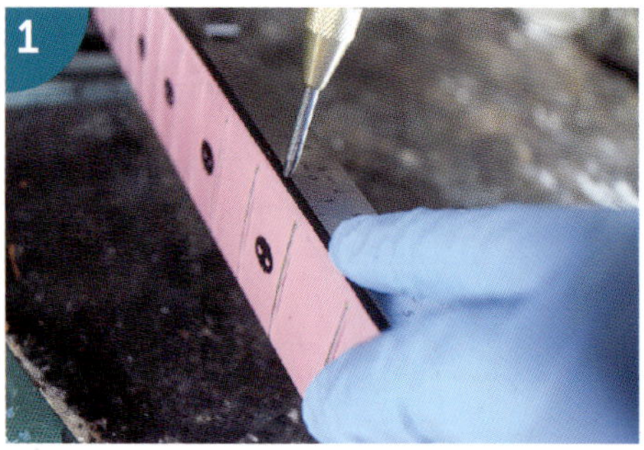

Whilst the neck is clamped in place, you can use the punch. A centre-finding rule is your friend.

Note how shallow the mark is. An aggressive punch can make a bigger mark, or chip the paint around the edge.

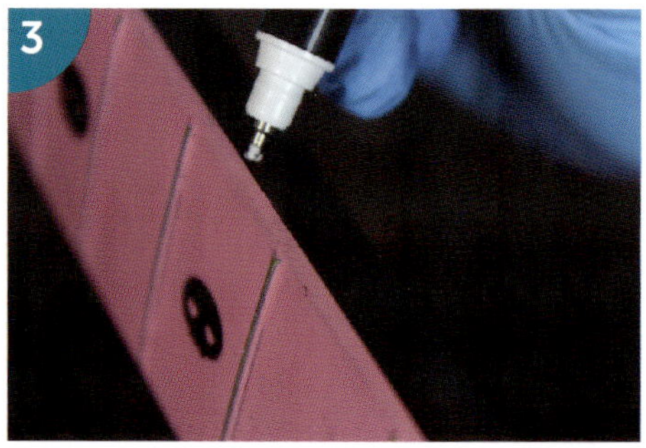

Using a paint pen or brush, drop in the paint to fill the bottom and sides of the hole.

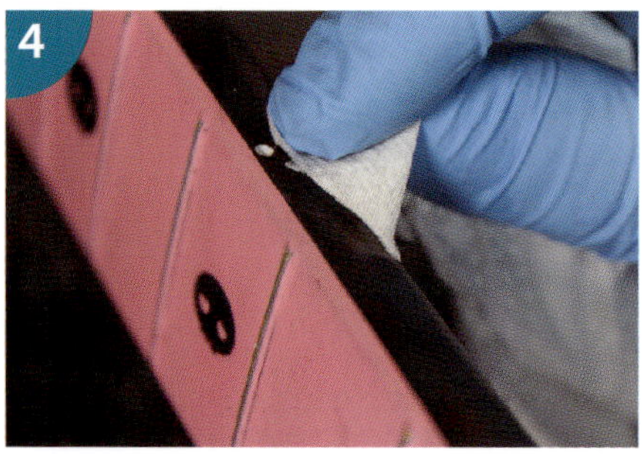

Wipe off the excess from around the edge.

Sometimes you will need to add more paint if the dot isn't clear enough.

A small drop of thin CA glue can help to fill before the clear coats. It may require levelling with a scalpel blade once dry.

HEADSTOCK LOGOS

The guitar logo is like an artist's signature on a painting. It's rare to find a guitar without one and most brands have a consistent way of doing it. If you're planning on customising multiple guitars, it's worth experimenting on scrap headstock-shaped pieces of wood to make sure that you get the best size and positioning. Don't forget that you are doing this before the hardware and strings are put on, so plan carefully as you don't want your logo to be obscured. String trees are your enemy here!

Many of the techniques in this book could be used to make a logo on the headstock, most to be applied after the main paintwork and before the topcoat. Alternatively, you may want to apply them to an unpainted neck before you finish it with a topcoat, wax or oil. It is sensible to run a test on a spare piece of wood for any of these if it's your first time.

INSPIRATION: FRANKLYN GUITARS

You will have already seen Franklyn Guitars in this book. The wax finishes that Chris uses on his guitars really made them stand out when I first saw a display of Franklyn Guitars, but it was his necks and headstocks that I most admired. There's a lot of detail in the way the wood has been layered and his logo looks really cool. Chris's technique is much the same as I have explained for embedding objects in the fretboard, but on a larger scale. Chris told me:

They're 'resin domed' stickers embedded in resin. The benefit of that type of sticker is they're rigid so don't distort as the resin cures and won't show the wood grain through them. They're also easier to handle. A tip is to glue them in with superglue first, or the heat of epoxy curing will melt the self-adhesive backing and it'll float up.

Rubber stamps

When I first started customising guitars, I had two rubber stamps made up of my logo. It's a very straightforward process of supplying a black and white image to the company (in reverse) and waiting for them to post you back your stamp. Lots of companies make them and also supply a range of inks. Look for an ink that is permanent and run a test to see how it reacts with your topcoat. You may find a thin first pass on the topcoat (of the three passes you will apply in one session) is a safe option to prevent the ink from running or lifting.

My original stamps. I don't use them often anymore as I prefer the stencil and waterslide methods, but I still stamp things with them. The stamp looks good on tags, certificates and other things you may want to supply with a guitar if you sell it.

I used small rubber stamps with numbers on them as side dots for my Ghostbusters-inspired Protoncaster guitars and basses.

Waterslide decals and vinyl stencils

Waterslide decals and vinyl stencils are two effective methods of creating and applying your logo.

I always print multiple logos, cut them out and physically place them to make sure I'm happy with the size before applying.

Using a vinyl stencil with a paint marker.

The area around the stencil has been masked off with tape and paper so that the logo can be sprayed.

The vinyl doesn't have to be the stencil; it can be the logo itself. Some people apply this at the end; others choose to put topcoats over it.

CASE STUDY: ARIA PRO II REFINISH

This was my first ever bass guitar, an Aria Pro II bought for me by my dad from a shop on Denmark Street in London around 1997. I love it, but like my first guitar it has been a test subject for different finishes.

The wine red showing through is the original finish, with a transparent black burst around the edges. On top of this I have done the Hammerite technique from this book, coating it in a blue acrylic paint wash then sanding back to nearly smooth. I sanded through in places to reveal the original finish. It then has another blue was on some parts, followed by multiple layers of Spray Max 2k clear it to give a smooth shiny surface.

I also painted the fretboard in the same way. The original fret markers were drilled out using the process described in this book. The holes then painted red and filled with UV resin.

All the hardware is new. It's been sanded back to give a rough look and exposing some of the metal under the chrome finish.

I've been thinking of selling it on, to give it a new life. At a recent guitar show a teenager tried it out and loved it, but it was a bit out of her price range for her second ever bass. Perhaps she'll buy this book and do it to her first one?

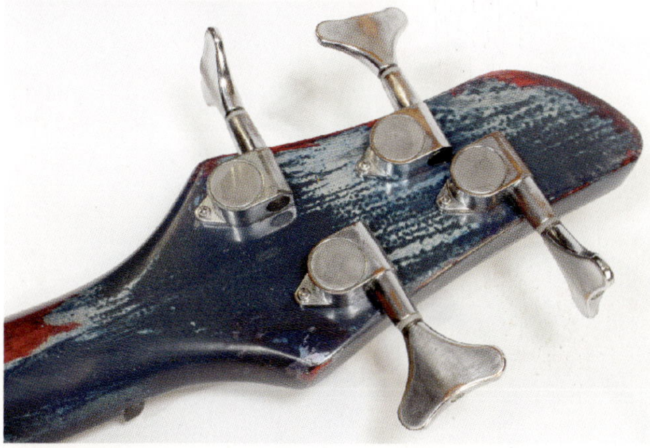

CHAPTER 7

HARDWARE

A simple way to customise a guitar is to change the hardware. There are so many options, including changing knobs, machine heads and bridges. There are companies like Guyker dedicated to producing components for upgrades, or you can buy parts made by guitar manufacturers themselves. There's such a good range in budget through to boutique parts that you can really spend what you want. However, there are some things you can do to your existing hardware pieces to make them unique to you and your custom design.

PAINTING PICKUPS

Most pickups have a cover, normally plastic, but also metal. Sometimes these will just slide off; occasionally they need a helping hand. Check the metal covers for a blob of solder that may be attaching them to the pickup, as this will need to be removed. If your pickup is potted (that is, has a waxy substance visible from underneath), the cover is likely to be held in place and removing it will damage the pickup.

If you can't remove the pickup cover, completely cover the wires. You can scrape paint off metal poles later, or mask them now. I use sticky tack for this.

Lightly sand the surface of the covers with 400 grit.

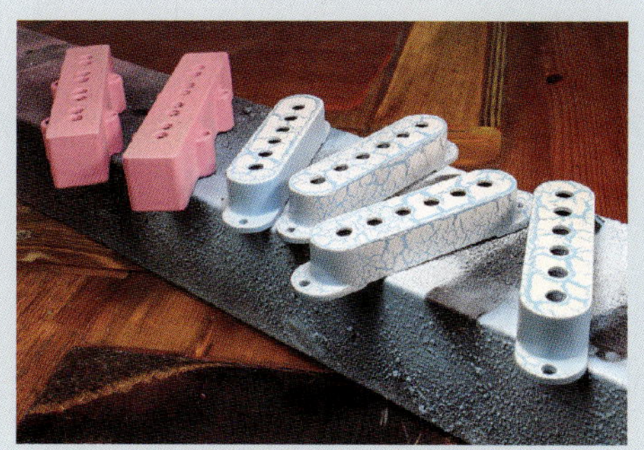

These covers have gone through the same processes as the body – prime, paint, topcoats.

MIND THE PICKUP COIL

The pickup itself has a coil of very thin wire around it, the ends of which attach to the thicker wire that links to the guitar circuit. This thin wire is often visible on single-coil pickups, so be careful not to break it. This is particularly an issue with many Telecaster neck pickups.

HUMBUCKER COVERS

Plastic humbucker covers are readily available, but check the size, as not all covers and pickups are compatible without having to clip bits off the pickups, which should only be done if you are confident that it won't damage the pickup.

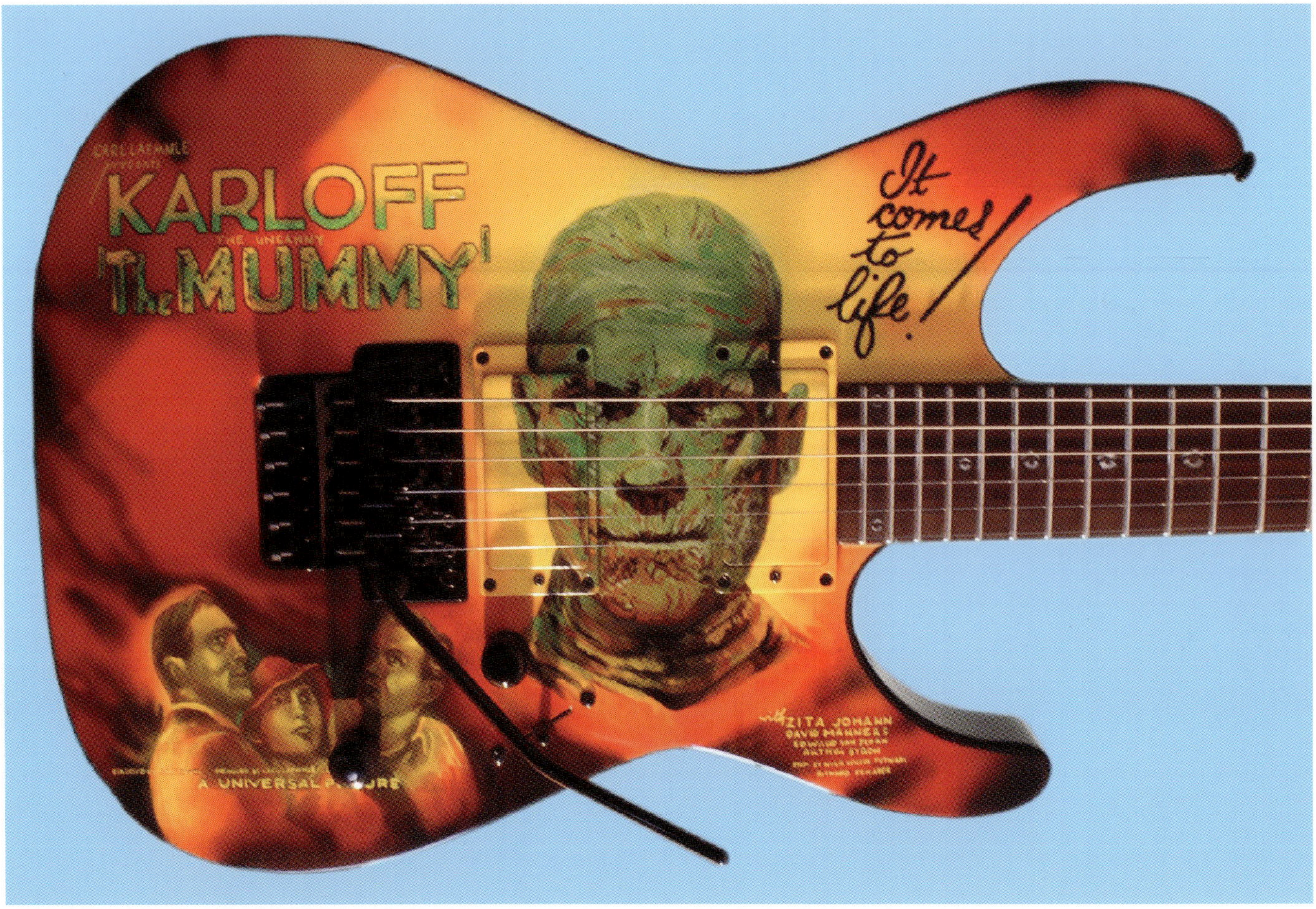

I made this version of the Kirk Hammett Mummy Guitar using a mix of waterslide decals, airbrushing and hand painting. The plastic pickup covers and surrounds allowed me to continue the artwork over a larger area.

INSPIRATION: MR GLYN'S PICKUPS

I've discussed in this book how the appearance of a guitar can influence playing style, stage presence and audience perception of the guitarist. One standout feature of Mr Glyn's pickups, beyond their sound quality, is their visual design. His Draig pickups, inspired by the heavy riffing guitar tone of Black Sabbath's Tony Iommi, are designed with all the genres encompassed by Doom Metal in mind. They feature a Dragon Breath finish that visually represents both the pickup and its sound, with *draig* being the Welsh word for dragon. The heat of the Dragon Breath is applied to chrome parts using a small gas blowtorch or pencil flame.

If you're inspired by Glyn's Dragon Breath finish, you can replicate it on any chrome hardware. When working on a pickup cover, remember first to remove it to avoid damaging the pickup itself. The cover is often soldered in place. Glyn's attention to detail means that all the pole pieces also receive the heat treatment. However, I would advise against doing this yourself unless you are confident in dismantling pickups. You can also buy pickup covers, but check the dimensions first, as not all pickup covers fit all pickups. For chrome bridges, dismantle them and avoid heating the springs. Remove the peg tops from chrome machine heads and set aside any small plastic washers.

SAFETY PRECAUTIONS

* Remember to wear the relevant safety equipment, especially heat-protection gloves.
* The metal sheet and grips could act as a heat sink, meaning that they will be hot and the effect could take longer to achieve.
* Everything will need somewhere to cool down.

Glyn has all the pieces on a sheet of metal, held by grips.

Keeping a close eye on what is happening allows Glyn to stop when the finish looks good.

I love this simple jig that Glyn uses to hold all the screws in place.

An assembled Draig bridge pickup with Dragon Breath finish.

PAINTING ON BRIDGES AND MACHINE HEADS

When painting on metal parts, especially those that are touched a lot and have moving parts, there is always the risk that the paint will wear in the long run. Lightly sanding the finish with 600-grit first, then priming and following with a 2K topcoat, is going to help, but it also makes the hardware thicker. For this reason, there are parts that should be masked off and shouldn't be painted. Don't forget to photograph everything before and during the dismantling stage to ensure you can fit it back together properly. Also, don't forget to lightly sand the edges of the painted surface where it meets the unpainted part with 800 grit to help smooth and protect them.

This machine head has been dismantled and masked. The small washers won't be painted.

The saddles on the bridge have had their sides and string grooves masked. Screws and springs won't be painted.

CASE STUDY: PUNISHER V

This is one of the four guitars I have customised for Zacharias from Inner Axis. It was originally a Dean Dimebag Darrell Razorback V, which I heavily customised to be a Marvel *Punisher* theme.

The bridge has been painted, but first I masked all the saddle sides except the outer two. I also painted the top of the fine tuners. The pickup covers and surrounds were in place when I painted the body to ensure that the design matches up.

All the additional parts are toys that have been screwed into routs I made to fit them. Milliput epoxy putty was used to smooth any joins. I made the knobs by sticking cut-down empty shotgun shells over volume knobs, cut to fit. I customised this guitar before I was confident about making my own fret markers, so these are stickers.

CUSTOM-TUNING PEGS

Many machine heads have tuning pegs that screw on. These can easily be replaced by anything that will allow the screw to pass back through.

The peg head was removed, elements added and moulded on to them, then they were reattached.

SCRATCHPLATES

Scratchplates can be painted on, but obviously they are designed to take a lot of wear, so it's likely that the paint would come off quite easily. One way round this is to buy a replacement in the colour you want, or, as I often do, in a transparent material and paint the back of it. This way, the colour shows through and won't be scratched when the surface is damaged. You can also make your own from scratch. Here are a few methods – you can easily mix and match elements from each process.

Designing a custom scratchplate

Some of the methods already covered in this book under the masking section can be used to design your own scratchplate. Stencil vinyl or Frisket film are great for laying over a body and seeing through. In the example with tape, I started with the tape on the body, drew a shape, removed the tape in one go to cut it, then put it back on the guitar for final adjustments. Multiple layers of tape help to keep it rigid. You can always draw on paper or work on a computer.

Making a copy of a scratchplate by hand

Simply stick the original scratchplate down using the masking-tape and cyanoacrylate-glue method (or double-sided tape). Cut as closely to the edge as possible, then sand the edges of the new material to match the original. Use the holes as a guideline. Note that this can damage the original scratchplate. As an alternative, you can draw around the original on to the new material and work from that. I find having the original as a physical guide is really helpful.

Tape an original scratchplate down to a new piece of material to use as a guide.

Once you have cut the new material, use the original as a sacrificial guide whilst you sand the edges smooth.

The original is useful drill guide.

USING A ROUTER TEMPLATE

Using a router template is the easiest method. You can buy them, or make them by drawing around an existing scratchplate, or by printing one on to MDF (some people prefer a thick, clear acrylic for templates).

It's important to cut as closely to the template as possible once it's stuck down. Routers are safer and more efficient with less material to remove. Always follow the router's safety instructions. I'm using a bench router, but a handheld palm router is good for this process too.

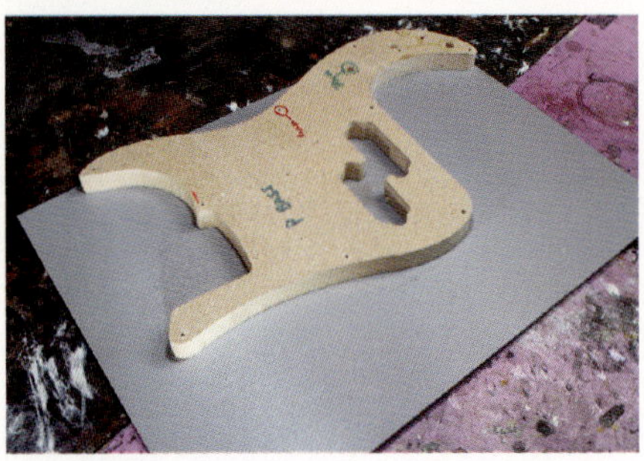

Customising an existing scratchplate

Chopping a piece off a pickguard is easy enough. Just use sandpaper to blend your cut back into the original edge. Bear in mind the cavity areas that the plate may be covering, as you won't want them exposed.

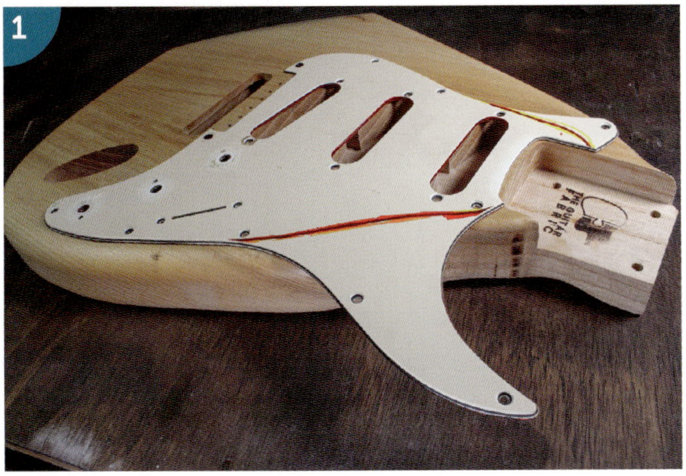

Mark the scratchplate in situ on the guitar.

Check the fit before sanding and smoothing out your cuts.

Cutting out a scratchplate

You can buy scratchplate material, or use sheets of acrylic or Perspex – 2–3mm is ideal. There's no reason not to use another material if you prefer.

If you are working directly on to the material because you are using a custom design and don't have the original scratchplate or a router template attached, there are a few things to note, as explained in the photos.

Cut out the shape by removing sections, as opposed to all in one go. I prefer using a bandsaw, but a powered fretsaw, hand fret or coping saw also work well.

Cutting the plastic with a powered tool can cause lumps of plastic because of the heat. This can easily be scraped off using a blade.

Use the edge of a scalpel to scrape the edge to an angle. This takes several passes. Don't angle at the neck pocket, or if there is a bridge shape like on a Stratocaster guard.

If using a router template and the scratchplate is face down, you can use an angled bit like this 45-degree chamfered bit from Radian Tools to bevel the edge.

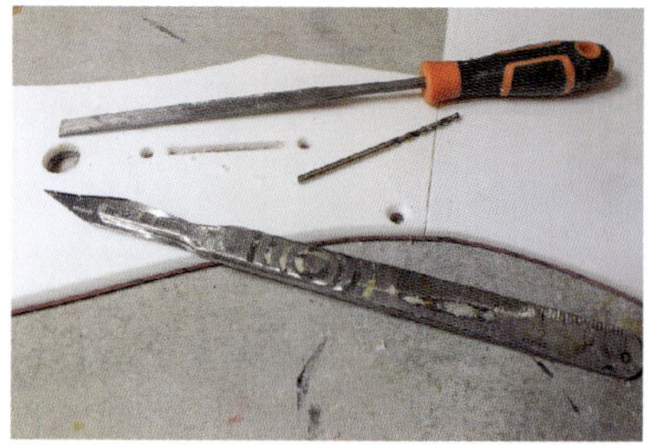

Drilling small holes in a line, then joining them by cutting with a scalpel and filing, is one way to make the pickup selector slot. Some people use a Dremel.

Screw holes

Don't forget to use a countersunk screw bit on all the screw holes where the scratchplate is held down to the body. The holes for pickup and switch screws aren't always countersunk – check the screws you have for these.

I bought this vinyl record three years ago, but never had an excuse to make it into a scratchplate until this book. Experiment with materials.

OTHER COVERS

There are others covers on your guitar too, such as the back control cavity covers and the truss rod cover. More canvas for your artistic expression.

CONTACTS

DEVIL & SONS GUITARS

You can find my how-to videos for setups, maintenance, building and finishing on YouTube: Youtube.com/devilandsons

For more on my own builds and customisations check out my website, www.devilandsons.guitars

I'm also on Instagram as @devilandsons and @devilanddaughters

Delve into the archive of my podcast, The Guitar Builders Collective Chat:

youtube.com/@GuitarBuildersCollectiveChat

Buy tools and jigs I have designed: guitarbuildingtools.com

INSPIRATIONAL PEOPLE

Here are the contact details for all the inspirational artists and builders mentioned and showcased in the book. Check them out and say hi from me.

Abhorrent Custom Electric Guitars
Abhorrent is a boutique brand for extreme guitars and basses.

Hand-crafted, human-designed and built from the finest materials

in the Forest of Dean, Gloucestershire, UK.

abhorrentguitars.com

instagram.com/abhorrent_guitars

ARY Guitars
Every guitar is unique in its own way. ARY guitars … a bit more. They paint unique guitars for the unique player. Stand out from the crowd.

aryguitars.com

instagram.com/arycustoms

Bonehead Guitars
Scott is my cohost of The Guitar Builders Collective Chat podcast. His YouTube channel is a video diary of his guitar builds for instructional and entertainment purposes.

https://www.youtube.com/BoneheadGuitars

instagram.com/bonehead_guitars/

Bonvillain Design Studio
Bonvillain Design Studio produces one of a kind instruments and customisations for performing artists, manufacturers and collectors. David Bonvillain has worked with a variety of manufacturers on limited-edition guitar designs including Ibanez, Dean, Spector, ESP, Strandberg and Fender/Jackson. He continues to work closely with Steve Vai and Joe Satriani.

bonvillain-design.com

Tobias Caspar
Tobias Caspar is a stabilised wood and resin supplier to a vast range of industries including luthiers, knife makers and more.

tobiascaspar.co.uk

instagram.com/tobiascaspar

Dom De Plume's Wasteland Guitars
Wasteland Guitars, created by Dom De Plume, is an art project where musical instruments become post-apocalyptic works of art. Each guitar is a testament to creativity and craftsmanship, with a unique dystopian style. Dom presents a collection of hand-painted guitars that tell stories of a future past.
wasteland.domdeplume.com
instagram.com/wastelandguitars

Nelson Faro
Artist for Marvel and DC. Teacher at School of Visual Arts. Founder and Frontman of the heavy metal band, MEGADROID, luthier and creator of cracked-mirror Iceman replicas.
facebook.com/nelson.f.decastro
@nelson-faro.bsky.social

The Guitar Builders Collective
The collective is also on social media.
facebook.com/groups/3350415801869100/
instagram.com/guitarbuilderscollective

Franklyn Guitars
Franklyn Guitars are dedicated to crafting meticulously handmade guitars and basses that feature a blend of contemporary interpretations of timeless designs, inventive combinations and experimental creations – all crafted to precise specifications.
https://franklynguitars.com
instagram.com/franklynguitars

Mark Gutierrez
Mark Gutierrez is a guitarist, producer and musician with a passion for creativity. With a design background, he brings a fresh perspective to guitar building, pushing boundaries and rethinking traditional methods. He forges his own path, creating standout guitars.
youtube.com/@MarkGutierrez
instagram.com/markgutierrez

Jamie Hewson
Guitarist, writer, producer, designer, husband, dad. Watch Jamie fumble his way through learning how to make guitars.
youtube.com/@fatpotanga
instagram.com/fatpotanja

Hilditch Handmade Guitars
Handmade guitars meticulously crafted in the heart of the Peak District.
Every musician has their own unique style and sound, so why shouldn't your guitar be unique too?
hilditchguitars.com
instagram.com/hilditch_guitars

Indra Custom Guitars
Indra provides a specialist custom guitar design and build service, working with their clients to create truly individual instruments that fulfil both sonic and aesthetic requirements like no other.
indraguitars.com
instagram.com/indra_guitars

K Ultimate Guitarworks
于溯 'Kayl' from K Ultimate Guitarworks shares his varied and unique guitar finishing techniques on Facebook and YouTube.
www.youtube.com/@suyek2045
https://www.facebook.com/profile.php?id=61568642649318
https://www.facebook.com/profile.php?id=100081464600319

LT Custom Guitars
Whatever your style, whatever your sound, there's a guitar waiting to be made for you ...
ltcustomguitars.co.uk
instagram.com/lt_custom_guitars

Maybury Guitars
A tribute to wood, tone and timeless craftsmanship. Their designs pay homage to the greats with a Maybury twist. Each guitar is a celebration of choice – be it wood, body style, pickups or scale length. No two guitars are alike.
mayburyguitars.co.uk
instagram.com/mayburyguitars

Milehouse Studios
Paul Richards, designing and building guitars inspired by everything, everywhere ...

youtube.com/@Milehousestudios
instagram.com/milehousestudios

Mord Guitar Works
Kalle Apps airbuses and finishes guitars, experimenting so you don't have to.

instagram.com/mord_custom_guitars

Mr Glyn's Pickups
Mr Glyn's Pickups are individually made near Auckland, New Zealand. From low-powered Vintage to powerful ROCK pickups. Designed combining experience, intuition and science. Road-tested by players on stage and in studios. Packaged with care for you and the planet. Food for amplifiers.

mrglynspickups.com
instagram.com/mrglynspickups

Court O'Reilly
Court is a self-taught Canadian pyrography artist and has been woodburning since 2016. She sustainably sources kiln-dried wood slabs that she cuts and sands into wood canvases for burning. She also works closely with local woodworkers to use their wood products for artwork such as hand-crafted canoe paddles, guitars and charcuterie boards.

hippienorth.com
instagram.com/hippienorth

Pherotone Studios
Helping you to fix things, make things and break things, all while having a laugh. With extensive guitar tone tests, guitar mods and entire guitar and speaker cab builds, their YouTube channel is the place to learn how to do something fun.

youtube.com/PherotoneStudios
instagram.com/pherotonestudios/

Richard Fay Swirls
Richard is an artist and guitar maker. He has been doing swirl paint finishes since the early 2000s.

richardfayswirls.com
facebook.com/SwirlPaintUK

Tasmaniak Guitars
Ray designs 3D printed guitars, a great resource for making bodies to experiment with.

http://cults3d.com/en/users/Tasmaniak/3d-models
instagram.com/tasmaniakguitars/

Tomas Tomas
The tattoo artist who worked on my arms, whose use of multiple coloured Sharpies to sketch out a design I now use, and hopefully you will too.

instagram.com/tomastomas108/

Uncle Death Guitars
Nick Adams (lead builder/owner) is a graduate of the Roberto-Venn school of Luthiery and a notorious volume and gain knob abuser. He incorporates a lifetime of guitar playing, woodworking and over fifteen years of professional automotive finish work into his builds. He is based in Salt Lake City, Utah.

uncledeathguitars.com
instagram.com/uncledeathguitars

Vertige Instruments by Fluid Alchemist
When visual symphony meets artistic mastery, every chord struck paints an outstanding example in elegance and design.

vertigeguitars.com
instagram.com/fluid_alchemist

SUPPLIERS

Although some suppliers may be based in certain parts of the world, many offer international shipping so it's worth checking them out.

All Parts
Parts and supplies for guitarists and luthiers.
allparts.uk.com and allparts.com

Axe Wax
Guitar care products, including polishing compounds and waxes.
axewax.co.uk

Chestnut Products
Supplier of wood-finishing materials.
chestnutproducts.co.uk

Crimson Guitars
Luthier tools, woods and finishing supplies.
crimsonguitars.com

The Guitar Fabrik
DIY guitar and bass kits, finishing products and hardware.
theguitarfabrik.com

Guyker
Hardware and parts upgrades.
guyker.com

GW Guitars and Woods
Jigs, tools, woods, and parts.
guitarsandwoods.com
Inlay Stickers Jockomo
Fret markers and vinyl decals.
https://www.inlaystickers.com/

Mars-Tronic Guitar Electronics
Guitar electronics upgrades.
mars-tronic.com

Montana Cans
Their website includes a store finder for you to source locally.
montana-cans.com

Nitorlack
Specialist in guitar varnishes and finishes.
nitorlack.com

Northwest Guitars
Finishing supplies, hardware and parts.
northwestguitars.co.uk

O3a
O3a is a dedicated range of cyanoacrylate adhesives specifically developed to meet the requirements of makers and crafters.
o3adhesives.co.uk

Pottery Crafts
The name of the company that was Tiranti and still sells their epoxy resin.
potterycrafts.co.uk

Stew Mac
Luthier tools and parts supplier.
stewmac.com

Tone Tech Luthier Supplies
Tone woods, building parts, paints, lacquers and luthier tools.
tonetechluthiersupplies.co.uk

INDEX

First published in 2026 by
The Crowood Press Ltd
Ramsbury, Marlborough
Wiltshire SN8 2HR

enquiries@crowood.com
www.crowood.com

British Library Cataloguing-in-Publication Data
A catalogue record for this book is available from the British Library.

For product safety-related questions, contact:
productsafety@crowood.com

ISBN 978 0 7198 4580 2

Typeset by Sergey Tsvetkov

Cover design by Envisage IT

Printed and bound in India by Nutech Print Services Pvt. Ltd.

Photographic credits
All photos are © Daniel Wallis except:
David Bonvillain/ Bonvillain Design Studio 11 (top four)
Neil A. Lim Sang 11 (lower two photos)
Maximilian Dawe /Tobias Caspar 53
Christopher Andrews/Franklyn Guitars 70 (bottom), 205 (bottom left)
Ali Yucel/ARY Guitars 74
Jamie Hewson 97
Lewis Trower/LT Custom Guitars 105
Sally Shaw Weddings 106, 120 (right side)
于溯/K Ultimate Guitarworks 120 (left side)
Jason Snelling/Maybury Guitars 122
Richard Fay Swirls 125
Cyrille Lefevre /Vertige Instruments by Fluid Alchemist 132
Charles Apps/Mord Guitar Works 138
Nicholas C Adams /Uncle Death Guitars 144
Paul Richards/Milehouse Studios 151
Nelson Faro 157
Richard Legg/Indra Custom Guitars 160
Mark Gutierrez 167-168
Alex Cook/Abhorrent Custom Electric Guitars 175
Court O'Reilly/Hippie North 178
Dominik Halbig/Dom De Plume's Wasteland Guitars 186 (bottom six)
Glyn Evans/Mr Glyn's Pickups 211